Irony and Outrage

Irony and Outrage

The Polarized Landscape of Rage, Fear, and Laughter in the United States

DANNAGAL GOLDTHWAITE YOUNG

OXFORD
UNIVERSITY PRESS

OXFORD
UNIVERSITY PRESS

Oxford University Press is a department of the University of Oxford.
It furthers the University's objective of excellence in research, scholarship,
and education by publishing worldwide. Oxford is a registered trade mark of
Oxford University Press in the UK and certain other countries.

Published in the United States of America by Oxford University Press
198 Madison Avenue, New York, NY 10016, United States of America.

Library of Congress Cataloging-in-Publication Data
Names: Young, Dannagal G., author.
Title: Irony and outrage : the polarized landscape of rage, fear, and
laughter in the United States / Dannagal Goldthwaite Young.
Description: New York, NY, United States of America : Oxford University
Press, [2020] | Includes bibliographical references and index.
Identifiers: LCCN 2019006859 (print) | LCCN 2019980569 (ebook) |
ISBN 9780190913083 (hardcover : acid-free paper) | ISBN 9780190913106 (ebook) |
ISBN 9780190913090 (pdf)
Subjects: LCSH: Mass media—Political aspects—United States. | Mass media and
public opinion—United States. | Television talk shows—Political
aspects—United States. | Radio talk shows—Political aspects—United States. |
Television in politics—United States. | Radio in politics—United States. |
Right and left (Political science)—United States. |
Political culture—United States. | Political satire, American.
Classification: LCC P95.82.U6 Y68 2020 (print) | LCC P95.82.U6 (ebook) |
DDC 810.9/93581—dc23
LC record available at https://lccn.loc.gov/2019006859
LC ebook record available at https://lccn.loc.gov/2019980569

9 8 7 6 5 4 3 2

Printed by Sheridan Books, Inc., United States of America

For Mike Young, whose infinite tolerance for ambiguity taught me to be comfortable in the not-knowing.

For Michelle Kennedy, whose high need for closure taught me to stop thinking and just do something goddammit.

Contents

Acknowledgments

COUNTLESS FRIENDS AND mentors made me feel that this project was worth pursuing and that I was the person to do it: Regina Lawrence, whose tireless mentoring and praise of my ideas convinced me that I know what I'm talking about; Sarah Sobieraj, who thinks and talks and brainstorms like an improviser in the best of all possible ways: "yes anding," building on offers to help you complete the scene—and the book. Michael Delli Carpini, who was excited about this idea from the start, and generously read a very early first draft, offering suggestions of where to tighten up the narrative. Lance Holbert, who has always been a champion of me and my work, even back when there wasn't very much work to be a champion of. My supportive colleagues and friends at the University of Delaware, with whom I've discussed these ideas (way too much) over the years; especially Scott Caplan, Lindsay Hoffman, Jenny Lambe, Paul Brewer, Steve Mortensen, Lydia Timmins, Tracey Holden, Phil Jones, Joanne Miller, Dave Redlawsk, Nancy Signorielli, John Courtright, Betsy Perse, and Kami Silk. My mentors from the Annenberg School for Communication at the University of Pennsylvania, including MXD, Joe Cappella, and Kathleen Hall Jamieson (who gave me invaluable publishing advice) and the brilliant Annenberg crew of the early 2000s, who inspire me every day: especially Kate Kenski, Jenny Stromer-Galley, Matt Carlson, Brooke Duffy, Jeff Gottfried, Talia Stroud, Scott Stroud, and Tresa Undem. The extraordinary women of political communication and political science (#womenalsoknowstuff), who are at once friends and colleagues: Amber Boydstun, Shannon McGregor, Katie Searles, and Jess Feezell.

For their generosity in taking the time to be interviewed, I would like to extend my heartfelt gratitude to The Committee's Alan Myerson, Ed Greenberg, and Latifah Taormina, comedy writer David Misch, documentary filmmaker Sam Shaw, and comedian Frank Lesser. Thank you especially to *Full Frontal*'s Ashley Black for entertaining these heady questions while still actively working on a popular political satire show in real time, and to Barry Lank for revisiting his memories of Air America to help fill out the picture of the early days there.

The thoughtful and generous Andy Chadwick introduced me to his editor, Oxford's Angela Chnapko. From the start, Angela made it clear that she shared the vision for this book and helped me see it through. Angela, thank you for believing in this project from our very first conversation! And to my copyeditor, Martha Ramsey: I would like to have you by my side every day to edit my every word.

Funding for some of the experimental work cited in the book came from two General University Research Grants awarded by the University of Delaware and from the University of Delaware's Center for Political Communication. Funding for books and travel to conduct interviews was provided by the National Institute for Civil Discourse at the University of Arizona.

I could not have begun to craft this line of argumentation without the formative work of other scholars and social psychologists, especially the contributions of Jeffrey Berry and Sarah Sobieraj, Nicole Hemmer, Alison Dagnes, John Jost, Jeffrey Jones, Geoff Baym, and Jonathan Haidt.

I should note that my approach is rooted almost exclusively in observations drawn in the context of American media and American electoral politics. The mechanism I propose in the book is rooted in underlying psychological, physiological, and likely even *genetic* predispositions. As highlighted by my non-American colleagues (Thank you, Cristian Vaccari!), if these underlying mechanisms operate as I propose, scholars should find these patterns in other cultural and geographic contexts as well. My hope is that my colleagues in political psychology, political communication, and humor studies from around the globe will be intrigued by (or reflexively opposed to) the propositions I advance here. I look forward to their explorations of these underlying theoretical mechanisms across diverse samples in various cultural contexts.

Without the experimentation and play of my favorite satirists, I would never have asked these questions in the first place. Thank you especially to Jon Stewart and Stephen Colbert. In 2000, while getting my master's at the University of Pennsylvania, I worked for 10 days as a production assistant for *The Daily Show* while they covered the Republican National Convention in Philadelphia (photo Ack.1). When I mentioned that I was deciding whether to continue toward the Ph.D. or move to New York to do improv, Stephen described the rampant rejection and uncertainty that fill the life of a young aspiring comic. He told me that if he had the chance to get a Ph.D. from Penn

PHOTO ACK. 1 Jon Stewart, Madeleine Smithberg, and the author backstage at *The Daily Show* during their Republican National Convention coverage in Philadelphia, August 2000.

studying something he loved, he would take it. So I did. I've been studying the psychology of satire ever since.

Thank you always to my mom and dad, Andrea and David Goldthwaite, for listening to me talk this stuff to death on the phone for hours. Mom, thank you for your passion for teaching and learning and thinking about things in new ways. Dad, thank you for being the very first reader of my very first draft, offering your keen insights, and being willing to become a part of the story. To my sister Jae Rock, for being my literal rock, who always makes sure my feet are on the ground, I'm taking care of myself, and using my "happy light," and to Kylee and Stephen for unconditional family love. To Crazy Susan Murphy, for your joy and friendship and for convincing me to write this book for real people. To my dearest Liz, for timeless laughter and affection from across the pond. To Heide for walks and talks and mindfulness. To Gracie for laughs and tea and faith. To David for keeping my head on straight. And to the Gallaghers: Nanny and Pop, Meg and Tom, Shan and Den, Kace and Bry, and Kev and

Lara. Everyone should be so lucky as to have a family that doubles as a personal pep rally. Especially you, Bryan Gallagher, for hitting me with the constant refrain "Write the book!" until I did it.

I am especially indebted to my ComedySportz family. You enrich my life and my scholarship through play and experimentation. The insights I have made about the connection between improvisation and a liberal psychology come from our collaborative explorations on stage. Thank you to Don Montrey, who is "featured in experimental stimuli" (i.e., plays the role of the comic) in one of my studies, which was recorded and edited by the talented Kevin Regan. And thank you to Emily Davis, who read early chapters and offered feedback. Indeed: "You guys have my back."

To my late husband, the brilliant improv comedy director Mike Young, who reminded us all that "There's always a reason to say no. The beauty is in finding a reason to say yes."

To Baxter and Edie: One day, I hope you'll see that your mom wasn't just a crazy lady who wrote to-do lists, made bad jokes, and limited your screen time. I love you always.

And finally, the greatest of all thanks to my husband, PJ Gallagher, the finest human being I will ever know, for his endless support and humor and intellect, and for putting everything back together.

Irony and Outrage

Prologue

"Melting hunk of uninformed apricot Jell-O."
"A demagoguing bag of candy corn."
"Sociopathic seventy-year-old toddler."

THESE ARE JUST a few of the colorful ways in which comedian Samantha Bee described President Donald Trump on her show *Full Frontal with Samantha Bee* in the early years of his presidency. On the half-hour program, airing weekly on TBS since it launched in February 2016, the former *Daily Show* correspondent offers passionate, unbridled liberal satire targeting Republicans, conservative policy positions, and of course, Trump himself.

Following the October 2016 release of the *Access Hollywood* audio recording in which then-candidate Trump bragged about "grabbing women by the pussy," Bee criticized Republican leadership for their delay in condemning their party's presidential candidate. To Paul Ryan, Speaker of the House, Bee proposed: "[Let's talk about] the idea that your petri dish of a political party allowed America's misogyny and racism to coagulate into a presidential nominee! Discuss!"

Bee's *Full Frontal* is the most recent iteration in the evolution of America's televised political satire genre. The show offers viewers a taste of Bee's authentic self, unabashedly critical of America's political right, focusing on issues related to women, reproductive rights, and social justice. That is why, following the election of Trump in November 2016, Bee's choice of interview guest was particularly unexpected by her predominantly liberal audience.

That guest? Glenn Beck. Glenn Beck of eighties-morning-zoo-radio-DJ-turned-political-pundit-fame. Glenn Beck of Obama-era-Fox-News-conspiracy-theory fame. Glenn Beck of chalkboard-flowcharts-where-all–roads-lead-to-Communism fame. Glenn Beck of now-regrets-his-divisive-rhetoric-from-his-Fox-days fame.

That Glenn Beck.

From 2009 to 2011, Beck had made a name for himself as the entertaining and incendiary pundit/conspiracy theorist on Fox News's *Glenn Beck Program*.

His inflammatory monologues railed against progressive community groups like the Association of Community Organizations for Reform Now (ACORN) (which he accused of trying to orchestrate widespread voter fraud in 2008);[1] and against President Obama himself, who had shown, Beck argued in 2009, "a deep-seated hatred for white people or the white culture."[2] Beck was an evocative performer whose emotional responses of outrage, horror, and sadness at the perceived malice of the left resonated with his audience, as evidenced by the two million–plus viewers who tuned in daily for his afternoon rants.

But after leaving Fox News, Beck went through an "awakening." In a 2014 interview with Megyn Kelly (then on Fox's *Kelly Files*), Beck lamented the role he had played in fostering the political polarization in the United States, stating: "I wish I could go back and be more uniting in my language, because I think I played a role, unfortunately, in helping tear the country apart."[3] By the 2016 presidential election, the Beck of 2010 was almost unrecognizable; the man who had once stated "Obama is a racist" had embraced the Black Lives Matter movement, praised Michelle Obama's powerful 2016 speech excoriating Trump's misogyny, and admitted that "Obama made me a better man.... There are things unique to the African-American experience that I cannot relate to.... I had to listen to them."[4]

In the December 19, 2016, episode of *Full Frontal*, the two opposing television personalities, clad in ugly Christmas sweaters, sat down opposite each other in an effort to explore themes of unity (photo Pro.1).

"Why would you have me on [your show] if not to mock?" Beck asked Bee.

Her response was slow and deliberate, "I think that our future is going to require a broad coalition of nonpartisan decency...."

Beck nodded in affirmation throughout Bee's talk of bipartisan coalition-building. "I believe you actually don't want to do damage," he empathized. "As a guy who has done damage, I don't want to do any more damage. I know what I did. I helped divide. I'm willing to take that. My message to you is, please don't make the mistakes that I made."

Samantha Bee appeared disarmed and confused.

"I hate to break it you," Beck continued, "See, I've been watching you and you've adopted a lot of my catastrophe kind of traits."

Bee, dubious and seemingly horrified, pondered aloud: "I'm a catastrophist?...In the mode of Glenn Beck?"

Beck then began an interrogation: "Let me ask you this...Do you believe there's a chance we fall into a dictatorship under Trump? Do you believe

PHOTO PRO. 1 Samantha Bee and Glenn Beck feeding each other cake on the December 16, 2016, episode of *Full Frontal with Samantha Bee* on TBS.

there's a chance that we lose our freedom of speech and press under this president?"

Bee, clearly uncomfortable with this line of questioning, rubbed her brow. "Jesus Christ. Glenn Beck is going to make me cry. What the fuck is happening?"

"I'm sorry." Beck shook his head and raised his eyebrows, "Somebody has to say it."

Bee replied spitefully: "How does it feel that *this*," she said gesturing to her own body, "is your legacy?"

"I'd never thought of it *that* way," he conceded.

Are Samantha Bee and Glenn Beck the same? Do they produce similar effects on their viewers? Put differently: can liberal political satire and conservative opinion shows—"outrage programming"[5]—be thought of as serving parallel purposes for their audiences? And if so, why do they look and feel so different?

Over the past decade, countless journalists have asked why political satire is so liberal. "Why does every 'conservative *Daily Show*' fail?" asked *Vulture*'s Josiah Hesse.[6] Jake Nevins at the *Guardian* has asked: "why can't rightwing comics break into US late-night TV?"[7] Josh Green at *Washington Monthly* put it a bit more bluntly, asking: "why aren't conservatives funny?"[8] Others, like

Jon Bershad at *Mediaite*, have framed the conclusion as foregone: "why conservative comedy doesn't work and likely never will."[9] Meanwhile, the *Atlantic*'s Oliver Morrison puts the issue a bit more artfully with the headline "Waiting for the conservative Jon Stewart."[10]

And while writers and commentators have wrestled with the question of why there is little successful satire on the right, they have also grappled with a similar conundrum on the other side: Why can't liberal talk radio succeed? *Forbes*'s Abram Brown analyzed "why all the talk-radio stars are conservative."[11] *Variety*'s Brian Lowry explored "how conservatives dominate the TV/radio talk game."[12] And after the liberal radio network Air America ended its five-year stint in 2010, *LA Weekly*'s Dennis Romero declared: "liberal talk radio a fail."[13]

So conservatives aren't good at satire and liberals aren't good at opinion talk shows. Why, though?

For a decade, it seemed that at every media interview and public lecture, someone asked me why political satire is so liberal. And I never had a satisfactory response. To be sure, this question has been answered by others in a number of ways, from conservative outlets proposing that conservatives are blackballed from the liberal-dominated world of comedy,[14] to writers who point to the liberal roots of today's satire in the 1960s counterculture, as if…that's just the way it has been and will always be.[15] Most common, though, is the argument that because satire tends to punch up at institutions and people in power, and because conservatives tend to support the status quo, satire will inevitably come more from the left than the right. Indeed, this was the answer invoked by popular satirist Stephen Colbert, when he was asked in 2006 why satire tends to be liberal. He replied: "going after the status quo is not necessarily a conservative thing to do; it's antithetical to the idea of conservatism. Comedy is all about change. So it's going to be a challenge for them."[16]

And while this reasoning makes sense, I never found it *that* compelling— especially in 2008–2010, when Democrats controlled both houses of Congress and the presidency. At some point during eight years of such a Democratic presidency, as liberal policies increasingly become law, doesn't liberalism become the status quo? I also found it increasingly difficult to argue that conservatives did not want to critique people and institutions in power when that was precisely what conservatives were doing on Fox News and talk radio every day of the Obama administration. It just so happened they were doing it through the format of opinion programming and punditry instead of satire, but they were still challenging the existing political establishment.

While I was attending the conference of the National Communication Association in New Orleans in 2011, I caught up with my old friend the political polarization expert Talia Stroud and her husband, Scott Stroud, who is a celebrated scholar of culture, philosophy, and rhetoric. I mentioned to them my frustration with this question about why there is no political satire on the right and admitted that my answers to date had been unsatisfying. Scott threw a wrench into my proposition.

"What if, for conservatives, Glenn Beck is a form of satire?" he proposed. "He's mockingly critical of the left. He uses hyperbole to emphasize his points. I'm just thinking that before you conclude that satire doesn't exist on the right, maybe rethink what satire is."

This one conversation started me on a six-year exploration. I've worked to reconcile the conceptual definition of satire with the way I measure and identify it. I've unpacked the psychological processes involved in comprehending and appreciating it. I've wondered if it makes sense to define satire not by what it looks like, or by who creates it, but by what it does, or maybe by how audiences perceive it.

This examination has brought me to the testable propositions that I explore in this book: first, that televised political satire and conservative political opinion programming, while *not the same*, serve similar needs for their audiences. Second, that televised political satire and conservative political opinion programming have parallel effects on their audiences. And most important: third, that televised political satire and conservative political opinion programming look different from each other due in large part to the different psychological frameworks of liberalism and conservatism, which account for distinct psychological traits and aesthetic preferences among their creators and audiences. Advancing these social psychological propositions would require that I acknowledge several historical realities: that televised political satire and conservative opinion programming both emerged as a response to the erosion of public trust in journalism through the 1980s and 1990s; and that both genres were made possible by technological and regulatory changes in media during that same time.

The difference between the political perspective that is most successfully communicated through satire and the one that is best communicated through "opinion talk" or "outrage" is inescapable. In this book, I explore the history of previous generations of political satire and "outrage" in the United States, which map nicely onto the liberal counterculture and the cultural and social conservative movements of the 1950s–1960s (chapter 1). I then explore the changes in media technologies, media regulation, and political polarization through the latter half of the twentieth century (chapter 2) and how these changes created the need and opportunity for a second generation of satire and outrage (around the year 2000) to thrive on the left and the right, respectively (chapter 3).

The book then turns to the internal structure and logic of satire, offering a deep dive into a consideration of how satire and irony are comprehended and appreciated in the brain (chapter 4) and how audience characteristics contribute to successful understanding and appreciation of humor (chapter 5). Chapters 6 and 7 visit the land of political psychology, where researchers have explored the psychological and physiological roots of political ideology. I look at psychological characteristics such as "need for cognition" and "tolerance for ambiguity" and how they correlate not only with social and cultural liberalism but also with appreciation of certain aesthetic forms, such as abstract art and stories that lack a clear plot resolution. I then connect these psychological correlates of both aesthetic preference and political ideology to liberal and conservatives' affinity for (and production of) satire and outrage (respectively), advancing my proposition that each of these genres is a logical extension of the underlying psychological profiles (and epistemological orientations) of people on the left and the right (chapter 8). To understand the parallel functions and outcomes of these two genres for their respective audiences on the left and right, chapter 9 chronicles why people consume satire and outrage programming and how they perceive it. This chapter summarizes the research on the effects of viewing satire and outrage and makes the case that many of the functions and consequences of satire for people on the left are quite similar to those of outrage for people on the right, despite contrasting content and aesthetics.

To understand those instances when liberals and conservatives have engaged (and have continued to engage) in the *other side's* preferred genre (though not particularly *well*), chapter 10 presents "playing against type," a look at the failed liberal attempt at outrage radio (Air America) and the failed conservative attempt at political satire (Fox's ½ *Hour News Hour*). Chapter 10 also introduces a consideration of how these two genres evolved under the Trump presidency. Chapter 11 advances a normative argument, proposing how citizens, scholars, and journalists should think about these genres and the ideologies of the people who create and consume them. Instead of hating or condemning the other side for holding contrasting views, one could think of these two ideologies and their accompanying psychologies as necessary subsystems that allow society to function as a whole. That being said, the capacity for exploitation of these two genres is not symmetrical. The internal logic of these genres and the nature of their audiences render conservative outrage a more viable vehicle for elite social and cultural propaganda. Liberal satire, by contrast, remains a more efficient vehicle for markedly *non*elite subversive experimentation and rumination.

Given that liberals and conservatives have different psychological profiles and accompanying aesthetic preferences, one should expect the ways that they explore and communicate their political belief systems to look different from each other in predictable ways. Because of their contrasting psychological needs and motivations, liberals and conservatives in the United States have frequently occupied distinct social and cultural spheres over the last century. As I will show, the forerunners of today's genre of conservative outrage arose from an explicit, organized rejection of liberal values by members of the conservative establishment. And today's liberal satire is the spiritual and ideological successor to radical comedy routines performed next door to frontally nude bearded men in evening gowns.

1

The Counterculture Comics versus the Hate Clubs of the Air

LONG BEFORE SAMANTHA Bee called Ivanka Trump a "feckless c*nt"—
and then, days later, apologized for using the word "c*nt";[1] long before Glenn
Beck called President Obama a racist with a "deep-seated hatred of white
people"[2]—and then, five years later, apologized for doing so;[3] long before we
knew of John Oliver and Trevor Noah, before we had heard of Sean Hannity
or Rush Limbaugh, America witnessed the birth of the first generation of the
genres of irony and outrage.

In the 1950s, America was on the cusp of a new political, social, and cultural order. Following World War II, in the advent of great economic prosper-
ity, with increased educational opportunities and homeownership facilitated
by the GI Bill, the country was changing. On the domestic front, economic,
racial, and gender hierarchies were shifting. On the world stage, leaders were
debating the merits of isolationism versus interventionism. As the 1950s gave
way to the 1960s, these tensions heightened. Americans witnessed the assassinations of prominent political and civil rights leaders, including President
John F. Kennedy, in 1963. In 1965, they saw the murder of the African
American activist Malcolm X. In 1968 came the assassinations of JFK's
brother Robert Kennedy, a Democratic senator and presidential candidate,
and of the civil rights leader Martin Luther King, Jr. Americans also watched
the buildup of troops in an increasingly bloody situation in Vietnam and took
sides in the debate over the nation's policies on race, from the Civil Rights Act
of 1964 to the Voting Rights Act of 1965.

In the face of such tumult, Americans had to choose: to embrace the
existing political and social order or . . . change. True to form, conservatives
chose the former, while liberals chose the latter. What is fascinating is the
way these two complex political philosophies, each of which embraced myriad issue positions and distinct orientations to the world, were communicated

through distinct informational genres. On the one hand were the strategic political persuaders on the right, like the anti-Communist, antiintegration John Birch Society and radio hosts like Clarence Manion, Dan Smoot, and H. L. Hunt, whose shows offered a steady drumbeat of doomsday predictions to prove that the United States needed to get out of the United Nations and impeach the chief justice of the Supreme Court, Earl Warren. On the other hand were scattered, experimental, not-operating-according-to-any-political-strategy radical liberal artists and performers, whose engagement with their political world was profoundly reactive, artistic, and improvised. It is in these distinct genres, born out of the tumult of the 1950s and 1960s, that one finds the origins of Sean Hannity and Rush Limbaugh, on the right, and John Oliver and Stephen Colbert, on the left.

Hate Clubs of the Air

On June 16, 2017, Fox News host Sean Hannity opened his Friday night program seated adjacent to a graphic stating: "Deep State Revenge."

"All right," began a confident Hannity, "so the unelected fourth branch of government is now being aided and abetted by the destroy Trump media, all in a massive effort to damage and destroy President Trump. Now, this week alone, we have seen unprecedented—and potentially criminal—leaks from the *deep state* to the liberal Washington Post."

The term "deep state" refers to the proposition that there is an unelected organization of power brokers who are running the government behind the scenes, having somehow infiltrated institutions from the White House to the courts, from the United Nations to media organizations. Although the notion gained increased currency after the election of Donald Trump, Sean Hannity was hardly the first proponent of the theory of an "invisible government" operating in the shadows.

Actually, *The Invisible Government* was—perhaps not so coincidentally— the title of the popular 1962 book authored by Dan Smoot, a former FBI agent turned conservative radio star. As described by media historian Nicole Hemmer, Smoot argued that the "Council on Foreign Relations—which included key members of JFK's administration—was in actuality part of an elaborate plot to prepare America for socialism."[4] Smoot began his conservative proselytizing through a limited-circulation newsletter with only a few thousand subscribers. His good fortune came with investment from the dog food magnate D. B. Lewis, an anti-Communist, antiinterventionist believer in the concept of the deep state (though he probably didn't call it that). He also liked Smoot's message and approach. As Hemmer tells it, Lewis believed that the American public was being brainwashed by the "liberal media." "The socialists have practically all the big newspapers and magazines and they control practically all broadcasting," he reportedly told Smoot in the 1960s.[5] With Lewis's financial backing, Smoot's radio show became one of the most popular of that era. The *Dan Smoot Report* boasted over 30,000 paid subscribers by its peak in 1965 and could be heard on 89 radio stations and 52 television stations across 31 states.[6] Smoot often used his program to rail against the dangers of the United Nations, calling the organization a "Soviet apparatus" and arguing that the shared goal of the UN and of Communism was the "creation of a world socialist system."[7]

Smoot was an active member of the conservative John Birch Society, an anti-Communist, antiintegration political organization launched in 1958 by retired candy manufacturer, Robert W. Welch. Throughout the 1960s, against the backdrop of a growing civil rights movement, the Birch Society's influence and popularity grew in small meetings over coffee and donuts in the living rooms of anxious conservative families across the country.[8] With Welch's candy fortune, the organization sponsored mass mailings and large billboards that were critical of racial desegregation and of global organizations like the United Nations. Across the South and the Midwest, the Birch Society's billboards dotted highways with messages like "Get US out! Of the United Nations" and a giant image of Dr. Martin Luther King, Jr., sitting in an audience with the heading, "MARTIN LUTHER KING at COMMUNIST TRAINING SCHOOL." One frequent Birch Society billboard called for the impeachment of Earl Warren: "Save our Republic! IMPEACH Earl WARREN!" (photo 1.1). Of the Supreme Court under Chief Justice Warren, Welch had stated: "[it] is now so strongly and almost completely under Communist influence that it shatters its own precedents and rips gaping holes in our Constitution in order to favor Communist purposes."[9] Smoot used his radio show to call for the impeachment of Chief Justice Warren, whom he, like Welch, accused of being a socialist.[10]

While Smoot was a popular voice heard in the homes and cars of conservatives across the country in the 1960s, he wasn't the only one. In *Messengers of the Right: Conservative Media and the Transformation of American Politics*, Nicole Hemmer traces the history of the vast conservative radio landscape that grew through the 1950s and 1960s, a story that centers on several key figures: chief among them Clarence Manion, a former dean of Notre Dame Law School and a short-lived Eisenhower administration appointee.

PHOTO I.I   A John Birch Society billboard calls for the impeachment of Chief Justice Earl Warren.

Like Smoot, Manion left his work with the government to become a commentator on the government. He was at odds with mainstream Republican politics of the time, favoring antiinterventionist approaches to America's future in a postwar world while the rest of the party was embracing the United Nations and America's prominent role in it. Smoot's vision for America was rooted firmly in American nationalism and American exceptionalism. In his 1950 essay "The Key to Peace," Manion "argued America's strength lay in its tradition of godly morality, individual liberty, and limited government."[11] His vision of America was one that focused not on America's obligations to the world, but on America's obligations to itself. Its traditions. Its people. Its way of life. "The need now is not for 'new concepts,' 'fresh approaches' and 'ingenious improvisations' in the cause of peace and unity," wrote Manion, "The need now is for rediscovery, and renewed understanding of the tried and true principle of Americanism"[12] Manion, also like Smoot, obtained financial support from D. B. Lewis. With Lewis's help, by 1962, Manion's radio show, *The Manion Forum*, "could be heard on around 270 radio stations and...seen on nearly 50 television stations, primarily on the West Coast."[13] In addition to stressing themes of antiglobalism and anti-Communism, conservative radio hosts railed against the "liberal media," the "left-wing columnists" who posed a problem for America, and more immediately, for conservatism. In fact, it was deep and growing concerns about liberal media dominance that launched this network of conservative media activists in the first place.

According to Hemmer's historical research, the roots of the conservative media establishment dated back to the 1940s, when conservatives rejected two core policies of the Roosevelt administration: (1) the New Deal, which used government resources and agencies to grow the economy, and (2) the postwar policies that placed the United States in complex international alliances, including the United Nations. Concerned about the interventionist direction of foreign policy, several students at Yale Law School created the America First Committee, which rejected America's new role in the world. While America First existed for just a year and disbanded after the United States entered World War II in response to the attack on Pearl Harbor in 1941, the group's influence was long-lasting, as the fiercest antiinterventionists became some of the strongest supporters of a new conservative media movement. In a 1953 meeting held at the behest of William Regnery, a Chicago-based publisher who had been a member of America First, a handful of conservative writers and thinkers were convened to think strategically about ways to counter the dominance of liberal philosophies and voices in the changing media environment. The answer, they decided, was to work strategically across media to argue for conservative principles and spread their word to the public. "Convinced that media were key to shaping public opinion and that public opinion was key to political power," Hemmer writes, "they launched a number of new media outlets to overcome both liberal dominance and conservative isolation."[14]

These efforts were part of a broader concerted effort to amplify conservative arguments and voices through print, radio, and television. In 1944 Regnery, along with former *Washington Post* editor Felix Morley and journalist Frank Hanighen, had launched *Human Events*, a newspaper designed to "look at events through the eyes that are biased in favor of limited constitutional government, local self-government, private enterprise, and individual freedom."[15] In 1955, William F. Buckley, Jr., a young conservative intellectual—whose book *God and Man at Yale* Regnery had published in 1951—launched the *National Review*, the conservative monthly magazine that is still influential today. Buckley appeared as a guest on Clarence Manion's radio show, *The Manion Forum*, which Buckley's father, William Buckley, Sr., had helped fund in 1954. Dan Smoot's radio show, the *Smoot Report*, was launched in 1957, and Texas billionaire oilman H. L. Hunt launched the conservative radio show *Life Lines* in 1958. Manion's, Smoot's, and Hunt's shows stayed on the air through the 1970s.

Most of these radio shows peaked in popularity in the mid- to late 1960s, both in terms of the number of syndicates carrying them and the number of listeners tuning in. Yet, for most Americans, conservative radio remained unknown—even during this time of peak popularity. In a 1964 *Nation* article, Fred J. Cook described these "Hate Clubs of the Air" for those members of the American public who were unfamiliar with the conservative radio movement. "For those outside of conservative circles," Hemmer writes, "Cook had uncovered a media world few Americans knew existed."[16] Cook's essay included a map of the United States dotted with icons denoting the locations of the various conservative broadcasts. Describing the resulting picture, he argued that "it looks as if the nation were seized with a virulent pox."[17] That "virulent pox" indeed spread across the nation but was concentrated in certain municipalities in Virginia, South Carolina, Alabama, Georgia, California, and Texas. In the Dallas region in the early 1960s, the political and cultural influence of broadcasters like Clarence Manion, Dan Smoot, and H. L. Hunt was palpable.

Journalists and authors Bill Minutaglio and Steven Davis document in careful detail the political, social, and cultural history of the city of Dallas through the years leading up to the Kennedy assassination in November 1963. As they describe it, the vitriolic political climate that served as the backdrop to Kennedy's murder was shaped by a number of factors: local leaders; active local chapters of the John Birch Society; Ted Dealey, the fiercely anti-Kennedy editor of the *Dallas Morning News;* and a steady stream of conservative talk radio. The conservative radio hosts of the early 1960s (consistent with the John Birch Society) concentrated on several key themes: a secret plot within the US Council on Foreign Relations to embrace socialism as a central political philosophy, the "dangers of racial integration," the need to get the United States out of the United Nations (which some conservative media hosts characterized as a mechanism to make socialism the dominant mode of government across the globe), and finally, President Kennedy's general systematic dismantling of the "American way of life."

So toxic was the environment at the time, write Minutaglio and Davis, that Vice President Adlai Stevenson, after a particularly contentious visit to Dallas in October 1963, told White House aide Arthur Schlesinger: "there was something very ugly and frightening about the atmosphere.... [Some in Dallas] wondered whether the President should go to Dallas [the following month].

And so do I."[18] On the morning of November 22, 1963, as people readied themselves for the passage of the presidential motorcade through downtown, H. L. Hunt's *Life Lines* could be heard on KPCN in Dallas. The show's host was painting a picture of the world that Kennedy and his "communist conspirators" wanted to bring to America:

> You would not be able to sing "The Star Spangled Banner" or state your Pledge of Allegiance to the American flag, because our stars and stripes would be replaced by the Hammer and Sickle. You would not be able to celebrate Independence Day, Memorial Day, or Labor Day. You would not be able to observe Thanksgiving as we know it today, thanking the lord for his blessings and fruitful harvest. You would not be able to celebrate any holiday of freedom. If communism were to come to America, never again would you be able to go off on hunting trips with friends. Private ownership and private use of firearms is strictly forbidden. No firearms are permitted the people, because they would then have weapons with which to rise up against the oppressors.[19]

Although radio commentators continued to decry what they described as an insidious Communist influence, their influence began to wane over the next decade. The decline of this first generation of conservative radio coincided with the rise of America's conservative think tank movement in the 1970s.[20] With the launch of the Heritage Foundation in 1973, and a neoconservative shift at the American Enterprise Institute in the 1970s, conservative intellectuals found ways of influencing public policy legislatively rather than just through the airwaves. And in 1980 many moderate conservatives found their worldview realized in two terms of President Ronald Reagan, followed by one term of President George H. W. Bush. Perhaps counterintuitively, "the conservative political movement [attained] its greatest success at the very moment conservative media was in decline," writes Hemmer. Counterintuitive at first glance, yes. But also quite understandable. The absence of outlets designed to amplify the most fringe elements of conservatism allowed Reagan to achieve legislative victories without the friction of a hostile media atmosphere. The "New Right"—the populist, nationalist version of conservatism that reemerged in the 1970s— certainly existed during Reagan's presidency, but it didn't have the media apparatus to pose too much of a problem to the administration. As conservative journalist and commentator Charles Sykes writes, it may well be that "the lack of a raucous Right media during the 1980s actually gave Reagan the space for maneuvering and ideological flexibility that his successors would not enjoy."[21]

Meanwhile, conservative intellectuals who continued their work in print media, like William F. Buckley, Jr., had long been at odds with the more fringe elements of the conservative movement, including Welch's John Birch Society. As detailed by Alvin Felzenberg, Buckley and Welch differed in the actors to whom they ascribed responsibility for "the military and diplomatic setbacks that befell the United States in the early years of the Cold War."[22] While Buckley attributed US failures in Korea, Eastern Europe, China, and Cuba "to misguided policies and lack of resolve among Western leaders," Welch considered them "the result of Soviet penetration into the highest echelons of the U.S. government."[23] According to Felzenberg, Welch believed that up to 70 percent of the country was under Communist control. Buckley had little respect for such simplistic and conspiratorial views of the world. He later wrote that Welch's "mischievous unreality...had placed a great weight on the back of responsible conservatives."[24]

As summarized by Sykes, Buckley recognized that "the problem that dogged conservatives was not stupidity; it was crackpotism."[25] In a section of his book titled "Purging the Crackpots," Sykes describes how the conservative establishment of the 1960s, under the leadership and gatekeeping of Buckley and with the prominence of the *National Review*, dealt with their "crackpot problem" by publicly identifying and rejecting people and points of view they deemed *outside* mainstream conservatism, from Robert Welch to Ayn Rand. The magazine was at the center of mainstream conservative values, policy proposals, and governance through the 1980s. Ronald Reagan reported reading *National Review* dating back to his days as governor of California.[26] Reagan and Buckley had a relationship of mutual admiration and respect throughout Reagan's years in the White House and beyond (photo 1.2).

In the words of conservative writer Matthew Continetti: "it was Buckley who for decades determined the boundaries of American conservatism." Continetti writes: "*National Review* is a great example of media gatekeeping theory: By exiling anti-Semites, Birchers, and anti-American reactionaries from its pages, the magazine and its editor determined which conservative arguments were legitimate and which were not. By denying a platform to quacks and haters, they broadened their potential audience."[27] But, while the conservative "hate clubs of the air" had all but disappeared by 1980, two changes—one regulatory, the other technological—revitalized the populist right-wing media establishment during the 1980s. The regulatory change was the Federal Communications Commission's (FCC's) repeal of the fairness doctrine in 1987, which had required broadcasters to be even-handed in their treatment of political and social issues. The technological change was the evolution of cable technologies that created new programming opportunities. The repeal of the fairness doctrine opened up the airwaves not just to

PHOTO 1.2   President Ronald Reagan and William F. Buckley, Jr., at the White House in 1988. Official White House photo.

conservative ideological speech but also to explicit partisan arguments *for and against* political policies and candidates. Rush Limbaugh, the most popular of all conservative radio hosts, launched his national radio program *The Rush Limbaugh Show* in 1988 and has spent the better part of the last three decades as the most listened-to radio host in the United States. Meanwhile, the advent of cable television and the proven success of Ted Turner's 24-hour news network CNN in the 1980s confirmed that television was a viable (and profitable) medium for political news and analysis. International media mogul Rupert Murdoch—with the help of his conservative founding CEO Roger Ailes—capitalized on the proven success of CNN as he launched in 1996 the Fox News Network, a forum for conservative programming that tapped into the same aesthetics and outrage as the early conservative radio voices like Manion, Smoot, and Hunt.

The History of American Political Satire: These Blobs Aren't Going to Go in a Straight Line

The history of conservative media in the United States is fairly straightforward. It reads like an organized, linear narrative because it is just that: an organized, linear narrative with a few key players working toward a clear political goal, with some fractures in the 1960s–1970s, but otherwise sharing a fairly common sense of political purpose. Telling the story of the history of satire in United States on the other hand is a bit like trying to put spilled blobs of mercury back into a thermometer. Every time you try to pick some up, it breaks into smaller and smaller little blobs. And there's definitely no way you're going to get that stuff to go into a straight line.

To make my meanings clear from here on, when I talk about the American political satire of today, I'm referring to the largely televised political satire programming by the personalities who dominate our attention: John Oliver, the host of *Last Week Tonight* on HBO; Samantha Bee, the host of *Full Frontal* on TBS; Stephen Colbert, host of *The Late Show* on CBS and former host of the critically acclaimed ironic political satire show *The Colbert Report*, on Comedy Central; Jon Stewart, former host of *The Daily Show* on Comedy Central and mentor to almost all of the personalities mentioned here; and Trevor Noah, the current host of *The Daily Show*.

I'm also talking about comedians like Bill Maher, who, for the last 25 years, has been a mainstay of televised political satire, from *Politically Incorrect* at Comedy Central and then ABC to his show *Real Time*, which has appeared on HBO since 2003. When I talk about televised political satire of today, I'm also talking more broadly about the social and political satire of *Saturday Night Live*, *MAD TV*, *Key and Peele*, and *Inside Amy Schumer*. I'm talking about the political, social, and cultural satire in the standup routines of Chris Rock and Dave Chappelle, Sarah Silverman and Louis C.K. I'm talking about the political satire of the network late-night hosts like Jimmy Kimmel, Seth Meyers, and occasionally Jimmy Fallon.

The term *satire* refers to a specific subgenre of humor. Satire is playful and is intended to elicit laughter, but it also articulates a political or social judgment in an antagonistic or aggressive fashion.[28] Satire advances critiques of society and institutions and in so doing forces its audience to examine their complicity. The target of satire might be political figures, institutions, or practices. It might be social or cultural conventions that have political implications. Or, it might just be us: the public.

While the history of political satire in the United States is slightly chaotic, I can say with confidence that there are several plot points that the story of satire does *not* include. It does not include a deliberate effort on behalf of politicians, former politicians, government officials, or party leaders to intentionally counter the influence of a competing political ideology. It does not include strategic political mobilization of audiences with an explicit goal of attaining or exerting political power. It does not include stories of dog food or candy company magnates working to fund the spread of an ideology. And it certainly doesn't include former FBI agents, law school deans, or White House administrative officials who abandon those insider positions to move public opinion from the outside. And while the history of conservative opinion media centers on a handful of key powerful players, the history of political satire includes too many people to count, let alone name.

Now, at the risk of excluding a whole lot of things…here are some core elements that the history of American political satire *does* include. It includes myriad eccentric characters: youths, misfits, pessimists, dreamers, and people using drugs—mostly marijuana and LSD. It includes stories of collaborations and rivalries, solo acts and ensembles. It includes experimentation and play, artistic expression and broad forms of social activism. It includes people of color and women—not in huge numbers, but they are there. And it plays out against the backdrop of major American cities in the north and on the coasts: Chicago, New York, San Francisco, and Los Angeles.

While the goals of the conservative media of the 1950s and 1960s were explicitly political, the goals of political satire from this same era can be characterized as experimental: play and artistic discovery designed to move people—making them (both the performers and audience) feel things. Yes, most political comics were seeking to deconstruct and challenge the dominant political and social order—but these objectives were typically guided by the spirit of play and experimentation, not by an explicit political goal.

Since I am not a historian but a social scientist, my historical understanding of these eras comes largely from accounts of others. These accounts vary in scope and focus. There is no definitive book on "the history of American political satire," mainly for the problems of mercury-being-impossible-to-put-back-into-a-thermometer that I referenced earlier. There are, however, several important accounts that have shaped my understanding of American political satire's history. Kliph Nesteroff's *The Comedians* offers the most thorough account of the history of American comedy.[29] Reading Nesteroff is a bit like sitting down with your grandfather and hearing disparate tales of the good old days, except it includes *lots of* days. Other comedy historians focus in on one particular comedy movement or one subgenre. For the history and spirit of improvisational comedy, Jeffrey Sweet's *Something Wonderful Right Away* offers a compilation of interviews with improvisational performers and directors from the founding members of The Second City and the Compass Players. For the definitive account of political stand-up comedy, Peter Robinson's scholarly work *The Dance of the Comedians* provides details and context to make some sense of this rather chaotic history. To provide a glimpse of the work of the radical political comedy group The Committee, documentary film producer Sam Shaw generously shared with me some early clips from his current project with Jamie Wright: *The Committee: A Secret History of American Comedy*. For some of the more vivid details, I rely on firsthand accounts from improvisational artists and comics from the 1960s, 1970s, and 1980s, like Alan Myerson, Ed Greenberg, David Misch, Latifah Taormina, and Debi Durst, all of whom gave time to be interviewed for this book.

The history of political humor is full of splintered narratives and countless characters; yet there is a key era when many of these stories seem to overlap. It is on this historical time and place where I focus my attention—to provide some understanding of the roots of contemporary American political satire and to contrast it to the roots of conservative media. The characters at the heart of this tale make up the core influences of today's political satirists— either directly, through mentorship, direction, and training, or indirectly, through the impact they have had on other performers, formats, and programs that have influenced the work of today's political satirists. What is most striking about this story is that it occurs *at the very same time* that Clarence Manion, Dan Smoot, and H. L. Hunt were creating a conservative political presence on radio networks across the country: the mid- to late 1950s into the 1960s. It was at this same moment that early counterculture comics like Lenny Bruce, Mort Sahl, and Dick Gregory, along with artists from improv groups like The Second City and the Compass Players, were experimenting with improvisational structures and content that were different in form and function from anything audiences had seen before. So, just as the disaffected antiinterventionists created a vast collection of "hate clubs of the air," a handful of experimental, boundary-breaking artists were creating entirely new forms of expression that would establish the foundation of the political satire of today.

The Comedy of the Counterculture

In the late 1950s and 1960s, San Francisco was the heartbeat of America's radical counterculture. The spoken-word and comedy routines coming out of San Francisco's coffeehouse scene included these satirists: Mort Sahl, Dick Gregory, and the infamous Lenny Bruce. Along with the groundbreaking work of these stand-up comics, a radical improvisational comedy theater venture called The Committee would come to embody and propel the spirit of that counterculture into American political comedy for decades to come. Many of The Committee's members would become writers and performers on *The Smothers Brothers Comedy Hour*, the short-lived variety show whose emerging political ideology in 1968 and 1969 placed it at odds with the White House and CBS executives. The Committee would also become the temporary home to Second City–trained improvisational guru Del Close, who later returned to Chicago's improv scene, where he mentored comedians from Bill Murray to Tina Fey, who would find fame on *Saturday Night Live* and in solo careers.

The Committee's founders, Alan Myerson and Irene Riordan, met in 1961 through their early work at Chicago's improvisational comedy theater The Second City. Throughout the 1940s, the influential theater instructor Viola Spolin developed acting exercises designed to help young performers discover characters and emotions organically on stage. Spolin's "theater games," as they were called, became the framework for the experimental improvisational theater launched by her son Paul Sills and several of his University of Chicago classmates. It was there—at The Second City—that Spolin's theater games became a central part of the American improvisational theater tradition. "Rather than telling the performer specifically how to behave," Jeffrey Sweet writes, "Spolin's [games] set up circumstances in which [an actor] would arrive at the right choice himself. Her belief was that an actor will absorb a lesson more readily if it is learned through his own experience than if it is spelled out by someone else."[30]

By 1962, Myerson and Riordan, now married, had left Chicago and The Second City and settled into a loose network of academics, psychologists, and artists in San Francisco. It was a natural pairing for the notably progressive city: an art form based on creating something from nothing: engaging in spontaneous collaboration on stage and infusing art with a spirit of radical politics and activism. With financial help from their diffuse network of acquaintances and admirers, in 1963 Alan and Irene opened a 300-seat improvisational theater in North Beach (photo 1.3). They called themselves The Committee.

According to Riordan (now Latifah Taormina), "it was the combination of the group ethic of our work...and the allusion to the House Un-American Activities Committee and its significance to San Francisco and Berkeley that made The Committee the perfect name for us."[31] The Committee's work was socially and culturally provocative and explicitly political. As Committee member Carl Gottlieb explains, "The Committee didn't dabble in politics. It had a political base from the first day it opened....The environment was always political. The Committee started as a group that was intent on doing more political satire than social satire. The Second City had made social satire their goal and they didn't dabble too much in politics."[32] Although the work of The

PHOTO 1.3 Members of The Committee standing in front of The Committee Theater, 622 Broadway, San Francisco (c. 1970). Courtesy of Ed Greenberg.

Second City had been informed by the politics of the moment and of their members, political activism was not at the center of their performances. But at The Committee, Myerson regularly brought a newspaper to rehearsal to allow the players to improvise scenes based on the headlines of the day. The political world shaped everything they did.

One of The Committee's best-known sketches, "The Star-Spangled Banner,"[33] was typically performed at the closing of their show. The sketch featured about a dozen members of the company standing in a line across the front of the stage, proudly singing the national anthem—except for one person, situated toward the center of the stage, who remained seated. The seated performer was usually one of the more innocent-looking, gentle-spirited company members. As the players began singing, they gently tapped the seated gentleman, encouraging him to stand and sing. The gentle tap turned into a sharp elbowing from both sides. The sharp elbowing then became violent tugging as other members across the stage approached him and urged him to stand for the anthem. As he continued to quietly refuse, the attempts to bring him to his feet grew more aggressive. Finally, as the anthem reached the climactic "Oh say does that star-spangled banner yet wave," the entire company dragged him from his seat, threw him to the ground, and proceeded to kick and "beat

PHOTO 1.4 The Committee's *Wide World of War* (1973), album artwork by Ernie Cefalu. Courtesy of Sam Shaw and Jamie Wright.

him to death." The act closed with the corpse lying there as the remaining performers continued to sing, hands over hearts, the final line: "O'er the land of the free and home of the brave," followed by a blackout.

The Committee blended genres and concepts in order to reveal—through metaphor—larger truths about politics, society, and war. One such work was an audio recording featured on their 1973 LP *Wide World of War*. The album's cover art features a running back in a military helmet, a marine in a football helmet, football players adjacent to military tanks, and corpses in wooden boxes (photo 1.4). The recording begins with the comic narrators describing a scene from "a broadcast booth high above the playing field in southeast Asia." They then narrate a military action in the quick cadence and varied intonation of a typical NFL announcer:

It's apparent that we're in for a scintillating contest here this afternoon! Both teams are really in tip-top shape for this one. And in the case of the 101st, that's due in no small part to their coach, Colonel William "Billy" Slocum, who has really—as they say—"got em up" for this one! That's obvious in everything they're doing out there: the way they come busting out of those helicopters; the way they begin shooting long before they've actually seen anything. This is not to take anything away from the Viet Cong, though. They're a rugged opponent at any time. They've had a wonderful season and no one can take that away from them.[34]

Although collaborative improvisational political satire was new to San Francisco, the city was a hub of artistic and musical experimentation and political expression. The Haight-Ashbury district was home to beatniks, hippies, artists, and musicians commingling with students from the University of California at Berkeley and the University of San Francisco—all navigating their way through the volatile McCarthy era of the 1950s. It was then that the city became home to a circuit of coffeehouses where spoken-word poets and comics made their mark. A *Variety* editorial highlighted the emergent coffeehouse scene as an incubator for entertainment talent: "there's every indication this newly created atmosphere will become an important spawning ground for new show business entities. It already has happened in San Francisco where a young comedian-satirist named Mort Sahl first found an audience."[35]

Mort Sahl was the Berkeley-based stand-up comedian who ruminated on matters political, social, and philosophical, clad in a red sweater-vest, speaking quickly and without pause. His material was cerebral, revolutionary, and largely devoid of punch lines. As Nesteroff recounts, Sahl "took credit for the [San Francisco club] circuit, [stating] 'I constructed a network of theaters where people can speak—they happen to be saloons, and people said it could not be done—in complete freedom...the whole climate has changed.'"[36] Chief among them was the "hungry i" nightclub in North Beach. It was there that Sahl was put on the map as a significant cultural voice and where comics from Joan Rivers to Bill Cosby to Woody Allen would develop their careers. And it was there that counterculture icon Lenny Bruce perfected his so-called sick comic style.

In his meandering but electrifying performances, Bruce talked about every topic Americans in the late 1950s and early 1960s were told *not* to talk about at the dinner table—or anywhere, really: religion, politics, race, and sex. His acts were filled with thick-accented characters engaging in fictional conversations; obscene language describing sexual acts; words to demean just about every kind of ethnic or religious subgroup while satirizing the very people who would use such slurs. He mocked the money-hungry corporate entertainment industry in "Adolf Hitler and the MCA," a sketch about a sleazy talent agent looking to cast Hitler in the role of dictator. He mocked whites' awkward treatment of blacks in "How to Relax Your Colored Friends at Parties." Bruce had a special contempt for hypocrisy, particularly that of self-proclaimed liberals who purported to stand for all that was good and tolerant: "liberals can understand everything but people who don't understand them. The liberal, the true liberal: 'I'm so understanding, I can't understand anyone not understanding me, as understanding as I am. I'm so liberal I've never had any *rachmones* for the white Southerner—"He tawks lahk that, he tawks lahk that"'—The poor schmuck probably doesn't even talk like that, but some schmuck in the Bronx wrote a screenplay with him 'tawkin lahk that' so the putz ends up tawkin lahk that."

At a time when any perspective that was remotely critical of Christianity was suspect, Bruce explicitly challenged the intentions of those who exploited organized religion:

> A lot of people say to me, "Why did you kill Christ?"
>
> "I don't know…it was one of those parties, got out of hand, you know."
>
> We killed him because he didn't want to become a doctor, that's why we killed him.
>
> Or maybe it would shock some people, some people who are involved with the dogma, to say that we killed him at his own request, because he knew that people would exploit him. In his name they would do all sorts of bust-out things, and bust out people. In Christ's name they would exploit the flag, the Bible, and…whew! Boy, the things they've done in his name!
>
> This routine always goes good in Minnesota, with about two Jews in the audience. But he's going to get it if he comes back. Definitely. He's going to get killed again, because he made us pay so many dues. So he's going to get whacked out. And you can tell that to the Jehovah's Witnesses, who have all those dates. As soon as he comes back, whacked out again.

Historian Peter Robinson writes: "Americans…in the later fifties and early sixties were [beginning to be] drawn to more radical standup professionals whose work had been considered beyond the pale for various reasons just a year or two before, but whose material now began to reverberate with shocking authenticity. Lenny Bruce had the greatest influence on this transformation, even though he largely avoided politics and remained unseen and unheard by most Americans."[37] Through the 1950s, Bruce's work transformed the essence of stand-up comedy. His style was simultaneously vulnerable, crass, and filled with narratives rather than jokes. His sets were largely improvised and always thrilling. A genre that had long been dominated by glib commentaries on relationships ("Take my wife...please!") and the banalities of daily life suddenly opened up to include a comedian's passions, vulnerabilities, and honesty. Lots of honesty.

"In a career that lurched from the anonymity of sleazy strip clubs to critical acclaim, then to arrests on obscenity charges, and finally to a drug overdose that killed him in 1966 at the age of forty," writes Robinson, "Bruce forced the debate over what political humor should sound like in an age of assassination, war, executive deceit, and presidential resignation."[38] Bruce would be arrested four times from 1961 to 1965 on obscenity charges (and several other times for other offenses, mostly drug related). At the site of his 1962 arrest at the Gate of Horn nightclub in Chicago, a young aspiring comic by the name of George Carlin was seated in the audience. "Lenny Bruce opened the doors for all the guys like me," Carlin said; "he prefigured the free-speech movement and helped push the culture forward into the light of open and honest expression.... Lenny opened all the doors, or kicked them down."[39]

Although Lenny Bruce made his name as a comic in the strip clubs of Las Vegas and Los Angeles in the 1950s, San Francisco was one of the cities he (occasionally) called home. It was also the city that served as the site of his first arrest on charges of obscenity in 1961, following an act at the Jazz Workshop that included the word "cocksucker" and references to ejaculation. The years when Lenny Bruce and Committee cofounder Alan Myerson overlapped in San Francisco were Bruce's later years: 1963–1966. Myerson describes Bruce as both a friend and an important influence on the work and spirit of The Committee. In fact, The Committee's first long-form piece, "The Fear, Guilt, and Impotence Collage" of 1965, was inspired by Bruce's club work. Kim Johnson describes this piece as "a compendium of sketches and improvisations, a slide show, primitive audiovisual material, as well as low-technology extras like a slide projector and a tape recording."[40] Myerson acknowledges that the content of this seminal work of long-form improvisation was directly influenced by Bruce: "The Fear, Guilt, and Impotence Collage was inspired by something that Lenny did once in a club. He was performing in San Francisco.

I had gone to see the show. He started riffing about '"what if such and such were such and such'...Making absurd metaphors. That became the inspiration for the fear guilt and impotence collage. Lenny inspired all of that."[41] "We in *The Committee* all looked up to [Lenny Bruce] tremendously," says Gottlieb. "He was influential in that he made it okay to riff onstage, to find material in performance, which is why improvisers related to him."[42]

I highlight Lenny Bruce's presence in San Francisco and his influence on Myerson and The Committee to illustrate the hybridity of the counterculture comic art of the 1960s. The Committee did not do stand-up comedy routines. Lenny Bruce never worked as part of a collaborative improvisational company. Yet the overlap in spirit and intent reflects the hybridity and collaborative spirit that defined much of the art of the 1960s.

Jeffrey Sweet writes:

> The late 50s and early 60s saw a remarkable explosion of social satire with the appearance of Lenny Bruce, Mort Sahl (satirical cartoonist) Jules Feiffer, *Catch-22* author Joseph Heller, and others. Not only were their perspectives similar, but their methods were analogous. To listen to Bruce and Sahl records is to hear two solo improvisational masters in action. Feiffer rarely knew the ending of a strip when he started drawing the beginning, but in a process analogous to improvisation, followed the pull of the internal logic established in the first panel to its relentlessly funny conclusion. Interviews with Heller indicate he followed a method not unlike Feiffer's in writing *Catch-22*.... The kinship between these satirists and the improvisers was further reinforced by frequent collaboration.[43]

The concept of "hybridity" is central to the work of the counterculture. Radical artists. Activist musicians. Guerrilla theater with political themes. Entertainment wasn't expected to "stay in its lane." It was expected—encouraged even—to blur the lines between fact and fiction, entertainment and politics, art and social justice. It was even expected to blur the lines of genre, with musical acts like Jefferson Airplane and The Warlocks (soon renamed the Grateful Dead) performing at benefit concerts organized by The Committee and other political theater groups in the city. Myerson describes this hybridity as a "cross pollination."[44]

The cross-pollination extended beyond the realm of art to the world of activism. The Committee Theater itself became a gathering place for activist groups to meet, organize, and just spend time together. It was an important and valued part of San Francisco's collective of radical movements. Myerson worked with the Artist Liberation Front, known for guerrilla-style works of art with political and social themes throughout the city. Myerson notes:

> *The Committee* was more than just a theater. It was a social phenome-
> non. We were the soup kitchen for the Red Guards and for the Black
> Panthers. The Diggers operated out of our place sometimes. San
> Francisco was a community. We were a community within it, around
> which many other communities circulated, which again seems to
> be…part and parcel of improvisation. Everybody on stage is there at
> some level to support the need of the other person. If you aren't there
> with that as your fundamental intention then there's no scene. Nothing
> happens. With all due modesty I think we were the best improvisational
> theater that came along.… What we were to each other. What we were
> to the city of San Francisco was a far more significant thing.[45]

Committee member Ed Greenberg described the salience of world events and politics at the time as "so big that you couldn't help but have it affect the work that you do." In an interview, Greenberg reminisced about the cultural moment that was late 1960s San Francisco. He emphasized the spirit of hybridity: the artists and performers, the activists and musicians. He described the aesthetic of the time as one that centered on fluidity and ambiguity. A favorite local radio station, KSAN, played the Grateful Dead, Jefferson Airplane, and Bob Dylan. The station's news reporter, Scoop Nisker, "would do these sound collages," Greenberg recalled. "They told the news in almost like a Harold [an improvisational structure] type of way. Linear structure was not at the center."[46] Near the Committee Theater was the radical drag show The Cockettes, featuring, as described by Greenberg, "men dressed in surreal makeup and evening gowns, with beards and their male genitals fully exposed." The show was so "out there," he explained. "It emphasized gender fluidity. It was really in your face in questioning 'what is gender,'" he recalled.[47]

The Committee's popularity exploded in the mid-1960s. They cast more players and staged shows in San Francisco and at the Tiffany Theater on Sunset Strip in Los Angeles, performing 13 shows each week at each venue. They even launched a temporary show on Broadway in New York City in 1964 (photo 1.5). Historian Stephen Kercher writes: "what won the admiration of student radicals and exurbanites alike were The Committee's satiric commentaries on the absurdity of the Cold War, racism, and the hypocrisy of white, middle-class liberals, among other topics."[48]

PHOTO 1.5 Playbill from The Committee's 1964 Broadway run. Courtesy of Sam Shaw and Jamie Wright.

As Myerson told Jeffrey Sweet in the 1970s, "of the original company at The Committee, there were only three college graduates. We were bright and informed, but we did not have the formal educations that the people in Chicago [The Second City] had, and our attitudes were bawdier and more raucous, which was more compatible to San Francisco than to Chicago. They are different kinds of cities and foster different kinds of attitudes."[49]

This description of the work of The Committee as "bawdy" and "raucous" speaks to the raw political and artistic culture of 1960s San Francisco. In his rich account of life in the Haight-Ashbury neighborhood in 1967, Nicholas Von Hoffman writes about the deeply felt politics that characterized the culture of the San Francisco: "it is a current of emotive, affective politics; it is politics of the gut, of feeling, of unqualified conviction, of the compulsion to act out the disposition of the soul in public and political ways. It is a politics that finds dichotomies damnable and hypocritical, that demands a perfect consistency between private and public life, a politics without distinctions of subtleties—without craft."[50]

Increasingly, through the early 1960s, the world of comedy became a reflection of such "affective politics." Dick Gregory, the African American stand-up comedian who started his career in the black nightclubs of the South, became increasingly political through the early 1960s. Gregory's comic routines dealt explicitly with civil rights, bigotry, and racism. Soon his identity as a political and social activist became more salient than his identity as a comedian. Speaking in reference to his speech at a voter registration drive in Jackson, Mississippi, Gregory said: "for the first time, I was involved. There was a battle going on, there was a war shaping up, and somehow writing checks and giving speeches didn't seem enough. Sure I could stay in the nightclubs and say clever things. But if America goes to war tomorrow would I stay at home and satirize it at the Blue Angel? I wanted a piece of the action now."[51] Gregory also stated without equivocation: "I'm a Negro before I'm an entertainer."[52]

As the counterculture's influence grew, so did the audiences of The Committee. As their audiences grew and The Committee staged regular shows in both San Francisco and Los Angeles, improvisers from around the country sought performing opportunities with them. Perhaps the most broadly influential of all the improvisers who joined The Committee was Del Close. A comic improviser who had worked with Myerson at The Second City in the late 1950s, Close went on to teach and direct some of the most important names in comedy through the 1970s and 1980s, including Tina Fey, Rachel Dratch, Bill Murray, Mike Myers, John Belushi, Chris Farley, and Dan

Aykroyd. "Del's great talents were as an inspirational teacher and evangelizer," Myerson observes. "He was a great salesman of improvisation. A fabulous salesman."[53] Such a fabulous salesman was Del that he was hired by Lorne Michaels at *Saturday Night Live* to serve as an on-site improvisational theater coach and had himself listed in the show's closing credits as "House Metaphysician."[54]

The Committee's influence was palpable with live audiences in San Francisco and Los Angeles. But their performances also influenced young comics and writers and emerging leaders in the entertainment industry. Gottlieb recalls: "we were a success across the board, full houses and doing great business, so much so that the Hollywood establishment all came to the shows."[55] Among the "Hollywood establishment" who came to see The Committee in 1967 and 1968 were the hosts of one of television's most popular programs at the time: Tommy and Dick Smothers.

The Smothers Brothers was a musical comedy duo consisting of the real-life brothers Tommy and Dick Smothers, whose wholesome look, affable personalities, musical talents, and comedic banter made them a hit on popular variety shows of the 1960s, including *The Jack Benny Program* and *The Jack Paar Show*. In 1967, CBS offered the brothers their own show, *The Smothers Brothers Comedy Hour*, a variety show featuring comedy sketches and musical guests from the emerging folk and rock scenes, from Joan Baez to The Doors. The show was an instant hit with young people. Robinson observes: "young people delighted in the smart writing, irreverent send-ups of popular folksongs, and appearances by top music acts."[56] The Committee (its performers and its sketches) were featured prominently on several episodes of *The Smothers Brothers* in 1968 and 1969, with Committee member Leigh French appearing regularly as a stereotypical free-loving counterculture hippie.

By the show's third season, produced in 1969, there was a marked shift in the tone of the writing of the sketches. Robinson explains: "the Smothers Brothers were not politically active initially; they achieved fame with material which echoed that of their mentors from mainstream comedy's golden age.... [But] as the Vietnam War waxed and the decade waned, however, they turned towards topical satire influenced both by their more radical contemporaries and by the daily headlines from the war and the civil rights struggle."[57] It was just prior to their third season that the brothers hired a handful of new writers who shared their political perspective, which was explicitly antiwar and pro–civil rights. These included Committee members Rob Reiner and Carl Gottlieb, as well as the stand-up comic and improvisational musician

Mason Williams. Williams soon brought on board a new writer, a young up-and-coming comedian named Steve Martin.

As the Smothers Brothers' facial hair and sideburns grew longer and more unruly, so did their sketches. Soon the brothers (mainly Tommy) found themselves regularly at odds with CBS network executives. "[The Smothers Brothers] were the first members of their generation with a prime-time pulpit, and they used it," writes TV critic David Bianculli. "Each season, the average age of their writing staff got younger, and the satiric edge of the material being televised—or censored—got sharper."[58] The network's close relationship with the White House made the increasingly antiwar angle of the show problematic from the network's standpoint. CBS's Standards and Practices Department (aka network censors) began to clamp down on the topics and wording in the show's sketches. They demanded advance scripts and copies of the taped shows prior to airing. What resulted was a fight over artistic expression that the corporate network giant—and Tommy himself—were both intent on winning. CBS canceled the show midseason in 1969, and the Smothers Brothers later won a $1 million settlement against the network for breach of contract.

While *The Smothers Brothers Comedy Hour* was only on the air for three seasons, the work of the Smothers Brothers and the writing of those politically minded young comics from Los Angeles and San Francisco helped shape the political satire genre of today. The show mainstreamed the music, comedy, and ethos of the counterculture for much of the American public. Robinson writes: "*The Smothers Brothers Comedy Hour* marked a significant transformative step in the final shift of political comedy performance from the tentative fringes of American popular culture to center stage."[59] More broadly, the ironic sensibility and progressive politics of the counterculture—Mort Sahl, Dick Gregory, Lenny Bruce, The Committee—once relegated to the smoky underground clubs and coffeehouses, were now prominently on display in America's living rooms.

2

Political and Technological Changes That Created Jon Stewart and Bill O'Reilly

JUST AS THE early 1960s marked an important moment for the first generation of American satire and outrage, 1996 was an important year for the second generation of these two competing genres. It was in 1996 that two shows at the center of this story launched on cable television. The first was *The Daily Show*, a news parody and satire program on Comedy Central that showed up in July. The second, appearing in October of that year, was a news "analysis" show featuring the conservative pundit Bill O'Reilly, which was introduced as an offering of the new 24-hour Fox News Channel.

The Daily Show, created by Lizz Winstead and Madeleine Smithberg, was initially hosted by comedian Craig Kilborn delivering mock news in a fake news studio. The show featured headlines from the day's pop culture news and introduced fictional correspondents in pretend "field segments" interviewing strange and eccentric people. With Kilborn at the helm, *The Daily Show* focused more on popular culture and celebrity news than it soon would under the more politically minded Jon Stewart, who was brought on as host in 1999. As Stephen Colbert explains, "it turned from local news, summer kicker stories, and celebrity jokes [under Kilborn], to something with more of a political point of view. Jon has a political point of view. He wanted us to have a political point of view, and for the most part, I found that I had a stronger one than I had imagined."[1] Stewart (and his executive producer and head writer Ben Karlin, a former *Onion* editor) transformed *The Daily Show* into a political satire vehicle in 1999, but the news parody atmosphere, aesthetic, and format of the show were created in 1996.

Just three months later, a few channels down (or up) the dial (cable box), a former tabloid television show host got his own show at the behest of media mogul Roger Ailes. On the new Fox News Channel, Bill O'Reilly, who had hosted the celebrity entertainment news show *Inside Edition* for six years, launched *The O'Reilly Report* (later renamed *The O'Reilly Factor*). From its inception, this show was positioned as a hybrid news and opinion program that quickly came to define the conservative television talk genre. It also dominated cable news ratings for well over a decade, up to O'Reilly's termination by the network following charges of sexual harassment in 2017.[2]

The twin births of *The Daily Show* and *The O'Reilly Factor* were no accident. Both programs are logical outgrowths of simultaneous changes in the economic and regulatory underpinnings of the media industry and the development of new cable and digital technologies. Books have been written on the structural changes in media industries in the 1980s and 1990s. Still more books have been written about the technological revolution caused by cable and the internet. I don't need to rewrite those books here. However, to explain how and why satirists Jon Stewart and Bill Maher and outrage hosts Bill O'Reilly and Sean Hannity within a period of just a few years all began hosting quasi-political entertainment programs (or quasi-entertainment political programs) I've got to talk media regulation, media economics, and media technologies.

At least for a minute.

The Reagan Era's Deregulation of Media

The story goes like this. In the 1980s the Reagan administration pushed to deregulate various industries. From the oil and gas industries to the financial sector, the notion was that reliance on the free market rather than government "interference" was the best way to grow the economy. Among the industries deregulated under Reagan was the rapidly growing media industry. In the 1980s under Reagan, the regulatory powers of the FCC over media content and media industry behaviors all but disappeared. The FCC removed requirements on the amount of informational programming that broadcasters had to supply and repealed the fairness doctrine, which had required that broadcasters give "equal time" to competing political voices. Under Reagan, the FCC also reduced limits on media ownership. These limits had previously restricted the quantity of media companies that could be owned by a single entity. For example, a single entity was permitted to own no more than seven television stations in 1981. By 1985, that number had increased to 12.[3]

These changes in the economic and regulatory underpinnings of media fueled a focus on profit—mainly because the potential for profit was just so huge. With few limits on the number of holdings allowed by the government, large conglomerates began to form, as media giants capitalized on economies of scale. Large corporations began to acquire smaller media enterprises at a record pace, thereby vastly increasing profits by increasing efficiency and eliminating redundant positions and departments. Putting multiple media holdings (television networks, movie studios, film distributors, cable networks, radio stations, publishing companies) all under the same roof also reduced costs as it allowed for cross-merchandising across these growing corporate empires.

Take, for example, Disney. In 2019, Disney owns ABC, the Disney Channel, ESPN, Marvel, theme parks, cruise lines, and 30 percent of Hulu (to name just a tiny few). By collapsing all these companies under the Disney umbrella, each of the smaller holdings is able to save money internally. Need marketing done? No problem. Need financing? No problem. Need production studios? Got it. Need capacity for distribution? Got it. Need to get a product in stores? Got it. Want to promote a new show on a family cruise line? Weird request, but sure.

And the real genius of the consolidation of media ownership (from a profit standpoint) is that it maximizes the owners' ability to promote their brands across their many holdings. Industry folks enthusiastically refer to this as "synergy." Synergy is when ABC airs the Disney parade, thereby promoting Disney theme parks to a national audience on their television network. Or when an episode of *Modern Family* (on ABC) features the Pritchett family enjoying themselves in Disneyland. Or when *Dancing with the Stars* (on ABC) has "Disney Night," when the dancing couples perform to famous songs from Disney's giant film archive, from *Alice in Wonderland* to *Beauty and the Beast*. Free marketing across the media empire. And yes, all of these cross-merchandising activities have actually happened.

The capacity for profit in media industries is so great that it fueled, through the 1990s and into the 2000s, the consolidation of ownership across our vast media landscape. For the better part of the twentieth century, each individual mass media industry—newspapers, film, television, magazines—was controlled by multiple medium-specific companies. Media historian Robert McChesney writes that each individual media industry was "dominated by anywhere from a few to a dozen or so firms."[4] As recently as 1983, over 50 different corporations owned most of American media. By the mid-1990s that number had dropped to 23.[5] And by 2000, the dire prediction by Ben Bagdikian, author of *Media Monopoly*, that a "half-dozen large corporations would own all the most powerful media outlets in the United States" had come to pass.[6]

In 2019, over 90 percent of American media is controlled by five corporations: Comcast, Walt Disney Corporation, 21st Century Fox, AT&T–Warner Media, and National Amusements (which includes Viacom and CBS). The latest trend in consolidation of media ownership is in the direction of vertical integration, in which corporations that own the dominant mode of distribution (the internet) are also acquiring content producers (the entities that make the stuff that goes on—or through—the internet). For example, during the writing of this book, AT&T (internet service provider) acquired Time Warner (content producer), making it a direct competitor with Comcast (internet service provider), which entered the content business back in 2009 with the acquisition of NBC Universal (content producer).

In sum: media deregulation means fewer—and much larger—corporate owners of media.

Profit-Oriented "Journalism" and Erosion of Trust in News

In *Rich Media, Poor Democracy*, McChesney included a section pessimistically titled "Farewell to Journalism." Here he explained how the "commercialization" fueled by the formation of media conglomerates in the 1980s and 1990s contributed to "the decline and marginalization of any public service values among the media, placing the status of notions on nonmarket public service in jeopardy across society."[7] In other words, in a corporate media world, concerns like "what we should do" or "what would be good for citizens" are trumped by considerations of profit. Hence, in the corporate media world, the practice of journalism itself becomes a bit of an afterthought. According to Bagdikian, "the immense size of the parent firms means that some of their crucial media subsidiaries, like news, have become remote within their complex tables of organization. That remoteness has contributed to the unprecedented degree to which the parent firms have pressed their news subsidiaries to cross ethical lines by selecting news that will promote the needs of the owning corporation rather than serve the traditional ethical striving of journalism."[8] In their canonical work *The Elements of Journalism*, Bill Kovach and Tom Rosenstiel outline normative obligations of contemporary journalism, or "what we should expect from those who provide the news."[9] Two obligations in particular are central to the problem posed by the consolidation of media ownership. Kovach and Rosenstiel contend that the owner/corporation at the head of a news organization must be committed to citizens first, and that journalists must have final say over the news. Kovach and Rosenstiel also propose that journalists' first obligation is to the truth and their first loyalty is to citizens.

By the accounts of media and journalism historians, this normative ideal actually was the model of journalism that dominated throughout much of the twentieth century. In a rare positive description of media practice, McChesney writes: "journalism has been regarded as a public service by all of the commercial media throughout [the twentieth century]. In particular, commercial broadcasters displayed their public service through the establishment of ample news divisions.... Professional journalism was predicated on the notion that its content should not be shaped by the dictates of owners and advertisers or by the biases of the editors and reporters, but rather by core public service values."[10] To be fair, though, William Randolph Hearst and Joseph Pulitzer did make a mockery of the idealized obligations of the newspaper industry with the "yellow journalism" of the 1890s, which included sensationalized and fabricated accounts of war atrocities that contributed to the United States' involvement in the Spanish-American War. And these practices were driven by a circulation race between these two media moguls. But in the wake of this disgraceful moment, the American Society for Newspaper Editors (ASNE) created a code of ethics for journalists (in 1923), consisting of canons that journalists should follow to protect the integrity of the practice of journalism. The spirit of this code of ethics remained at the heart of the practice of journalism at newspapers and networks for decades. The code says: "the primary function of newspapers is to communicate to the human race what its members do, feel and think. Journalism, therefore, demands of its practitioners the widest range of intelligence, or knowledge, and of experience, as well as natural and trained powers of observation and reasoning. To its opportunities as a chronicle are indissolubly linked its obligations as teacher and interpreter."[11] The code contains the following canons: responsibility to the public welfare; freedom of the press; independence from private or partisan interests; sincerity, truthfulness, and accuracy; impartiality; fair play, and decency.

Based on the high rates of trust in news in the United States through the 1960s and 1970s, it would seem that the ASNE code was successful in fostering public trust in journalism at the time. The Roper Center for Public Opinion Research and the American National Election Study data show that in the 1950s–1960s, 65–70 percent of Americans thought the news was "fair." In 1972, Gallup reported that 68 percent of the public said they had "a great deal" or "a fair amount of trust" in news organizations to "report the news fully, accurately, and fairly." The Watergate scandal of 1972–1974 highlighted the "watchdog" capacity of the press, with fierce investigative reporting by Bob Woodward and Carl Bernstein at the *Washington Post*. When Gallup asked their "trust in news" question in 1976, 72 percent of the American public reported trusting news organizations—a historical high.

Through the 1990s and into the 2000s, though, those numbers took a precipitous turn. By 2016, the portion of people who reported trusting news organizations had dropped to 32 percent. The Pew Center for the People and the Press reports that when they began asking questions about trust in media in 1985, 72 percent of Americans viewed news organizations as "highly professional" and only 34 percent said they believed that "news stories are often inaccurate."[12] By 2011, only 57 percent of Americans saw news organizations as "highly professional," and the percentage of Americans who believed that "news stories are often inaccurate" had risen to 66 percent. Perhaps most relevant to this discussion is the percentage of Americans who reported believing that news organizations are "influenced by powerful people and organizations," a Pew statistic that rose from 53 percent in 1985 to a shocking 80 percent in 2011.

It is not a coincidence that this plummeting faith in news and growing sense that news organizations are "influenced by powerful people" happened just as media industries were deregulated and facing intense demands for profit. Put simply: profit-oriented changes in the newsrooms of the 1980s and 1990s degraded the practice of journalism. As Kovach and Rosenstiel explain, with corporate ownership, "business practices were put into the newsroom that ran counter to journalism's and citizens' best interests."[13] McChesney laments that "by the 1990s, traditional professional journalism was in marked retreat from its standards of the postwar years, due to the tidal wave of commercial pressure brought on by the corporate media system."[14] Journalism professor Herbert Gans describes the problems of postmodern journalism as "[stemming] largely from the very nature of commercially supplied news in a big country."[15]

A quick survey of research on the state of news over the past century includes countless historians, journalists, and media theorists all pointing to the same problem: corporate media. Corporate media's intense focus on profit undermines the function of journalism. Gans writes: "the crucial question about chains and conglomerates as opposed to traditional news firms is profit: how much profit are the news firms expected to deliver, and what effects do the pursuit and expenditure of profit have on the journalists? The more profit the firm demands, the less money is available to be spent on journalists and news coverage, the more bureaus have to be closed and the more shortcuts taken."[16] What kind of profits are we talking about? According to former *Washington Post* editors Leonard Downie, Jr., and Robert Kaiser, authors of *The News about the News: American Journalism in Peril*,[17] "media owners are accustomed to profit margins that would be impossible in most traditional industries."[18] Whereas General Motors might consider a profit margin of 5 percent of total revenue to be "a very good year," Downie and Kaiser describe desired profit margins of 30 percent and even 50 percent at newspapers and local news stations, respectively. "Protecting such high profits," they write, "can easily undermine the notion that journalism is a public service."[19]

Part of this dysfunction is due to the complicated economic model that supports the media industry. Unlike a "normal" economic model in which people go into a store and buy a good or service and money changes hands in exchange for that good or service, the news itself is not the product that is bought and sold in exchange for money. Sure, you pay $2 for *USA Today* at a newsstand (which itself is a quaint notion), but the actual money that is sustaining the paper comes from advertisers. And the advertisers are paying the newspaper or television network not for journalism but for access to audiences.

Kovach and Rosenstiel write: "in short, the business relationship of journalism is different from traditional consumer marketing, and in some ways more complex. It is a triangle. The audience is not the customer buying goods and services. The advertiser is. Yet the customer/advertiser has to be subordinate in that triangle to the third figure, the citizen." So if "journalists' first obligation is to the truth, and journalists' first loyalty is to the citizens,"[20] then any efforts to elevate the importance of advertisers or profits over citizens is antithetical to the purpose, function, and obligation of journalism—and, unfortunately, is what corporations do best. That is not intended to be read as a glib dig at corporations. That is an honest assessment of what corporate institutions are designed to do. They are designed to make profits. Their "fiduciary responsibility" is to their shareholders, full stop. McChesney writes: "the main concern of the media giants is to make journalism directly profitable, and there are a couple of proven ways to do that. First, lay off as many reporters as possible.... Second, concentrate upon stories that are inexpensive and easy to cover, like celebrity lifestyle pieces, court cases, plane crashes, crime stories, and shootouts."[21]

Is McChesney right? Is this really what journalism became in the 1990s and 2000s under pressure for corporate owners to cut costs and maximize profits? Celebrities, court cases, plane crashes, crime stories, and shootouts?

According to Downie and Kaiser, former *Washington Post* editors who had been with the paper since the mid-1960s, McChesney isn't too far off. In their 2002 book *The News about the News: American Journalism in Peril*, they describe a news industry squeezed for profits, producing at the whim of news "consultants" brought in to newsrooms to tell journalists "what audiences want." They detail the vast cuts to investigative journalism and a reduction in foreign bureaus and correspondents across the globe—at both newspapers and television news organizations alike. They describe a shift in favor of cheaper content, including the rise of television "pundits," people talking about news in lieu of journalists investigating and reporting news, or, as they put it, "the substitution of talk, opinion, and argument for news."[22] Downie and Kaiser see this dire situation as the result of corporate motives prevailing unchecked across the media landscape. As they put it, "much of what has happened to news has been the by-product of broader economic, technological, demographic and social changes in the country. Most newspapers, television networks, and local television and radio stations now belong to giant, publicly owned corporations far removed from the communities they serve. They face the unrelenting quarterly profit pressures from Wall Street now typical of American capitalism."[23]

The first time I was introduced to these problematic aspects of news was through the work of University of Washington professor W. Lance Bennett, author of *News: The Politics of Illusion*.[24] This book, which I read as an undergraduate at the University of New Hampshire in 1998, was first published in 1983. Its tenth edition was published in 2016. In it, Bennett explores the importance of journalism to democratic health and the latest trends in news dissemination and reception. In spite of the many revisions to Bennett's text over time, what has remained consistent over most of its 30-year life span is its articulation of four major "information biases" present in news: personalization, dramatization, fragmentation, and the authority-disorder bias.

According to Bennett, stories about individual people and personalities predominate over stories about systems and policies in mainstream news content, a phenomenon called "personalization." The focus is on stories—narratives constructed with a beginning, middle, and end—to satisfy audiences' supposed need for conflict, closure, and yes, drama ("dramatization"). Bennett explains that "news dramas emphasize crisis over continuity, the present over the past or future, and the personalities at their center. News dramas downplay complex policy information, the workings of government institutions, and the bases of power."[25] These stories are presented as discrete, self-contained entities, with little, if any, exploration of how they are connected. These little nuggets of chaos are absent historical, economic, polit-ical, or cultural context, so "the impression is created of a world of chaotic events and crises that seem to appear and disappear because the news picture offers little explanation of their origins" ("fragmentation").[26] Finally, a dance in news content moves back and forth between disorder and chaos on the one hand and authority and order on the other (the "authority-disorder bias"). As outlined by Murray Edelman, news programs construct "a series of threats and reassurances" that repeatedly scare people and then tell them everything is fine.[27] Bennett, heavily influenced by Edelman's work, puts it a bit more con-cretely: "writing dramatic endings for fragmented stories often becomes the highest imperative in the newsroom. Sometimes authorities save the day, and order is restored to some corner of society. Sometimes authorities fight val-iantly, but the forces of evil are simply overwhelming, and disorder seems to prevail."[28] The four information biases Bennett describes can be viewed as a direct result of the profit pressures already discussed. Information biases help illustrate the answer to questions like these: What does news look like when news organizations chase what they think the public "wants," while trying to simultaneously reduce production costs? What does news look like when news organizations gut their investigative units and so increasingly rely on official sources for information? What happens when journalists are under pressure to entertain audiences, to captivate them in an effort to keep them coming back?

Personalization, dramatization, fragmentation, and authority-disorder bias offer a way to categorize the systemic trends in the selection and framing of news programs that are an outgrowth of an industry focused on ratings and cheap production routines. Bennett discusses these information biases as part of a trend toward commercialism that has contributed to "the fall of jour-nalism."[29] "News organizations are being driven into the ground by profit pressures from big corporations that now own most of them," he writes, pointing to the fact that this trend "has been in motion for over 20 years, with devastating effects on the reporting of so-called 'hard news.'"[30]

Why Political Polarization? (And No, It's Not All the Media's Fault)

While the erosion of the practice of journalism was certainly to blame for some of the decline of faith in news that has occurred over the last 30 years, it's not entirely the fault of a profit-centered media system. At least part of this decline can be attributed to the nation's political polarization. This trend, characterized by a more consistently liberal Democratic Party platform, a more consistently conservative Republican Party platform, and an eroding ideological middle, has made news viewers—and citizens—harder to please. Political communication scholars have documented a "hostile media effect," in which viewers perceive balanced news reporting to be hostile toward their own ideological position, an effect that is especially concerning in a sharply divided political climate.[31] But political polarization is is also the result a complex series of structural, political, and technological factors.

If you live in the United States, partisan gridlock, "all-or-nothing" politics, and compromise as a "dirty word" characterize your political world. Indeed, the Democratic and Republican parties are farther apart from one another on the issues than they have been in decades.[32] The average Democrat and the average Republican are both more homogenous in their own issue positions than they were in the 1990s, with fewer Democrats holding at least some conservative issue positions and fewer Republicans holding at least some liberal issue positions. According to data from the Pew Research Center, the ideological placement of the average Republican has moved to the right while that of the average Democrat has moved to the left. What this leaves is an ever-shrinking political "middle" and a reduced possibility of bipartisan compromise. And while the parties move farther apart ideologically, an increasing number of Americans are describing themselves as politically independent rather than identifying with a political party. If viewed in the context of polarization as a movement of the two major parties to the extremes, this increase in American "independents" is quite logical. The rise in independent voters should be seen at least in part as an outcome of the polarization of the Democrats and Republicans, which leaves those in the ideological middle without a political home.

The roots of America's political polarization don't just go back to the 1990s, however. They don't start with the partisan cable news networks. Instead, this movement away from ideological moderation in the direction of ideological extremity and homogeneity dates back to important social and cultural shifts, as well as changes in the party nominating processes and in the media environment. In the 1960s, as civil rights took center stage in American politics, the two parties' positions on issues related to race began to crystallize. This phenomenon, referred to by Edward Carmines and James Stimson as "issue evolution," transformed the Democratic Party into the party of civil rights and the Republican Party into the party of states' rights.[33] Meanwhile, over the past 40 years, the parties were also in the process of distinguishing themselves on so-called social issues; most notably abortion, gay rights, and other matters relating to the separation of church and state. As described by Geoffrey Layman, Thomas Carsey, and Juliana Horowitz, "cultural polarization began in Congress, in party platforms, and among party activists, and then was translated into growing divisions between the parties' mass coalitions."[34] In other words, party elites staked out their "policy territories," and then strong party identifiers followed suit.

Polarization between the parties has also been exacerbated indirectly by changes in the way primary elections are conducted—and in how candidates have changed their behaviors as a result. After years of party nominees being selected by party insiders behind closed doors, progressive reformers in the 1910s and 1920s sought to reduce the power of party bosses and bring transparency to the process. By shifting the selection of party nominees to voters through primary elections, the thought was that the process would become less opaque and would reduce corruption in party politics. It was a laudable goal, and a completely reasonable set of expectations. In practice, though, the primary process, while reducing shady insider dealings, has had the unintended consequences of increasing polarization—in two ways.

First, very few citizens actually vote in primary elections. And those who do are more politically engaged and ideologically extreme that most party members. Less than 30 percent of eligible voters typically participate in primary elections. In 2016, that number was 28.5 percent.[35] General election turnout is bad enough (usually between 50 and 60 percent), but less than 30 percent? People who vote in political primaries tend to be highly engaged and attentive to politics (which is great), but they also tend to be strong party identifiers who are farther to the left than the average Democrat and farther to the right than the average Republican. This pushes the pools of Republican and Democratic primary voters farther away from the middle than the rest of the American public. This in turn contributes to the election of party nominees who are farther left and right than average party members. Second, recent research also suggests that the "extremity" of the primary electorate is not necessarily fueling polarization on its own.[36] Rather, in anticipation of "extreme" primary voters, candidates may change their behavior and positions accordingly. Anticipating more ideological and strident primary voters, candidates strategically adopt issue positions that are more ideologically extreme, hence exacerbating this phenomenon.

All of these historical factors contributing to America's political polarization have been compounded by the growing influence of outside interest groups. Issue-driven interest groups and super PACs help fund candidates who best represent their positions on the issues—positions that tend to be more extreme and less moderate. The 2010 *Citizens United* ruling by the US Supreme Court allowed for unlimited funds from individuals, corporations, and unions to flow into campaigns and elections. According to the Center for Responsive Politics, over the last decade, aided by the *Citizens United* ruling, outside spending in American elections has increased from about $500 million in 2010 to $1.7 billion in 2016, with about 99 percent of those funds coming from groups that are politically liberal (44 percent) or politically conservative (55 percent). In 2016, *only 1* percent of outside group spending came from groups that were bipartisan or neither left nor right.[37]

Of particular concern in this equation is the increasing role played by "nondisclosing groups": 501(c) nonprofit organizations that are not required to disclose the identities of their donors. In 2004, such nondisclosing groups contributed less than $6 million to US elections. By 2016 that number had risen to $180 million. And the ideological breakdown of these nondisclosing groups is astounding. In 2016, $141.9 million came from conservative nondisclosing groups, $34.4 million from liberal ones, and a paltry $2.1 million from "other" groups. Needless to say, the money that is flooding into elections isn't coming from moderate, bipartisan groups seeking compromise and middle-of-the-road approaches to public policy. Can you imagine someone willing to throw millions of dollars into a campaign because they are *really passionate*...about *moderate* issue positions?

It is worth noting that while ideological political polarization is clearly happening, political scientists are not in full agreement on whether or not this "party sorting" is a bad thing in itself.[38] This homogeneous sorting process is actually quite rational. It demonstrates the emergence of more internally consistent and constrained belief systems, which political scientist Phil Converse lamented were largely absent in the American electorate of the 1950s.[39] Converse feared that without internally consistent belief-systems, Americans' political decision-making processes were largely random, driven by group loyalties or "issues of the moment" in ways that could be easily manipulated or exploited.

While political scientists disagree on whether party sorting itself is inherently good or bad for democracy, one thing that political scientists generally agree is bad is the affective polarization that has accompanied this party sorting.[40] The term "affective polarization" ("affective" meaning emotional or feeling-based) captures Americans' increasing hostility toward members of the opposing party. Americans rate members of the opposing party less favorably

now than they did 50 years ago. They even disapprove of the mere suggestion of their child marrying someone from the opposing political party more
than they ever have. And this is true of Democrats and Republicans alike. So
polarization isn't just about the parties moving apart on matters of policy.
This is about Americans increasingly loathing members of the opposing
political party.

Political scientist Jonathan Ladd suggests that rather than thinking of
today's political media environment as one of low trust and high polarization,
one should look at the 1950s–1970s as an era of uniquely high trust and low
polarization. By all measures, though, trust in journalistic institutions has
gone down over the last 70 years. Political polarization has increased over that
same time. And these two contemporaneous trends have contributed to some
rather unhealthy aspects of contemporary American politics: partisan vitriol,
legislative gridlock, a reduction in political participation, and increasing reach
and influence of political disinformation. As I will show, this lack of trust in
news also contributed to the emergence of alternative sources of political
information in the late 1990s.

Cable and Digital Technologies Create New Programming Opportunities

Media deregulation and political polarization might not have had much of an
impact on the political information landscape without concurrent changes in
media technologies at the close of the twentieth century. If media deregulation and political polarization contributed to the erosion of public trust in
news, it was the advent of cable and digital technologies that made alternative
political information sources possible. These new technologies expanded the
breadth of the information landscape. With new outlets came increased
opportunities for experimental programming—where new hybrid genres (a
little news, a little entertainment) could test the waters in a low-risk setting.
Cable created a place for politically minded comics and entertainment-minded
pundits. It made it possible to have entire networks dedicated to comedy and
entire networks dedicated to "news."

The technology of cable originated as far back as the 1940s in the United
States. Community Access Television, was a way for people in rural areas,
whose television signals were typically obstructed by natural terrain, to import
the signals from distant network affiliates using tall community antennas
placed atop mountains or hills. These giant community antennas could pick

up television broadcasting signals that were too remote for ordinary home antennas. Coaxial cable lines could bring those amplified signals from the community antennas into local homes, increasing the distance that urban affiliates' signals could reach.[41] Residents of rural areas in the 1960s and 1970s paid for cable subscriptions for access to clear signals from nearby network affiliates. The result? Folks like my mom and dad, tucked in between New Hampshire mountains, previously unable to receive any broadcasting signals with their roof antenna, were finally able to receive a clear picture from WCVB out of Boston.

The possibility of "importing signals" through community antennas opened up programming possibilities. If signals could be amplified and imported from distant locations, why not just import the best quality programming out of Los Angeles and New York to everywhere else in the country? Well, because the FCC at the time said you couldn't. Both the 1966 and 1972 FCC rules required that cable subscriptions "must carry" a market's local network affiliates, and the 1972 rules prohibited cable companies from "'leapfrogging' nearby stations in favor of large-market independent stations."[42] But throughout the latter half of the 1970s, many of these regulations were loosened. Networks soon began using new cheap satellite technology to amplify their signals, which were then picked up by community antennas and sent through existing cable lines into homes. The FCC's Open Skies policy on satellite technology made it possible for just about anyone to launch a communications satellite, "thus leaving cable networks free to use satellite as a means of nationally distributing programming."[43] In the early 1970s, a young Ted Turner owned and operated a small independent television station, WTCG out of Atlanta. In 1976, he capitalized on the cheap combination of satellite and cable to help carry his station's signal nationwide. This new "superstation," renamed WTBS in 1979, proved highly lucrative. In 1980, using the same basic model, Turner launched the Cable News Network (CNN), the first 24-hour cable news station.

With the passage of the 1984 Cable Act, which focused on deregulating the cable industry, cable experienced explosive growth. The number of cable programming networks increased from 28 to 70 over the 1980s. The five years from 1980 to 1985 saw the birth of Black Entertainment Television (BET), CNN, Bravo, Showtime, Music Television (MTV), the Disney Channel, Lifetime, Playboy, the Financial News Network, the Weather Channel, the Discovery Channel, the Home Shopping Network (HSN), Arts & Entertainment (A&E), and American Movie Classics (AMC).[44]

"Breaking Up America"

The cable landscape was vast and growing vaster every year. As it grew, the giant mass audiences that broadcast networks had been able to reach since the 1940s began spreading out and shrinking, a process that media scholars call "media fragmentation." Instead of a handful of giant audiences consuming the same television fare, cable technology created dozens—soon hundreds—of smaller audiences consuming a whole bunch of different things. In 1951, the beloved CBS sitcom *I Love Lucy* dominated the ratings, "with 11 million families tuning in every week (and that was when there were only 15 million TV sets in the country)."[45] Can you imagine? Seventy-three percent of Americans with televisions all watching the same show at the same time. In 2017, the most watched regularly airing program, according to Nielsen, was *Sunday Night Football*, with 19 million viewers;[46] but with 301.7 million people living in homes with televisions,[47] that means that only 6 percent of folks with televisions were actually watching that "top-rated" show—a far cry from the 73 percent watching Lucy and Ricky back in 1951.

Media scholars refer to this shift rather hyperbolically as "the death of the mass audience."[48] As viewers spread themselves across an ever-widening array of programming options, the audiences of each individual program shrink. Joseph Turow explores the consequences of this "media fragmentation" in his book *Breaking Up America*, positing that because the economics of television relied so heavily on advertising revenue, it was the advertising industry in this "fragmented" media world that came to dictate what programming began to look like.[49] Yes, cable technologies—and digital technologies in the late 1990s and 2000s—increased the number of outlets and opportunities for new programming, but as Turow explains, the deliberate segmentation of audiences according to demographics and psychographics was driven by advertisers and media executives.

With hundreds of new media outlets, the question of how and where to advertise to a promising market became exponentially more complicated than it had been in the days of ABC, NBC, and CBS. Advertisers couldn't count on the efficiency of a national or local ad campaign the way they could in the 1970s. Since the products bought and sold in media economics are the audiences sold to advertisers, cable technologies rattled the economic underpinnings of the entire television industry. Advertisers scurried to find their customers across this diffuse new landscape. Media executives were stymied as well. The existence of their networks was contingent on advertising revenue. How do you sell advertisers on the idea of marketing to your cable network's really tiny audience?

According to Turow's research, media executives sold the desirability of their smaller audiences to advertisers using two claims: "the claim of efficient separation" and "the claim of a special relationship."[50] The claim of efficient separation suggested that media outlets could promise advertisers a small, homogenous audience, without the advertisers having wasted money on any-one they didn't want to try to reach. And the claim of a "special relationship?" This is the notion that because these new outlets were programmed with spe-cialized "niche" content designed for a "specific kind of person," their audi-ences were loyal, engaged, and eager to receive everything that came to them through that trusted outlet—including advertising.

The resulting media and advertising content effectively "signaled divi-sions" between Americans—based on hobbies and interests, yes, but also on race, class, lifestyle, and culture.[51] These "efficient separations" of distinct sub-groups with whom networks cultivated "special relationships" certainly helped the specificity and efficiency of advertising campaigns but also contrib-uted to cultural and even political divisions. While programming executives figured out how to put sports fans in one box (ESPN) and home décor hobby-ists in another (HGTV), they also figured out how to segment news-obsessed partisans into boxes, by means of ideologically driven 24-hour news networks that provide news and "analysis" all while supporting a particular worldview. Meanwhile, astute program developers at a new network called Comedy Central realized that young, politically knowledgeable, largely male viewers were up for grabs, too. For them, Comedy Central offered foul-mouthed "pup-pets making crank phone calls,"[52] as well as cutting—largely left-leaning—political satire.

Cable television was not created with the explicit purpose of dividing audi-ences into socially, culturally, and politically distinct enclaves. Those outcomes were merely a by-product of the economics of the new technology. But cable's emergence against the backdrop of low public trust in news and an increas-ingly polarized electorate positioned it well as the place where media producers could develop new programming genres that would satisfy their audiences' political information needs: outrage on the right and satire on the left.

3

Outrage and Satire as Responses and Antidotes

JUST AS THE first generation of irony and outrage—the counterculture comedy on the left and the "hate clubs of the air" on the right—occurred concurrently in response to the political upheaval of the late 1950s and early 1960s, the second generation of irony and outrage have a parallel history as well. The outrage programs that rose to prominence in the 1990s (radio shows like *The Rush Limbaugh Show* and cable news shows like *The O'Reilly Factor*) came on the scene at the very same time as satire shows such as *The Daily Show* and *Politically Incorrect* on Comedy Central. Both outrage and satire were articulated as reactions to perceived problematic aspects of the political information environment. Both genres were fueled by the rising political polarization and media distrust that had exploded in the last third of the twentieth century. And both genres were made possible by new media technologies of the late 1990s. In the face of political polarization and a reduction of trust in journalism, conservative talk radio's Rush Limbaugh and Fox News's Roger Ailes created programming to deconstruct the ideological bias they perceived in mainstream news. Meanwhile, comedians worked to deconstruct the bias that *they* saw in the profit-driven news of that era; not an ideological bias but a bias in favor of strategy, spin, and partisan jargon. In response, shows like *The Daily Show* and *Politically Incorrect* offered their own "antidote" to the artificial mediated political world. Using satire, parody, and irony, they would deconstruct the "political spectacle."[1]

Response Option A: Outrage

"Outrage programming": *noun*. Political commentary, typically presented on television, radio, or the internet, that is guided by the spirit of anger and indignation. In their 2014 book *The Outrage Industry*, Jeffrey Berry and Sarah

Sobieraj chronicle the growth of a new genre of political programming through the 2000s; programming that places a charismatic host at its center and employs tactics like hyperbole, sensationalism, ad hominem attack, and extreme language to "prove" that political opponents are hypocrites and like-minded viewers are morally superior.[2]

In their exploration of the roots of the so-called outrage industry, Berry and Sobieraj detail some of the same technological and regulatory changes I outlined in chapter 2. They write: "outrage has been propelled by a synergistic confluence of economic, technological, regulatory, and cultural changes that converged to create a media environment that proved unusually nurturing for outrage-based content."[3] In other words, outrage programming did not just appear out of nowhere in the 1990s. It was made technologically possible by cable and media fragmentation. It was made economically viable by political polarization and a drop in public faith in news. And was made permissible by regulatory changes that arose during that same era.

Chief among these regulatory changes that facilitated the rise of outrage was the repeal of the fairness doctrine in 1987. That act of deregulation removed the FCC's requirement that broadcasters had to present multiple points of view in the presentation of issues to the public. Rush Limbaugh's nationally syndicated radio show was (not coincidentally) launched in 1988.[4] Having been a radio DJ and politically minded radio talk show host since the 1970s, Limbaugh was well-positioned to take advantage of the FCC's ruling. *The Rush Limbaugh Show* immediately became radio's most listened-to program. For 30 years, it has retained that spot (photo 3.1). In 2018, Limbaugh continues to attract about 14 million listeners per week.[5] And he was doing this long before Fox News commentators expanded the outrage genre to television. Hemmer writes: "for the better part of a decade, from his national syndication in 1988 to the launch of Fox News in 1996, conservative media *was* Limbaugh."[6]

Limbaugh's show was and is an overt rejection of liberalism. The show's audience is decidedly conservative. According to National Annenberg Election Survey data from 2004, Limbaugh's listeners are older (53 was the mean), and overwhelmingly: male (67 percent), white (93 percent), Republican (78 percent), and conservative (85 percent).[7] As a prime illustration of Berry and Sobieraj's description of the outrage genre, the show places Limbaugh at the center, as the charismatic personality that drives the show's political perspective and orientation to the world. His tone is brash and unapologetic, riddled with ridicule of the left. He strategically uses "emotionally evocative language"—graphic descriptions of key political issues (especially in the context

PHOTO 3.1 Rush Limbaugh addressing, via satellite, the Conservative Political Action Conference, Washington, DC, February 19, 2010. Courtesy of Gage Skidmore via Wikimedia Commons.

of abortion)—designed to horrify and anger his listeners.[8] His terminology ("class envy," "econazis," "environmental whackos," "femi-Nazis," "reporter-ettes and info-babes") is deliberately designed to discredit liberals and journalists (especially female journalists). And research has shown that it works. Kathleen Hall Jamieson and Joseph Cappella document several outcomes of a person's exposure to the Limbaugh "echo chamber," including increased "moral outrage" aimed at the behavior of Democrats, increased distrust of mainstream news outlets, significant distortion of one's understanding of politicians' issue positions, and more extreme conservative issue positions.[9]

The success of Limbaugh's show served as "proof of concept" for 54-year-old Roger Ailes. Ailes had started his career in the entertainment business, as executive producer of the popular (and Emmy-winning) variety show *The Mike Douglas* show in the 1960s. By the late 1960s, Ailes had shifted his attention to politics, serving as media consultant to Republican presidents Nixon, Reagan, and George H. W. Bush. But in 1993, Ailes returned to television.[10] As Gabriel Sherman writes, in the wake of Clinton's 1992 victory, "Ailes came around to the breakthrough insight: the media industry was a much more powerful platform to spread a political message.... [He] discovered he could achieve his political goals by changing roles. Instead of being at the mercy of the networks that controlled the airtime, he could control the message by *joining* the media."[11]

Ailes's first—quite logical—move was to serve as an executive producer on Limbaugh's radio show. Soon after, in an effort to bring the success of talk radio to television, NBC brought Ailes on board as president of a new business and talk news cable network, CNBC. Part of Ailes's charge at NBC was the development of a new 24-hour television channel dedicated to opinion talk. For Ailes, a populist who had always had a disdain for elites, an all-talk political channel seemed a natural fit.[12] At the new network, called America's Talking, Ailes created programming that tackled political issues according to the language and sensibility of regular people, and he used technology to invite those regular people to become a part of the show. The formula had worked for Limbaugh, and now Ailes sought to bring the same guiding philosophy to cable.[13] In an interview with the *Los Angeles Times*, Ailes described the spirit of America's Talking: "Our society has speeded up, but the government has slowed down and our institutions are not dealing with the nation's problems. I'd like for our business shows to give viewers what I call 'take-aways,' additional information that helps them live successful lives. Talk shows are personality-driven, but I'd like to find more ways to deal with the issues that are driving people crazy."[14] Ailes's experiment was widely panned as a failure—even before it officially launched in 1994. "Many felt that the network had a down-market, public access feel," Sherman writes. One of the junior producers described the show as "very Wayne's World-ish."[15] And by 1996, America's Talking was gone. It had been transformed into MSNBC.

I should note here that while the MSNBC of 2019 is a left-leaning cable news outlet that features liberal outrage programming, that iteration of the network is quite new. When it replaced Ailes's failed America's Talking experiment in 1996, MSNBC began featuring talk shows and news analysis shows from across the political spectrum. In fact, several conservative outrage personalities, including Fox News's Tucker Carlson and Laura Ingraham, as well as conservative pundit Ann Coulter, started their cable news careers at MSNBC. After about a decade without a clear programming niche and trailing in the cable news ratings war, in the mid-2000s the network pivoted to the left and positioned itself as a liberal alternative to Fox.

Once America's Talking was replaced by MSNBC in 1996, Ailes took his reactionary populist philosophy to yet another 24-hour news channel. In partnership with conservative global media mogul Rupert Murdoch, Ailes embarked on the creation of a conservative news network, something he had talked about for years. As Hemmer recounts, "while Murdoch saw the channel as an alternative to what he saw as biased reporting in the news, it was Ailes who brought a fierce and unrelenting partisanship to the table."[16] After an unsuccessful bid to purchase CNN from Ted Turner, Murdoch opted for the next best thing, launching a cable network competitor to erode CNN's market dominance. Murdoch saw Fox as an opportunity to get back at Turner while simultaneously challenging the norms of contemporary television news.[17] Sherman writes: "together, Murdoch and Ailes were embarking on a holy mission to lay waste to smug journalistic standards. . . . Murdoch [shortly after hiring Ailes] spoke of 'a growing disconnect between television news and its audience . . . an increasing gap between the values of those that deliver the news and those that receive it.'"[18]

Ailes openly discussed his belief that liberals dominated the media. "There are 18 shows for freaks," he told Associated Press in 1995. "If there's one network for normal people it'll balance out."[19] Just as the values to which Murdoch was referring were obviously conservative values, the freaks to whom Ailes was referring were obviously liberal freaks. Statements like this expressed not just political values but psychological values as well: wanting a sense of order. Wanting to feel secure and comforted. Wanting to feel like you understand the world. "Viewers don't want to *be* informed; they want to *feel* informed," Ailes's longtime creative mentor Chet Collier would tell Fox producers.[20] This amalgam of Fox News's ideology and aesthetic emerged in Ailes's 2001 interview with Marshall Sella for the *New York Times*:

> Sitting at dinner one night at Patsy's, his favorite Italian joint in Midtown, Ailes links his channel's claim to neutrality with his own common-man posture. "There's a whole country that elitists will never acknowledge," Ailes says. "What people deeply resent out there are those in the 'blue' states thinking they're smarter. There's a touch of that in our news." Never having lost the taste for regular-guy food from his blue-collar Ohio upbringing, Ailes says he orders mac-and-cheese from the kiddie menu when staying at five-star hotels. But Patsy's carbonara is a swell substitute, and he takes tiny bites as he talks.[21]

The emotional feel of Fox News's programming was always at the center of its mission. Internal memos from the early days of the network detailed the ways it would be distinct from CNN. Instead of CNN's format, which placed news at its center, Fox would be about "personality and programming, produced information, appointment TV, news plus human interaction that was both convenient and interesting . . . with attitude."[22] Delivering news was hardly the primary goal that Fox News was setting out to accomplish. They boasted only nine news bureaus compared to CNN's 30, a staff of 700 compared to CNN's 3,500, and a budget roughly one-tenth the size of CNN's.[23]

Fox News was positioned more as a referendum on the other news channels than as a news channel in itself. In an effort to tap into the populist spirit that Ailes had championed for years, the network adopted the catchphrase "We report, you decide." It also disparaged other news networks that it characterized as spoon-feeding liberal perspectives to their audiences. In a 1996 news conference, Ailes announced the now infamous Fox News slogan: "Fair and Balanced." Since ABC, CBS, NBC, and the elite newspapers all leaned so consistently to the left, the logic went, Fox News, by positioning itself even slightly to their right, was offering a corrective to offset that "systemic ideological bias." Ailes said: "in most news, if you hear a conservative point of view, that's called bias. We believe if you eliminate such a viewpoint, that's bias. If we look conservative, it's because the other guys are so far to the left. So if we include conservatives in our promos sometimes, well...tough luck!'"[24] Internal documents from the network characterized Fox's market position thus: "By reporting stories that competitors don't cover, Fox would become a haven for viewers looking for relief from the one-sided reporting by competition."[25] But inside the network, the slogan "Fair and Balanced" was always stated with a "wink and a nod."[26]

Since "personality" and "attitude" (rather than newsgathering) were the priorities at Fox, the network stacked its programming with charismatic hosts from the entertainment world rather than journalists. By creating programming focused on charismatic people who shared the network's ideological worldview, Ailes had created an entire network to explore and cultivate the genre of "outrage." Ailes wasn't interested in A-list hosts. Ever the populist, Ailes, as Sherman writes, "valued authenticity over talent."[27] His sense was that starting the network with lesser-known talent would fuel viewer loyalty. Plus he had contempt for the coiffed, TV-head look. He believed viewers would find accessible "regular" hosts more likable and credible.[28]

Two of the outrage landscape's most notable exemplars, Bill O'Reilly and Sean Hannity, were created by Ailes at the birth of the Fox News Network. Before coming to Fox, O'Reilly had been a local news anchor turned entertainment television personality, cohosting the Hollywood celebrity gossip program *Inside Edition* through the early 1990s. At Fox's launch in 1996, Ailes gave O'Reilly his own show, one of the network's many "analysis" programs on which hosts shared their opinions on current events. On *The O'Reilly Factor*, O'Reilly would give his perspective on current events, controversies, and headlines of the day. In a segment called "Talking Points," he railed against the "liberal media," the notion of "white privilege,"[29] and "the totalitarian left on college campuses."[30] He chastised progressives for removing "Christ from Christmas" and for being "pro-illegal immigration."[31] Until the show's cancellation in 2017 after allegations of sexual harassment, *The O'Reilly Factor* was consistently one of the top-rated cable news shows. Emily Steel and Michael Schmidt of the *New York Times* write: "for a generation of conservative-leaning Fox News viewers, Mr. O'Reilly, 67, was a populist voice who railed against what they viewed as the politically correct message of a lecturing liberal media. Defiantly proclaiming his show a 'No Spin Zone,' he produced programming infused with patriotism and a scorn for feminists and what he called 'the war on Christmas,' which became one of his signature themes."[32]

Sean Hannity had garnered notoriety early in his 1980s career after being fired from his college radio station for insulting a lesbian mother on air and then adding: "anyone listening to this show that believes homosexuality is just a normal lifestyle has been brainwashed.... These disgusting people."[33] It was the American Civil Liberties Union that fought to restore Hannity's show to the station's broadcasts, citing the station's violation of Hannity's First Amendment rights. But Hannity, instead of returning to college radio, used the scandal as a marketing opportunity for his firebrand style and was quickly picked up by a radio station in Alabama, where he built an audience and a reputation as a regular-tough-talking-guy-angry-at-liberal-fascists.[34] Hannity's populist approach was especially appealing to Ailes, who invited him to join the new cable network in 1996.

While solo-hosted shows have become a mainstay of Fox News programming, until 2009 Hannity was actually featured alongside a liberal cohost. But even then, Hannity was the alpha that drove the duo's agenda, tone, and perspective. So much so, in fact, that until the network had landed on a suitable cohost, Hannity's program was affectionately entitled "Hannity and LTBD" (liberal to be determined).[35] Since 2009, however, Hannity has been a solo outrage host, and *Hannity* has earned top ratings across cable news for months on end. During the Trump administration, *Hannity* has become must-see conservative television and the source for Trump supporters' daily dose of outrage (photo 3.2). Echoing Dan Smoot's allegations of a Communist "invisible government" working in the federal government, Hannity rails against the so-called deep state, a secret powerful liberal cabal working to undermine the Trump administration at every turn. He has even suggested that the Clintons, Comeys, and Muellers are "obvious Deep State crime families trying to take down the president."[36]

PHOTO 3.2 Sean Hannity at the Conservative Political Action Conference, National Harbor, Maryland, November 5, 2015. Courtesy of Gage Skidmore via Wikimedia Commons.

In 2009, Fox brought on board a solo outrage host who would take the genre to an entirely new level. Glenn Beck, who had been a popular "shock jock" radio personality through the 1990s, had broken into television in 2006 with his program *Glenn Beck* on CNN. The show was an instant success and became CNN's second most popular show, with almost 400,000 viewers at 7 p.m. and another half million at 9 p.m.[37] In January 2009, Beck took his conservative views to Fox. This move coincided with the swearing-in of President Barack Obama, and Beck's show made Obama's domestic policies—which Beck labeled "socialist," "Marxist," and "Maoist"—the center of its ire. "Look in your rear-view mirror," Beck told the *Los Angeles Times*; "we just passed France. I think our country is on the verge of disintegration."[38] Beck would use his program to expose "dirt" on various Obama administration officials, like White House science and technology policy director John Holdren, who, Beck claimed, "has proposed forcing abortions and putting sterilants in the drinking water to control population."[39] Beck purported to reveal the "truth" about various Obama policies, for example his false claim that the Affordable Care Act actually provided insurance for dogs.[40]

Fueled by this sort of disinformation, Beck's show catapulted Fox's outrage programming into a new stratosphere of outrage—one in which the truth

value of the claims was a distant second consideration to their emotional prov-
ocation. Importantly, Beck's untruths, fearmongering, and chalkboard-con-
cocted conspiracy theories worked. Within a month of his move to Fox, he was
earning 2.2 million viewers in his time slot, more than all the other cable news
networks combined.[41] Beck's success served as a roadmap for online conspiracy outlets like *The Gateway Pundit* and *Alex Jones InfoWars*, whose popularity
has surged thanks to political polarization and social media algorithms.

Beck left Fox in 2011, reportedly after network executives told him to "stop
talking about God."[42] In a shocking twist, in 2016 he began a sort of apology
tour. A strong opponent of President Trump, he began to acknowledge the
role he himself had played in sowing seeds of Obama-hate that had contributed to Trump's rise. The *Atlantic*'s Peter Beinart writes: "the same doomsday
sensibility that helps [Beck] appreciate the menace posed by Trump led him to
massively exaggerate the menace posed by Obama—and thus to breed the
hateful paranoia on which Trump now feeds." But, Beinart writes, "Beck says
he's sorry for all that."[43]

"I played a role, unfortunately," Beck told Megyn Kelly during a 2014 interview on Fox News, "in helping tear the country apart."[44] Hence his 2016
appearance on Samantha Bee's *Full Frontal* described in the introduction.

In 2018, Fox boasts an entire lineup of similar news "analysis" (read: outrage) shows, all featuring tough-talking solo hosts who dissect the news of the
day through an accessible, conservative, angry lens. On *Tucker Carlson Tonight*,
the founder of the *Daily Caller* challenges liberal critiques of "toxic masculin-
ity,"[45] declares the concept of "white privilege" to be racist,[46] and calls liberal
feminists "insincere."[47] He talks openly of the changing demographics of the
United States as a trend that many Americans—rightfully, according to him—
find troubling. "Though most immigrants are nice...this is more change
than human beings are designed to digest," he stated, later asking: "How
would you feel if [an increase in immigrants and minorities] happened in your
neighborhood?"[48] Carlson has also become more brazen in his suggestion
that mainstream news outlets not only are "biased" but "are lying." In June
2018, the Justice Department's inspector general released a report that contra-
dicted President Trump's allegations of FBI malfeasance in the investigation
of Secretary of State Hillary Clinton's use of a private email server. On his
show, Carlson suggested that all other news outlets were misrepresenting the
report's findings, saying: "IF you're looking to understand what's actually
happening in this country, always assume the opposite of whatever they're
telling you on the big news stations. That is certainly the case here. They
are lying."[49]

On the *Ingraham Angle*, former Republican speechwriter and talk radio host Laura Ingraham criticizes proimmigration "amnesty fanatics," points to "gun rights provocateurs" trying to "repeal the 2nd amendment,"[50] calls progressive efforts to take down confederate memorabilia "Talibanesque,"[51] and suggests that professional athletes should stop talking about politics and social issues and instead just "shut up and dribble."[52] She faced advertiser boycotts after mocking 18-year-old David Hogg, Parkland School shooting survivor and gun reform activist, tweeting: "David Hogg Rejected By Four Colleges to Which He Applied and Whines about It."[53]

By placing solo outrage hosts at the helm, Ailes had succeeded in creating a "news channel" that, consistent with its mission, eschews actual journalism in favor of "personality" and "attitude." The programs define who holds in- and out-group status, remind the audience of salient threats (including liberals, immigrants, feminists, and gun control activists), and reaffirm a conservative worldview. The network identifies what events or subjects to cover, thereby "making news" out of otherwise banal events. The network also plays fast and loose with facts, frequently earning negative scores from fact-checking organizations. According to Politifact, for example, 61 percent of fact-checked claims at Fox News were deemed mostly false, false, or "pants on fire," compared to only 21 percent of the fact-checked claims at CNN.[54] While the hosts maintain that they are scrutinizing current events and illuminating truths, Berry and Sobieraj contest that claim: "because of the approach used in outrage venues, the ensuing attention offers something more akin to the captivating distortions of a funhouse mirror than to the discriminating insights of a microscope."[55]

Even as outrage hosts imply that they are the truth-tellers, they simultaneously claim that they should not be held to the same standards as actual "journalists." After all, Fox categorizes shows like these under the label "analysis programming," which they insist is distinct from their "news programming" (a label reserved for the noneditorializing news programs like the one hosted by Shep Smith, for example). But the extent to which viewers are actually making the distinction between news and analysis on Fox (or MSNBC or CNN for that matter) is questionable. For all of Hannity's claims that he is "not a journalist" but "a talk show host,"[56] his show certainly has all the trappings of news. Former CNN reporter Frank Sesno, the director of George Washington University's School of Media and Public Affairs, has this take on the issue: networks like Fox have succeeded in blurring the lines between news and analysis to the point where this distinction is moot. According to Sesno, "one of the dangers is thinking that people know the difference between the editorial page and the front page, between a commentator or pundit commenting on something alongside a reporter who's supposed to be providing facts. In this environment, when you have news, talking points and opinions all colliding, it can be really disorienting to the audience."[57] New research from Pew Research Center confirms this suspicion.[58] When given five factual and five opinion statements and asked to determine which was which, "roughly a quarter [of respondents] got most or all wrong." Most important, "Republicans and Democrats are more likely to think news statements are factual when they appeal to their side—even if they are opinions."[59]

Regardless of whether viewers can—or want to—make the distinction between news and analysis, Fox's outrage programming is hugely successful. The network's total revenues more than doubled over the course of the Obama presidency (fig. 3.1).[60] And there is reason to believe that this particular correlation might actually illustrate causation. As Berry and Sobieraj explain, successful outrage hosts tell stories that allow them to "position themselves or their political compatriots in the role of the hero or to taint enemies, oppo-

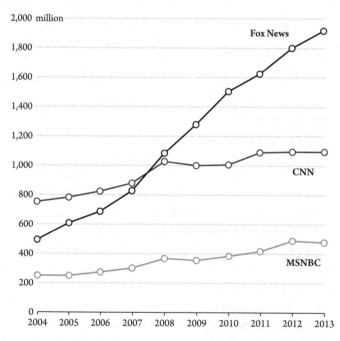

FIGURE 3.1 Cable news networks' revenues in dollars, 2004–2013. All figures are estimates.

Source: SNL Kagan, a division of SNL Financial, LLC. Courtesy of Pew Research Center.

nents or policies they dislike as dangerous, inept, or immoral."[61] Hence, outrage is designed to be "reactive"—to respond to the events, topics, and people of the day. Naturally, the Obama presidency proved to be an exceptional foil—and fuel—for Fox's outrage-centered business model.

Response Option B: Satire

In 1992, the fledging cable network Comedy Central sought to mix politics and humor in their playful coverage of the 1992 presidential election, dubbed "InDecision 92." The success of their election night programming motivated them to develop a political entertainment talk show featuring then 37-year-old political comedian Bill Maher. The show, *Politically Incorrect*, which launched in 1993, featured a comedy monologue by Maher, followed by spirited political conversation between four B-list celebrities from the worlds of television, film, and music, alongside political personalities and journalists. The success of the politics-entertainment-comedy-talk show catapulted it from cable network Comedy Central to "network"-network ABC in 1997, where it served as a staple of late-night programming until 2002.[62]

With the birth of *The Daily Show* in 1996, producers Lizz Winstead and Madeleine Smithberg set out to create a parody program that commented not just on the politics of the day but on the emerging cable news landscape that "produced" politics as entertainment. In a recollection published in *The Cut*, Winstead described sitting in a bar, watching Gulf War coverage on CNN: "we were all watching the Gulf War unfold and it felt like we were watching a made-for-TV show about the war. It changed my comedy—I started writing about how we are served *by* the media."[63] Buoyed by the spirit of experimentation and the need for content that came with the new 24-hour-cable landscape, Comedy Central signed a one-year contract for Winstead and Smithberg to "do a news satire where the genre itself was a character in the show."[64] Without a pilot and with a guaranteed year on the air to "learn, grow, and make mistakes," the producers and writers had the freedom to explore, caricature, and comment on the tropes of cable news, hence creating a template—and foundation—on which later comedy writers, producers, and hosts could build.

Just as the development of outrage at Fox was inspired by political, technological, and regulatory changes, so was the development of satire at Comedy Central. According to Jeffrey P. Jones, as a result of these changes, "television producers recognized the weaknesses in the system and began to offer new forms of political talk programming that they believed audiences were interested in seeing. Any objections that these new forms of political talk programming would be illegitimate because of their using celebrity hosts, or allowing people who were not experts to talk, or producing an entertainment spectacle all seemed moot, because of what pundit television itself had become."[65] Like Jones, I see these simultaneous trends in the rise of "new political television" like *Politically Incorrect* and *The Daily Show* and the personality-driven and populist ethos of early Fox News programming as inherently connected. They are both logical outgrowths of the political and media climate that emerged in the 1990s.

In his 2010 book *From Cronkite to Colbert*, Geoffrey Baym connects the rise of political satire to the increase in profit-seeking news that was failing in its journalistic responsibilities.[66] Baym describes Comedy Central's satire programming of the 2000s (*The Daily Show with Jon Stewart* and *The Colbert Report*) as reactions to journalism's abandonment of its "high-modern" investigative ideal. Baym chronicles the shift from the sober investigative journalism of the 1970s, replete with journalistic authority (think CBS's Walter Cronkite telling Americans at the end of each broadcast "This is the way it is"), to ratings-driven postmodern journalism, big on flash and short on substance. Baym's account focuses on how the news media of the 1990s turned away from offering news people needed in favor of news people wanted. As a consequence of the profit-seeking motives of news executives coming out of the 1990s, Baym argues, entertainment-oriented shows like *The Daily Show* and *The Colbert Report* actually embraced the spirit of "high-modern" journalism even more than the so-called news shows of the time that were failing in their journalistic mission. He writes: "*The Daily Show* holds out the hope of reinvigorating political journalism and public discourse, celebrating the quite modernist hope that we might be able to reason our way out of the predicament in which we have been mired for too long."[67]

Both Jones and Baym suggest that the political satire of the 2000s was not just emblematic of a new genre of political information but was created with the goal of challenging elite approaches to politics. Maher's show, in particular, marked a rejection of elite political discourse in a manner similar to the populist philosophy of Fox News under Roger Ailes. Maher's show was designed to put regular people, actors, journalists, and other celebrities in a conversation about politics using the language and framework that normal people use when thinking about their political world. (Sounds very much like Ailes, doesn't it?) And in perhaps the oddest illustration of the parallel histories of satire and outrage, guess who served as a celebrity guest during Maher's first taping of *Politically Incorrect* back in 1993?[68]

Roger Ailes. Yes. *That* Roger Ailes.

The missions of both genres—satire and outrage—took on new meaning and intensity in the wake of the 2001 terrorist attacks. Fox's outrage programming in the 2000s offered a consistent ideological perspective, critiquing journalism's perceived liberal bias and offering a conservative frame around world events.[69] Meanwhile, *Daily Show* host Jon Stewart, who took over from the original host, Craig Kilborn, in 1999, was positioning this news parody program as a response to his perception of the failures of mainstream journalism. Along with executive producer Ben Karlin, who had served as editor of the satire newspaper the *Onion*, the show developed a strong political point of view. In the wake of the 9/11 attacks, as the United States launched wars in Iraq and Afghanistan, Stewart's *Daily Show* offered critiques of—and a response to—the dysfunctional, symbiotic relationship between politicians and the press. The show tackled everything from the embedding of journalists with US military units in the Middle East to the failure of the White House Press Corps to adequately challenge the Bush administration on claims of weapons of mass destruction in Iraq.

Like Fox News on the right, *The Daily Show* identified perceived failures of the press while offering its own remedy to them. Stewart explicitly identified and critiqued aspects of mainstream news that he found absurd or troublesome. The parody segments on *The Daily Show* often mocked the very aspects of cable and network news programming that media scholar W. Lance Bennett described as problematic: overpersonalization, dramatization, and fragmentation. In my 2008 essay "*The Daily Show* as New Journalism," I argued that the show used irony and parody to criticize practices of the postmodern newsroom that were troubling journalism scholars like Bennett. One example from the 2004 election illustrates how Stewart was explicitly critical of cable news shows' penchant for the dramatic and personalized.

In a confident and didactic tone, Stewart introduced the program's headlines.

"So now the debates are over, both candidates have staked out their positions on domestic policy, the war on Iraq, the war on terror, and the media can finally help the American people focus in on the important issues that will help them make an informed decision on their choice for president."

The program then cut to nine different clips from news sources ranging from NBC to FOX to CNN, including such well-known newspeople as Wolf Blitzer, Katie Couric, Judy Woodruff, Bill O'Reilly, and Jack Cafferty. In each clip, the reporter referred to [Vice President Dick

Cheney's daughter] Mary Cheney's "sexuality," her being "gay" or a "lesbian." Taken together in rapid succession, the banality of the topic becomes clear. Mary Cheney's sexuality is not an issue that will 'help the American people make an informed decision on their choice for president.'" Instead it represents the dysfunctional press bias towards the personal and the dramatic.[70]

In December 2003, *The Daily Show* deconstructed the sensationalized cable news coverage of the discovery and capture of Saddam Hussein. In the US military's Operation Red Dawn, the ousted president of Iraq was found at the bottom of a deep underground hole in a town outside Tikrit. Stewart's coverage of Hussein's capture was dominated by his criticism of the way media organizations had covered the event.

> The capture of Saddam Hussein was obviously a huge story. But here's the problem from the point of view of the 24 hour cable news standpoint: it's only one story. It happened and now it's no longer happening. There's still 24 hours to fill. So how are you going to do it? Well...[cut to various computer models shown on CNN and Fox] 48 hours of nonstop computer simulations that boil down the concept of "guy in hole" to something even they layman can understand. But computers are so cold, impersonal, so...accurate. [Cut back to Stewart] Is there some theatrical, cheesy, low budget, perhaps way of doing this? ah yes...MSNBC [cut to MSNBC clip of female reporter in high heels and a suit standing in and then crawling down into a plywood model of Saddam Hussein's "spiderhole"].[71]

Stewart was an outspoken critic, in interviews and on the lecture circuit, of the exploitation of news programs by partisan pundits and surrogates. He saw the norm of "he said/she said" journalism as serving the interests of politicians, candidates, and parties while undermining the ability of news reporting to serve the public and democracy. In a 2004 interview with Ted Koppel on *Nightline*,[72] Stewart argued that news hosts, in pitting representatives of the left and the right against each other without challenging the arguments they made, were failing to do their job: "she throws out her figures from the Heritage Foundation and she throws her figures from the Brookings Institute, and the anchor, who should be the arbiter of truth says, 'Thank you both very much. That was really interesting.' No it wasn't! That was Coke and Pepsi talking about beverage truth. And that game is what has, I think, caused people to go, 'I'm not watching this.'"[73] At a 2004 forum held at the S. I. Newhouse School of Public Communications at Syracuse University, Stewart articulated what he thought journalists ought to be doing: "I think there is a responsibility within the media to help. You could create a paradigm of a media organization that is geared towards no bullshit—and do it actively—and stop pretending that we don't know what's going on. And stop pretending that it's a right/left question. I don't buy that the world is divided into bi-chromatic thought like that."[74] On October 12, 2009, *The Daily Show* featured a montage of cable news hosts abruptly ending uninterrogated political "debate" between surrogates from the left and right, concluding: "we have to leave it there." The camera cut to Stewart, incredulously asking: "why would you leave it there? There is a terrible place to leave it!?!" Stewart went on to explain how the cable news shows neglect their responsibility to play "arbiters of truth" in an effort to appear "objective": "it's called 'balance.' It works like this: Basically you get two crazy bald people [cut to reveal Democratic strategist James Carville and Republican operative Ari Fleischer] one representing the right and one representing the left and since those are the only two functional and rational points of view, the anchor [cut to reveal CNN's Anderson Cooper] helps them come to a golden consensus. [Cut to montage of shouting match between Carville and Fleischer which Cooper interrupts with 'We're going to have to leave it there.'] Leave it where? [Pleading] I don't even know where we were!" Stewart often explored the trouble with so-called media objectivity. In a *Daily Show* segment about the media coverage of the allegation by Swiftboat Veterans for Truth that John Kerry had not served honorably in Vietnam, Stewart asked comedian-correspondent Rob Corrdry about the role of the journalist in examining contradictory claims:

STEWART: Here's what puzzles me most, Rob. John Kerry's record in Vietnam is pretty much right there in the official records of the U.S. military and hasn't been disputed over the past 35 years.

CORRDRY: That's right Jon—and that's certainly the spin you'll be hearing from the Kerry campaign over the next several days.

STEWART: That's not a spin thing. That's a fact—it's established.

CORRDRY: Exactly, Jon, and that established incontrovertible fact is one side of the story.

STEWART: That's the *end* of the story! I mean you've seen the records, haven't you? What's *your* opinion?

CORRDRY: I'm sorry...my "O-PIN-ION?" I don't have "O-PIN-IONS" [air quotes]. I'm a reporter, Jon. My job is to spend half the time repeating what one side says and half the time repeating the other. Little thing called objectivity—might want to look it up someday.

STEWART: [Incredulous] Doesn't objectivity mean objectively weighing the evidence and calling out what's credible and what isn't credible?

CORRDRY: Whoah! Well well well! Looks like someone wants the media to act as a *filter*. [Switches to high-pitched mocking tone] "Oooh! This claim is spurious! Upon investigation this claim lacks any basis in reality! [pinching his nipples] MMMMmmmm! MMmmmm!" Listen, buddy—not my job to stand between the people talking to me and the people listening to me.[75]

The Daily Show, as it offered a critique of contemporary journalistic practices, also offered a remedy for those failures by scrutinizing political elites' claims and challenging doublespeak and hypocrisy. *The Daily Show* produced a series called "MESS-o-potamia" dedicated to satirical takes on the wars in Iraq and Afghanistan, often juxtaposing past comments by President Bush and Defense Secretary Donald Rumsfeld with the administration's present positions to illustrate arguable hypocrisy, dishonesty, or opportunism. It also featured interviews with journalists, politicians, and experts, with whom Stewart would try to unpack the underlying logic for the United States' involvement in the Middle East (photo 3.3). While civil and playful, Stewart's interviews were

PHOTO 3.3 Navy admiral Mike Mullen, chair of the Joint Chiefs of Staff, being interviewed by Jon Stewart on *The Daily Show*, September 12, 2011. Courtesy of Wikimedia Commons.

not the softball interviews politicians would typically expect from a late-night comedy host. Stewart often pressed his Democratic and Republican guests on their talking points, asking them to go beyond their practiced sound bites, something to which they were clearly unaccustomed.

So, while Stewart's humorous segments offered satirical critiques of contemporary news practices, the show also created a template for the alternative: Pushing beyond the information from the White House. Scrutinizing the dominant narratives of elites. Asking questions that were simultaneously respectful but challenging. Jeffrey Jones summed up the role played by *The Daily Show* through the years of the Bush administration this way: "it was the confluence of these two forces—masterful information management techniques and fear-mongering by the Bush administration and a television news media that helped facilitate these political deceptions and ruses through its weak reporting and tendency toward patriotic spectacle— that made *The Daily Show* the perfect vehicle for interrogating the truth."[76] By the time Stewart left the show in 2015, it had earned two Peabody Awards and won the Emmy for Outstanding Variety Series for a record 10 years in a row.[77]

In the interest of intellectual honesty, though, I cannot ignore the fact that, for all of Jon Stewart's substantive critiques of the failures of journalism, he never actually explored the systemic reasons for those failures. His critiques often suggested that journalistic failures were the responsibility of journalists or the fault of "the cable networks." But he didn't explore why cable news fails in the ways it does. He never tackled media deregulation or the consolidation of media ownership. He never discussed the conundrum posed by journalism being charged with serving the public good and simultaneously being squeezed for corporate profit. He never discussed the democratic threat posed by five megacorporations owning the nations' entire media landscape, or the fact that his own network, Comedy Central, was owned by one of them (Viacom). This always bothered me. If you're going to go there…why not really go there? Maybe it was the fact that his network was part of the corporate media landscape. Or maybe he thought that the abstract nature of corporate media ownership couldn't be easily mined for comedy. I must note that in recent years, John Oliver (on subscription-supported HBO, owned by AT&T Warner Media) and Samantha Bee (on advertiser-supported TBS, owned by AT&T Warner Media) have both tackled the troubling economics of investigative and local journalism. Oliver (perhaps liberated by the absence of advertisers) has dedicated entire segments to issues like the dangers of corporate consolidation and the failures of corporate for-profit journalism.

I write in such detail about Jon Stewart's time at *The Daily Show* because of its profound influence on the contemporary satire genre. Not only did the show establish the template for television satire, but it served as an incubator for some of the most popular and critically acclaimed talent in the genre. *Daily Show* correspondent Stephen Colbert launched *The Colbert Report*, his ironic parody of a conservative pundit show, in 2005. Stewart cocreated *The Colbert Report* with *The Daily Show*'s head writer, Ben Karlin. Stewart also served as the show's executive producer until its last season in 2014, when Colbert left to prepare for his new role as David Letterman's replacement on CBS's flagship late-night program, *The Late Show*.

The Colbert Report was an entirely new genre of television programming. Performed totally in ironic persona, four nights per week, Colbert's show offered an O'Reillyesque take on the news of the day but through a wildly underinformed, arrogant, faux-conservative lens. Colbert's show featured interviews with journalists, academics, political figures, and authors, all while

PHOTO 3.4 Stephen Colbert accepting the 2012 Peabody Award for *The Colbert Report*'s coverage of super PACs and campaign finance laws. Courtesy of Anders Krusberg/The Peabody Awards, via Wikimedia Commons.

Colbert occupied the character of an ignorant but exceptionally confident ego-tistical pundit. As Colbert described it to NPR's Terry Gross, he typically pre-pared interview guests backstage, telling them: "I do the show in character, and he's an idiot, and he's willfully ignorant of what you know and care about. Please just honestly disabuse me of my ignorance. Don't let me put words in your mouth, and we'll have a great time out there."[78] *The Colbert Report* won the 2013 Emmy for Outstanding Variety Series, putting an end to *The Daily Show*'s winning streak and providing endless fodder for a fake dispute between the two show hosts.[79] *The Colbert Report* also earned two Peabody Awards (photo 3.4). Since Colbert's CBS debut in 2015, Jon Stewart has served as an executive producer of *The Late Show* with Stephen Colbert, where Colbert con-tinues to hone his skills as a playful, yet biting, satirist.[80]

British comic John Oliver served as a correspondent on *The Daily Show* from 2006 until 2013 (photo 3.5). While Stewart was working on a film project in the summer of 2013, Oliver replaced him as host, proving that he had the

PHOTO 3.5 John Oliver addressing the audience at the Seventh Annual Crunchies Awards, San Francisco, February 10, 2014. Courtesy of Steve Jennings for TechCrunch, via Wikimedia Commons.

chops to host a show of his own. In 2014, Oliver launched his own late-night satire program on HBO. His Emmy-winning weekly program *Last Week Tonight* is yet another iteration of the postmodern satire program. Free from advertising breaks and advertisers' pressures, the show capitalizes on the work of researchers and writers to dive deep into lesser-known political issues. Oliver's "investigative satire" has tackled such topics as for-profit universities, payday loans, net neutrality, and school segregation, earning the show a Peabody Award in 2014 and again in 2018.

For 11 years, Canadian comic Samantha Bee served as a correspondent on *The Daily Show*. In 2015, she launched her own satire show, *Full Frontal*, on the cable network TBS. The weekly program features political satire segments and interviews through an explicitly feminist lens. Tackling such controversial issues as sexual harassment, rape, and abortion, Bee's show pushes the genre of television satire in yet another new direction, one that has evolved under the Trump administration—as I will discuss in later chapters—into a combination of feminist satire and outrage.

From network late-night shows to HBO, from Comedy Central to TBS, *The Daily Show*'s impact on the spirit and aesthetic of contemporary political satire has been palpable. Palpable and...kind of familiar. When asked about his comedy influences, Stewart consistently cites several of key players from the comedy landscape of the counterculture, including Lenny Bruce, George Carlin, and Steve Martin.[81] The forum for the political satire of the 2000s was certainly different from that of counterculture satire (cable networks rather than smoky nightclubs). The specific targets had changed (Iraq and corporate media norms rather than Vietnam and social mores). Yet political satire's ideology and aesthetic were—and still remain—very much the same. Just as Limbaugh and Hannity bear a striking resemblance to their forebears, the 1960s "hate clubs of the air," today's political satirists share the same liberal ideology and ironic hybrid aesthetics of the counterculture comics. As I will outline in the coming chapters, the tendency for liberals to articulate political critique through satire and for conservatives to do so through outrage is not a fluke. What if there really is something inherently *liberal* about satire and something inherently *conservative* about outrage—not as industries but as aesthetic forms that tap into and appeal to unique psychological characteristics—characteristics that are themselves tied to political ideology?

4

The Psychology of Satire

IN CHAPTER 3 I proposed that outrage and satire both emerged as responses to the political, technological, and regulatory changes of the 1990s. In this chapter I dive deep into the content and psychology of the satire genre, to delineate what it is, how it works, and why it is so frequently expressed through irony. According to humor scholar George Test, satire is defined by four characteristics: aggression, play, laughter, and judgment.[1] "Aggression" is the notion that satire embodies the spirit of attack. "Play" refers to the fact that humor operates like a riddle that must be solved, often including allusions to silly or strange constructs (think: giraffe, spatula, Chihuahua, rutabaga). "Laughter" captures the mirth anticipated by, and derived from, a satirical message. "Judgment" is the notion that satire presents a valenced, evaluative argument aimed at a target—usually an institution, a policy, a practice, or society as a whole. According to Test, aggression and judgment are the two criteria that distinguish satire from other kinds of humor: "satire ultimately judges, it asserts that some person, group, or attitude is not what it should be. However restrained, muted, or disguised a playful judgment may be, whatever form it takes, such an act undermines, threatens, and perhaps violates the target, making the act an attack."[2] The targets of satire, and the judgments it levels, are broad—aimed at society, systems, and the audience itself. Rachel Caufield proposes that "most political humor is aimed to entertain the audience by poking fun at outsiders—political candidates, government officials, or public figures. In contrast, satire's target is broader—it is meant to attack political institutions, society's foibles, or public vices. Put simply, conventional political humor is often geared at making the audience laugh at others, while satire is designed to make the audience laugh at itself as well as others, therefore allowing the audience to realize a larger set of systemic faults."[3] In other words, jokes that mention political topics and people might be satirical, but it's just as likely that they are not. If a political joke doesn't critique policies, institutions, or social convention—if it doesn't make its audience think about how they themselves, as a society, need to do better—then it's probably not satire, according to this definition.

Underlying the two criteria of "play" and "laughter" is the broader concept of humor itself. Digging into the logic and psychology of humor is a bit like trying to track and predict the path of wild squirrel. It's difficult to impose order and rules onto something whose entire modus operandi violates order and rules. Yet for more than a century some very serious people who have referred to themselves as "humor scholars" have tried to do just this. At the center of all of the scholarly definitions of humor is the notion that humorous texts are themselves incomplete without active participation by the audience. Henri Bergson, writing in 1911, emphasized that humor results from two incompatible ideas that the listener recognizes as overlapping in some way. "A situation is invariably comic when it belongs simultaneously to two alto-gether independent series of events and is capable of being interpreted in two entirely different meanings at the same time," he wrote.[4]

Perhaps the most exhaustive (and exhausting?) consideration of such "incongruity" in humor comes from the writer and journalist Arthur Koestler. In his 1964 work *The Act of Creation* Koestler considers various aspects of the imagination and the human need to create—music, art, fiction, and humor.[5] He argues that humor is created when a text (like a joke) activates one frame of reference in a person's mind, which is then followed by the introduction of a totally different frame of reference that seems fundamentally at odds with the first. To understand what the humorous text means, it is up to the listener to bring something to bear on the gap in between the two frames. Only then can the listener reconcile the incongruity. Humor involves perceiving "a situation or idea, L, in two self-consistent but habitually incompatible frames of reference, M1 and M2.... The event L, in which the two intersect, is made to vibrate simultaneously, on two different wavelengths, as it were. While this unusual situation lasts, L is not merely linked to one associative context, but bisociated with two" (see fig. 4.1).[6]

Take, for example, the pun-based joke that was a favorite of my son at a young age:

How do you make a tissue dance?
Put a little boogie in it.

The first frame of reference activated by this riddle concerns ideas and con-structs related to tissues, including head colds, sneezing, and runny noses. This set of thoughts is quickly interrupted and complicated by the concept of

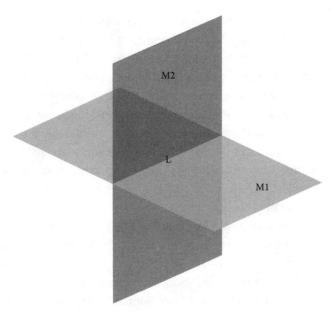

FIGURE 4.1 Graphic visualization of Arthur Koestler's concepts of incongruity and bisociation. Adapted from Arthur Koestler, *The Act of Creation* (London: Hutchinson, 1964).

"dance," which is unlikely to be related to tissues in your mind. According to Koestler's diagram, the two unique frames of reference (which he illustrates as planes) run perpendicular to each other and intersect at the moment when the listener is able to reconcile that gap between tissues and dancing. The punchline, "put a little boogie in it," allows you to do just that.

Although it seems to happen rather easily, what is happening in the brain is quite complex. The brain is accessing an idea that is simultaneously residing within two very different informational networks in memory; one related to tissues and the other related to dancing. Since we know tissues are used to wipe "boogers" from our noses, and "the boogie" is also a kind of dance, we experience mirth after having reconciled this gap. The term "mirth" is important here, as it captures the fleeting feeling of a positive mood or emotional state, but in response to a humorous stimulus (like a joke).[7]

When audiences work to bridge the gap in a humorous text, they can do so through various cognitive activities: (1) interpolation—in which you fill in the missing links (as in the "boogie" joke above); (2) extrapolation—in which you elaborate on the idea presented and you extend it, often to an absurd conclusion; or (3) transformation—in which you reinterpret the initial information through some formula to result in a parallel concept. All of these processes of reconciliation require intense engagement with the text from the start. If you are not paying attention, not actively bringing to mind the relevant constructs, you will not be readily able to bridge the gap to get the joke. This enhanced cognitive activity as people encounter humor increases their recall of information in the message.[8] Since understanding and appreciating humor requires one's attention and cognitive energy, people are more motivated to think about the funny part of a message, and are more likely to remember it later.

Puns are an easy way to demonstrate how humor is processed in the brain, and why humor increases attention and processing motivation. But what about political satire, which is arguably a bit more subtle and complicated than my son's beloved "boogie" joke?

Consider this joke made by Conan O'Brien in August 2016: "Donald Trump has dropped to second place in a national poll. On the bright side, he's still polling Number 1 among Germans of the 1930s." The mental network of information first activated here concerns Trump and public opinion polls, in particular his dropping to second place nationally. The incongruity is introduced with the reference to Trump "polling Number 1 among Germans of the 1930s," a historical impossibility since the joke was delivered in 2016. The second network of information that you retrieve from long-term memory as you listen to this joke relates to "1930s Germany." This frame of reference (or network of information) includes concepts like Nazism, Hitler, and the popular rise of the Third Reich at that time. You still have to fill in the blank, though. If Trump is polling Number 1 among those people at that time, that means _____. This is Koestler's moment of extrapolation/ interpolation, where you draw information from long-term memory to make sense of the joke.

If Trump is polling Number 1 among Germans in the 1930s that means he is…a Nazi? Hitler? Maybe. But at the very least…it means that he is racist.

If Trump is polling Number 1 among Germans in the 1930s that means that the *voters who support Trump* are…white nationalists? Nazis? Supporters of Hitler? Maybe. But at the very least…it means that they are racist.

This joke, although brief, invites the listener to issue a substantive and biting critique of Trump, Trump's supporters, and the American public. After all, if Trump is in second place in national polls and is a racist or a white nationalist, then what does that say about the people who vote for him? The riddle aspect makes it playful and the reconciliation of the incongruity produces laughter, but the most important elements are the aggressive and sweeping judgments advanced implicitly through this joke, forcing *the audience* to come up with the argument: Trump and his supporters are racists.

Cognitively speaking, this is the aspect of satire comprehension that sets it apart from other kinds of discourse. The argument that is made through the joke is never made *in* the joke. It is the listeners who come to the argument or proposition themselves.

A Note on Improvisation and Humor

According to Immanuel Kant, writing in 1790, "laughter is an affectation arising from the sudden transformation of a strained expectation into nothing."[9] This idea of a surprising violation of expectations is at the core of what makes things funny. It also accounts for the close relationship between improvisational theater and comedy. In improvisation, as an art form that is created in real time, with performers collaborating in the creation—and discovery—of a fictional world onstage, everything is a surprise. But nothing is treated by the actors as though it is surprising at all. When a character reveals that she is actually her scene partner's mother, the audience is surprised, but the actors act like they knew it all along. When characters finally identify the location of the scene, and the audience learns that the intense romantic conversation they've been witnessing has been taking place in a spaceship, the audience is flabbergasted, while the performers don't flinch because it is their accepted reality. When characters immediately accept the offer of their scene partner, they show zero hesitation in the face of the absurd. Instead, they accept, build on, and heighten the offer they were just given. These moments onstage violate the audience's expectations not only of the plot but also of the ways humans typically respond to unexpected information.

Improvisation is a breeding ground for humorous constructs because the entire practice relies on performers defying expectations. Improv was also a place where many satirists, including Stephen Colbert, Seth Meyers, Samantha Bee, and many of their writers, got their starts in comedy. Improvisers move confidently in the direction of a shared and ever-changing reality, which they discover collaboratively onstage. This in itself violates expectations and results in the audience experiencing laughter and mirth. In *Something Wonderful Right Away*, an oral history of The Second City, Sweet relates a description of improvisational theater given by director Del Close:

> In a workshop, Del Close, the co-director at *The Second City*, has drawn an analogy between improvising and a sporting event. In both improvisation and sport, what grips the audience is the fact that the outcome is truly in doubt. The players in both have, through arduous training,

developed skills with which to deal with the unpredictable; but these skills cannot tame the unpredictable, they can only give the players a better chance of not being routed by it. And, in both, the audience's enthusiasm is a major part of the experience. The football crowd cheers a terrific pass, the audience at *The Second City* applauds the line or bit of business which springs in startled and wide-eyed perfection out of the logic of the situation.[10]

Irony: A Contrast Between "What Is and What Ought to Be"

Political satire is frequently presented through irony—literally stating one thing while meaning the opposite. Bergson described ironic juxtapositions as contrasting "the real and the ideal" or "what is and what ought to be."[11] Simply put, when you describe things that are obviously bad as though they are good, or describe things that are obviously good as though they are bad, you are inviting your listener to question why things are bad in reality or, conversely, why things are not good in reality.

Given this, it's understandable why irony would be such a useful device of the satirist. As literary scholar Dustin H. Griffin argues, "the business of the satirist is to insist on the sharp differences between vice and virtue, between good and bad, between what man *is*, and what he *ought to be*."[12] What easier way to do this than saying that something is awesome when it is obviously a catastrophe? Paul Simpson, a linguist at the University of Liverpool, posits: "it is the concept of *irony*, more than any other device, which tends to be regarded as the central mechanism in the production of satire."[13]

The most iconic example of ironic political satire in the United States over the decade may very well be Colbert, who performed in ironic persona four nights a week for nine years on *The Colbert Report*. Created in the spirit of Bill O'Reilly (whom Colbert affectionately referred to as "Papa Bear"), Colbert's character was an arrogant, bloviating buffoon who would "feel the news at you" and never let facts get in the way of his opinions.

As Colbert said to Terry Gross in a December 7, 2005, episode of NPR's *Fresh Air*:

[my character] is passionate. He is closely attached to and invested in the stories he's talking about and the themes that he's talking about. He cares deeply about what happens in this country and…he just doesn't *know* a lot about what happens in this country. He gets little glimpses of things. He has little snatches of information and then he makes broad generalizations from that.…He's not a huge fan of facts. It's really more about what you feel in your gut.....It just...it makes sense that the world is flat and that the sun goes around us. I look up, I see the sun move. I don't see us move.[14]

Throughout his years on *The Colbert Report*, Colbert pretended to believe passionately in the things he said, but with a subtle wink and a nod he signaled to his audience that he believed quite the opposite. Take, for example, this joke on topic of the death penalty from April 2014: "folks, I love capital punishment. It sends a clear message. We as a society think it is depraved to take a human life and to prove it we're going to kill you." When Colbert says "I love capital punishment," viewers familiar with his show and his intended meaning know from the start that he actually opposes it. But the paradox introduced in the second half of the joke also helps reveal his ironic intent: "We think it's depraved to take a human life and to prove it we're going to kill you."

But, by killing you, aren't you taking a human life?
Yes, you are.
And didn't he just say it is depraved to do that?
Yes. Yes, he did.

This inherent contradiction that Colbert literally states (with the arrogant conviction of a politician at a campaign event) invites you to unpack this assertion, requiring you to consider the underlying logic, utility, appropriateness, and morality of the death penalty as federal policy. All because he said he loved it and revealed an internal contradiction in his reasons for doing so. Like the Conan joke about Trump polling number one among Germans in the 1930s, this joke doesn't explicitly issue the judgment Colbert wants the audience to take away from it. The audience must come to the conclusion themselves: capital punishment is a hypocritical, unethical, and illogical policy.

Although irony as a form of communication has many different subcategories, making it difficult to identify, scholars do agree that irony is a way of inverting your intended meaning to issue a judgment about something by saying the opposite. To clarify how this is done, I will summarize the five "irony factors" detailed by Christian Burgers, Margot van Mulken, and Peter Jan Schellens.[15]

Irony Factors

According to Murgers, van Mulken, and Schellens, irony includes five elements: evaluativeness, incongruity, valence, a target, and relevance to the current context.[16] First, irony is evaluative in that it issues a valenced judgment (good or bad) about something. Second, irony relies on an incongruity between the literal and actual meanings of a text. Third, it also requires an inversion of valence (meaning positive assessments are really negative and negative ones are really positive). Fourth, irony is always aimed at some target. Finally, irony must be directly or indirectly relevant to the situation or context in which it is introduced.

Put simply: irony is a relevant, context-specific form of judgment, aimed at a target; and its literal and intended meanings are at odds with one another.

Irony is a way of saying something really harsh by saying something kind: "very good, darling son. By all means...leave your dirty plates on the kitchen table for me to clear. After all, as your mother I am your devoted servant. I am only here to do your bidding, sir." It's a way of saying something positive by saying something negative: "An A+ on your biology test? Is that all you could do? Come on. Work harder next time." As these examples reveal, yes, I occasionally use irony when parenting. And for the record, I would not recommend using irony when parenting.[17]

By saying the opposite of what you mean, irony doesn't just offer an opportunity to decode a riddle. It forces you to ask what the alternative (literal) meaning signifies and why that contrast is important. In the case of the "leave your dirty plates on the table" example, the implication is that if that were my intended meaning, it would signify that I am my child's servant, only there to do his bidding. By rejecting this premise through irony, the implication is clear: there's no way in hell that I am my son's servant, so he better get his rear end back in the kitchen and bring his dirty dishes to the kitchen sink. In the case of the "An A+? Is that all you could do?" the implication is that if that were my intended meaning, I would be an unbearable, cruel parent with unreasonable expectations of my child's academic performance. After all, there is no grade higher than a perfect score. By rejecting this premise through irony, the implication is that my kid did a stellar job, couldn't possibly have done any better, and so I am extremely pleased.

Irony is a strange form of discourse, when you think about it. Why on earth would you say the opposite of what you mean? Isn't the role of language to communicate information efficiently and clearly to allow people to function collectively as a society? So why do people riddle one another with irony? Human beings use humor (and irony) to look good, to signal cognitive sophistication, to make each other feel good, to make society work more easily, and to tackle difficult subjects without making others angry (more on that in a minute).[18] Humor is an advanced form of communication that fulfills social and status-related needs and gratifications. Being able to successfully use humor is a sign of leadership, authority, and intelligence.[19] It's a way of promoting social cohesion among small groups of people, allowing groups to thrive and work productively together. Humor also creates temporary feelings of happiness—also called mirth—among audience members. These feelings often get projected onto the speaker or the person who created the humor, creating what is known as a "halo effect," through which audience members feel good about the person who made them feel good. (Like the opposite of the "shoot the messenger" effect.)[20]

So, people use humor because it makes them look good and because it helps them get along with each other. But humor has unique persuasion-related functions as well. First, there is the fact that humor requires such attention from its audience that it increases their recall of information central to the joke.[21] Second, humor allows you to imply a judgment (remember, inviting the listener to make valenced judgments is what satire and irony do best) without the typical risks associated with regular—serious—discourse. Humor helps you say critical things without angering people (as much). Philosophers have known this. Medieval court jesters knew this. Spouses know this.

How many times have you been offended by a friend or loved one (or political figure) who claims, after the fact: "but it was just a joke. I was just kidding!" As maddening as it is, the "I was just joking" defense is a smart strategy. If you can get someone to agree to treat something as humorous, they will probably not get angry at it. But why does this happen?

Can We Laugh and Be Angry at a Joke at the Same Time?

In 2006 and 2007, I was working on publishing the theory I developed for my dissertation: sometimes called the "resource allocation theory" of humor, it accounts for why arguments made through jokes elicit less resistance than arguments made through regular serious discourse. I submitted my study of this theory to the journal *Media Psychology*, where then-editor Robin Nabi, a professor at the University of California at Santa Barbara, was instrumental in helping me develop the piece. Robin had graduated from the University of Pennsylvania's Annenberg School nine years before I had, had studied under the same dissertation advisor I did (Dr. Joseph Cappella), and was working on similar questions relating to the processing of media messages. As it turns out, our shared academic roots had led us to a very similar line of work, unbeknownst to one another. The theory Robin and her colleagues came up with is often referred to as the "discounting cue" hypothesis.[22] It says that people perceive humor differently from serious discourse and choose to apply different rules when processing it. Instead of treating it seriously, people see humor as "just a joke," in which case scrutinizing the message or challenging the speaker about what the speaker is saying is not "appropriate." The discounting cue hypothesis is based on the idea that people choose whether or not to scrutinize messages—and in the case of jokes, usually decide not to.

The theory I was developing proposes similar effects of humor but through a different psychological mechanism. Remember the detailed diagram Koestler created to explain the work audiences have to do to reconcile the incongruity in humor? The more I studied the psychology of humor comprehension and appreciation, the more convinced I became that these "mental gymnastics" tax people's working memory. It might not feel like work, but the cognitive processing required to make sense of even the most basic joke is quite burdensome. There is also something powerful about a text insinuating something without actually saying it. The meaning of a joke is implicit, forcing the listeners to add the appropriate information from long-term memory to make sense of it themselves. If you are spending so much cognitive energy just getting and appreciating a joke, I thought, how on earth are you going to have the mental energy left over to scrutinize or challenge whatever argument the joke is suggesting?[23] This is the premise of my Counterargument Disruption Model of Humor, also called the "resource allocation" hypothesis.

Work coming out of neuropsychology over the last decade has confirmed that processing humor is not a simple feat. For example, fMRI studies show that joke comprehension involves an advanced level of cognitive processing. People reading jokes must (1) activate discrepant information simultaneously, (2) draw from long-term memory, (3) hold information in working memory, and (4) do all this while their reward centers are activated in anticipation of the payoff associated with getting the joke.

Seana Coulson of the University of California, San Diego, has completed several studies that capture the activity of the brain while processing humor. Coulson's findings are remarkably consistent with the theoretical process Koestler outlined back in 1964. When understanding humor, Coulson and Marta Kutas suggest, the listener engages in a process of frame-shifting, "in which the listener activates a new frame from long-term memory to reinterpret information already active in working memory."[24] Their findings highlight the unique and complex brain functioning that occurs in the context of humor.[25]

This process of suppressing information that was just activated in working memory and then replacing it with a different schema (or frame of reference) that the listener has to retrieve from long-term memory is hard work, a contention with which many neuroscientists agree. "Jokes presuppose the speaker's ability to interpret language against background knowledge," Coulson and Christopher Lovett write.[26] "The cognitive processes underlying the resolution of verbal jokes seem to be a part of executive functions such as schema shifting," Yu-Chen Chan and her colleagues conclude.[27] Coulson and Robert Williams go so far as to call joke comprehension "a high-level language phenomenon that underscores the functional asymmetry in the language processing capacity of the two hemispheres."[28]

The resource allocation theory proposes that because humor requires so much work aimed at comprehension and appreciation, people become less able to actively argue against whatever is being proposed in the joke itself. In essence, your cognitive resources have been allocated to getting the joke, so you have few resources left over to scrutinize or critique the argument made *in* that joke.

The premises of the resource allocation theory, like much work on information processing, are that (1) people are "cognitive misers," unlikely to expend more cognitive energy than is absolutely necessary, and (2) the capacity for information processing in working memory is limited.[29] In the context of humor, in anticipation of the reward of "mirth" from getting a joke, it may seem worth it to expend enough cognitive energy to get the payoff of the punchline, but it's unlikely to seem worth it to think much beyond that. People are both *not very motivated* to think hard and not particularly *able* to think about multiple things at the same time. As it turns out, and as multitasking experts can attest, humans' brains have a limited capacity to process information, which leaves people unable to think about and actively process multiple things simultaneously.[30]

Try this exercise: Have two people calmly and clearly tell you two different stories in each of your two ears for a period of two minutes.[31] How much of each story are you able to process and recall? What kinds of things do you miss? Obviously this activity is also about the limitations of people's attention, not just processing capacity, but it helps to illustrate the difficulty in simultaneous processing of discrepant information. Rather than simultaneous processing, what is actually happening is more likely a rapid form of "task-switching," in which you change cognitive tasks, alternating back and forth between the two sets of information.

The resource allocation theory proposes that in the context of humor there are two tasks that are incompatible with one another: (1) getting and appreciating a joke (processing the funny stuff), and (2) scrutinizing and critiquing the argument presented through that joke (processing the serious stuff). That right there is the special sauce of humor. In traditional persuasive communication, if you get people engaged in a message, you run the risk of increasing their scrutiny of your argument, which could backfire if your argument is not particularly strong. But if you can suspend their critical thinking, you can get them to judge the message based on superficial things like how attractive the source is, how much they like the music, or whichever primal emotion the message ignites inside them. This is why, as I always say to my students, if you are hired to create a persuasion campaign and you don't have strong arguments working on the side of your product or your cause (first, ask yourself why you're working at this place at all, and then...), do whatever you can to get the audience members distracted from what it is you're really trying to say in the hopes that they will suspend their scrutiny of your weak (or nonexistent) arguments.

But in humor, the dynamic is quite the opposite. The more invested the audience members are in the funny component of what you're saying, the less likely they are to judge the underlying strength of the argument. Imagine that: the more engaged they are with (the humorous part) of your message, the less likely they are to critique it.

While Nabi's and my theories both predict the same outcome (that humor will result in less scrutiny and less counterargumentation than nonhumor), we differ in the mechanism through which this outcome is thought to happen. In the discounting cue hypothesis, Nabi suggests that people are less likely to counterargue jokes because they don't really want to—which goes to their motivation. In the resource allocation hypothesis, I argue that people don't counterargue jokes because they can't—which goes to their ability. Why does this distinction between ability and motivation matter? Well, if Nabi is right and people just choose not to counterargue jokes because they are "just jokes," then it's up to the listener. The person getting the joke has the agency—the power to treat the joke as a joke or not. But if I'm right and people literally are less able to counterargue things presented in joke form, then it is not up to the listener. The audience has no agency. If humor undermines their ability to scrutinize a message, then the power is entirely in the hands of message sender.

So who is correct? It seems that both of us are right and it depends on the nature and complexity of the humor. Scholars have found evidence for both processes. Nabi found support for her theory in a study of audience responses to the stand-up comedy of Chris Rock. Yet my former student Jeremy Polk found evidence that when a humorous message is more complex and sophisticated (like irony), it is more likely that the humor undermines the listener's ability to counterargue,[32] a finding corroborated by Heather LaMarre and

Whitney Walther in 2013.[33] Work by Mark Boukes and his colleagues shows that the more "absorbed" audiences are in a humorous segment, the less they counterargue, also providing some support for the resource allocation hypothesis.[34]

Given that satire is a specific form of humor that deliberately advances an argument (albeit implicitly), the idea that political humor might reduce audiences' counterargumentation seems pretty consequential.

Remember that satirical joke by Conan O'Brien? "Donald Trump has dropped to second place in a national poll. On the bright side, he's still polling Number 1 among Germans of the 1930s." Now picture O'Brien showing up on his program and saying, without a hint of humor: "Trump and the people who like him are white supremacists." People would freak out. Even political moderates might find this kind of statement inappropriate and would condemn him for saying it. But the joke he told back in August 2016 didn't even cause a stir.

Not a headline, not a single angry Fox News story. Nothing. It was just another late-night joke.

Maybe listeners discounted O'Brien as "just a funny late-night comedy host," so no one should bother getting their knickers in a twist. Or maybe the process of understanding the joke (activating information from long-term memory and bridging the gap) took enough mental energy that people weren't able to question whether the allegation of Trump's white nationalism was fair. Or, most likely, a little bit of both. Regardless of the reason why, the capacity of satire to introduce biting and sweeping judgments without angering mainstream audiences is truly remarkable.

Of course, one joke implying that Trump and his supporters are Nazis isn't going to suddenly persuade someone that Trump and his supporters are actually Nazis. But getting an audience to entertain such a proposition without explicitly making that argument could be a powerful step in the persuasive process, as is getting an audience to entertain that proposition while suspending their resistance to it. This means that listeners are required to articulate the argument in their own minds—in this case, "Trump and his supporters are racist"—thereby activating those ideas in working memory. It also means that the listeners, with suspended counterargumentation, now have their guard down and so are less likely to dismiss that proposition out of hand.

But it doesn't always work this way, does it? There are times when humor fails to disrupt listeners' scrutiny of an argument. Examples are when a speaker is unfamiliar with the audience and the kinds of topics they are willing to treat in a humorous way, or when a speaker doesn't really understand the art and logic of humor. For humor to encourage people to entertain certain ideas while suspending their ability to counterargue those ideas, the argument advanced through the joke must be implicit. That is to say, the argument or proposition advanced through the joke must come from the audience themselves as they do the work to bridge the gap. The main argument of O'Brien's Trump/1930s Germany joke is never explicitly stated. The audience comes up with it in their own minds through the process of interpolation, which likely helps reduce their resistance to its underlying argument.

Here's another joke worth dissecting: "people look at the Statue of Liberty and they see a proud symbol of our history as a nation of immigrants, a beacon of hope for people around the world. Donald [Trump] looks at the Statue of Liberty and sees a 'four.'" (Source withheld temporarily for dramatic effect.) The joke requires that listeners first activate the idea of the Statue of Liberty and all that it represents including freedom, opportunity, and patriotism. The incongruity is then introduced by the statement that Trump sees the statue as a "four." The audience must activate knowledge structures related to Trump, and his past statements critical of women's looks, including his derogatory statements about Rosie O'Donnell or his statements, on Howard Stern's radio show, about rating women's appearances on a scale of 1 to 10.

To reconcile the incongruity, one must activate this knowledge from long-term memory and bring it to the text, to answer the implicit question: "Why is Trump calling the Statue of Liberty a four?" The implication is that Trump only sees women as objects and only thinks of their purpose and value in terms of their physical appearance, even when that woman is the Statue of Liberty. This joke is able to get the audience to make this assertion themselves through the process of getting the joke. And through that process, so much mental energy is spent "getting the joke" that there is little energy left to then scrutinize whether or not the claim of Trump's misogyny is fair or well-evidenced. By the time the laughter has subsided, the speaker is on to the next joke.

That speaker, in the case of this Statue of Liberty joke, was none other than the 2016 Democratic candidate for president, Hillary Rodham Clinton, addressing the crowd at the October 20, 2016, Alfred E. Smith Memorial Foundation Dinner, an annual fundraiser held in New York that supports Catholic Charities. For almost 70 years, the Al Smith Dinner has served as a venue where presidential candidates exchange lighthearted barbs just prior to the general election. Presidential candidates usually enlist the help of comedy writers and staff members in crafting their addresses, typically 15–20 minutes long, and use the opportunity to poke fun at themselves and their opponents.

Before Secretary Clinton gave her address at the dinner, Trump gave his own. After thanking the Archdiocese of New York, Trump opened his speech by referring to his reputation as someone who has trouble poking fun at himself, ending with the punchline "many people tell me that modesty is perhaps my best quality."

He then delivered an expertly crafted self-deprecating joke; self-deprecating, except that it was actually at the expense of his wife, Melania: "the media is even more biased this year than ever before—ever. You want the proof? Michelle Obama gives a speech and everyone loves it—it's fantastic. They think she's absolutely great. My wife, Melania, gives the exact same speech—and people get on her case." The joke referenced the speech Melania Trump delivered to the 2016 Republican National Convention, which was found to contain whole passages lifted from the speech Michelle Obama had delivered to the Democratic National Convention in 2008. Typically, if two people do the same thing, they should be treated the same—unless that "same thing" is the delivery of an "original" speech that is supposed to represent the speaker's own words and ideas. The joke implies that Trump and his team are owning the plagiarism allegation, acknowledging it and deriding themselves for having allowed it to happen. Listening to the joke is disarming. It is harder to have contempt for the act of plagiarism when it is acknowledged in this way.

In contrast, about halfway through his 15-minute address, Trump made a joke at Clinton's expense. And the joke failed. Unlike the joke made at Melania's expense, this joke didn't follow the formula for humor that would reduce the audience's ability and motivation to counterargue. Recall that jokes work best when the argument is constructed *by the audience* through the process of incongruity-reconciliation. With this in mind, now read Trump's joke: "Hillary is so corrupt...she got kicked off the Watergate Commission. How corrupt do you have to be to get kicked off the Watergate Commission? Pretty corrupt." The joke was met with loud booing and heckling from the audience before he even got to the punchline. He had ignored the formula that gives jokes their special sauce. Instead of crafting a joke through which the audience must infer the argument, he started with the explicit argument: "Hillary is so corrupt."

He basically "Yo-mama-so-fatted" his political opponent.

The type of joke Trump used here is referred to by linguists as "scalar humor." Benjamin Bergen and Kim Binstead explain that "scalar humor is the manipulation of a conceptual scale," often through exaggeration or hyperbole.[35] Examples provided by Bergen and Binstead include: "Yo' mama's so old, she was a waitress at the Last Supper." And "Yo' mama's so fat, she broke her arm and gravy poured out." Unlike irony, which requires an inversion of valence, such that what you say is the opposite of what you mean, in scalar humor, hyperbole, and exaggeration, the literal and intended valence is the same:

Yo mama is so old/fat = negative statement about the age/size of your mother.

This kind of joke does involve a semantic incongruity, in that "Yo mama" and "the Last Supper" typically do not occupy the same mental framework. But the mental effort necessarily to reconcile those kinds of incongruities is straight-forward. You simply draw the scalar inference. The Last Supper was a very long time ago, so she must be really old.

Most important, the first mental framework activated in this kind of joke tells the listener exactly what the scalar inference is going to be. "Yo mama's so old" = a joke about your mom being really old. "Yo mama's so fat" = a joke about your mom being really fat. These jokes explicitly tell the listener what the judgment is from the start. When a joke's main premise is stated from the outset, the resource allocation process simply doesn't work. If the argument is explicit (Hillary is so corrupt), then the audience does not have to allocate any cognitive resources to figuring out what the underlying argument actually is, so all the audience's mental resources are still available to scrutinize the claim that "Hillary is so corrupt." Which means they're able to get mad. And boo. And heckle. As they did even before the joke was over.

Next time, President Trump, maybe try something along these lines: "A thief, a liar, and a cheater walk into a bar. The bartender, wiping the counter, turns and says, 'Good evening, Mrs. Clinton.'" This joke doesn't explicitly make the argument that Clinton is a thief, a liar, and a cheater. The audience does.

So why did Trump get it so wrong? Why did he undermine his own joke's ability to do the magic jokes do? It seems that Trump's failed attempt at a humor is probably emblematic of something bigger than Trump himself. As I will detail in the chapters that follow, the successful creation and reception of humor is related to personality and psychological traits of the audience, traits that are themselves correlated with political ideology.

5

Who Gets the Joke?

ABOUT 20 YEARS ago, I had just moved to the Philadelphia area from New Hampshire. A neighbor, Rob, asked if I'd tried a local dish called "Scrapple."

"What on earth is scrapple?" I asked.

"It's a loaf of leftover pork parts that you can cut into slices, fry in a pan, and then eat."

"Ah-ha. So, it's a low-fat healthy dietary choice," I joked.

"No. Quite the opposite. It actually contains huge amounts of fat and sodium. "

Blink blink blink.

"Oh. OK," I said, looking at unflinching Rob, "I'll probably avoid it then. Thanks."

We've all met folks like this. The woman to whom you say, on a dreadfully cold and rainy day, "Great weather we're having, huh?" and she looks at you quizzically, as if to say "Do you not see that it's pouring rain?" The student who asks, "Professor, I was out all last week and was wondering if you covered anything important in class?" You tilt your head and tell her, "Nope. Not a thing. Since you were absent all week, I decided to only teach the class things that are useless and irrelevant to the course." The student responds, "Oh, good. Thanks," and leaves your office.

Why is it that some people just do not grasp irony—or even humor in general?

Believe it or not, entire subdisciplines have been dedicated to the study of humor comprehension and appreciation. Linguists and psychologists, communication scholars and neuropsychologists all have tried to figure out how people understand and appreciate humor and why some people just don't get or appreciate a joke. As described in chapter 4, understanding and appreciating humor requires quite a heavy lift in working memory—especially in the case of satire and irony. The more I studied the psychology of satire, the more interested I became in what kinds of people might be more able, or less able, to comprehend and appreciate humor at all. Equally fascinating, I've learned, is the question of who might be more *motivated* to comprehend and appreciate humor. The questions at the heart of this research are: Which kinds of people *can* get the joke and which kinds *can't*? And which kinds of people *want to* get the joke and which kinds *do not*?

First, some key terms. "Humor" (defined and explicated in chapter 4) is the broad category under which satire and ironic satire both fall. "Humor comprehension" refers to the understanding of a humorous text. "Humor appreciation" refers to whether—and to what extent—a person finds a humorous text funny. Everyone knows that you can understand a joke and still not find it funny. This, of course, is humor comprehension without humor appreciation.

Why did Cinderella throw the clock out the window?
Because she wanted to see time fly.

I can understand the play on words "time flying" versus time literally flying through the air, and still just not find this joke funny, much to my eight-year-old daughter's dismay. But can you appreciate a joke if you don't understand it? In most cases, the answer is no: you generally need to comprehend a joke to find it funny.[1] What makes this proposition challenging, however, is that the harder a joke is to understand, the funnier people tend to find it.[2] As the incongruity requires more and more cognitive work, the payoff gets bigger. Zhihui Wu summarizes it this way: "complexity seems to increase the degree of perceived humor so that if a joke contains several hidden violations, and claims for more reasoning efforts, it will be funnier than if fewer are noticed and less intellectual efforts are devoted to the incongruity resolution."[3] But this only works up to a point. Research in the 1960s and 1970s concluded that the relationship between humor complexity and humor appreciation could be represented by an "inverted-U shape": the more difficult the joke, the funnier people find it until the joke becomes too difficult to comprehend, at which point, appreciation decreases.[4] A team of experimental psychologists at Oxford University confirmed this inverted-U finding.[5] After examining participants' reactions to popular stand-up comics, they concluded: "[our findings] seem to suggest that professional comics cannot afford to tell jokes of such complexity that they leave the audience baffled."[6]

Attardo's Criteria for Humor Appreciation ("Funny Factors")

Humor scholar Salvatore Attardo outlined key criteria that determine how funny a humorous text will be perceived to be by an audience.[7] He writes: "all other things being equal, a humorous text will be perceived as humorous if the incongruity/resolution is: non-threatening, not too complex or too simple, based on available scripts/knowledge, unexpected, surprising, and occurs in a playful mode (the situation must be framed as humor)."[8]

But wouldn't these criteria depend an awful lot on the person listening to the joke? Different kinds of people might be more able, or less able, to perceive a joke in a way that meets each of Attardo's criteria. Different kinds of people might also be more *willing*, or *less willing*, to perceive a joke in a way that meets each criterion. I will discuss several of Attardo's "funny factors" (my words, not his) and explore the kinds of audience characteristics that might affect each.

Not Too Complex or Too Simple

While the inverted-U shape between humor complexity and appreciation sets up a framework for predicting how funny a joke will be based on how hard it is to understand, the mere concept of complexity depends on who is listening to the joke. What is complex to some may be simple to others. What is too simple or obvious to some may be daunting to others. At dinner recently, my kids and I were coming up with jokes based on puns. I was pretty proud of the one I came up with: "A glass of milk, an ice cream cone, and a stick of butter go to a slumber party. What game do they play?" My son said immediately, "Truth or *Dairy*!" Since he was able to predict the punchline himself, my son barely found it funny at all. My eight-year-old daughter, who took a few seconds before it "clicked," thought this joke was hilarious. The role of cognitive ability here is obvious. If someone doesn't have the working memory processing capacity to reconcile an incongruity, the joke will remain incongruous, and no humor will result. If someone is able to reconcile the incongruity with little to no effort, perhaps predicting the punchline before it even arrives (as my son did here), very little humor will result.

Studies from neuroscience show that the right hemisphere of the human brain plays a key role in the reconciliation of humorous incongruities. Patients with damage to the right frontal lobe are significantly less likely to comprehend or appreciate humor.[9] This lack of appreciation stems from their inability to reconcile the incongruity at all, a finding that is consistent with the role of the right frontal lobe in inference-making, or drawing conclusions from incomplete information.[10] Based on Koestler's outline of how a joke is understood in the brain, it seems that "drawing conclusions from incomplete information" is at the heart of joke comprehension.

Perhaps the most complex humorous texts are those that utilize irony. In the case of irony, the audience must be able to properly identify ironic intent and then reconcile that incongruity. And here, the reconciliation of the incongruity itself is quite complex, as understanding irony requires that listeners process the literal meaning of a text first ("Gorgeous weather we're having!") before using context clues to signal the need for an ironic inversion (it is pouring rain outside, so the speaker must actually mean the opposite).[11] And none of this process will happen properly if the ironic intent of the speaker goes unrecognized.

Several ability factors that predict successful comprehension of irony relate to the listener's social and communication abilities. Individuals with autism spectrum disorders have been found to have significantly more trouble in identifying speakers' ironic intent.[12] Especially in the context of face-to-face communication, in which nonverbal cues such as facial expressions and vocal patterns are used to subtly signal ironic intent, individuals with autism spectrum disorders show reduced brain activity "in those regions that respond selectively to face and voice,"[13] illustrating how and why an autism spectrum disorder would reduce an individual's ability to comprehend—or even recognize—irony.

Together these studies, on patients with right frontal lobe damage and individuals with autism spectrum disorders, illustrate how perception of humor complexity relates to the audience's processing abilities. But research on individual personality and psychology suggests that your motivation to process certain kinds of information might shape your perceptions of complexity, as well. One such trait is need for cognition. Developed by John Cacioppo and Richard Petty in the early 1980s, "need for cognition" captures people's enjoyment of thinking.[14] Need for cognition isn't about how intelligent you are but how much you actually enjoy the process of solving problems and working through information.[15] According to Cacioppo and Petty, high need for cognition signifies a high motivation to engage in effortful processing, whereas a low need for cognition signifies little motivation to think too hard.[16] Put simply: individuals high in need for cognition are more motivated to process complex information and form complex judgments. They also tend to engage thoughtfully in message processing, mentally elaborating on incoming information more than people with lower need for cognition do.[17]

People with different levels of need for cognition tend to differ in countless other ways as well.[18] People low in need for cognition are more likely to be dogmatic and are more aware of social comparison cues. They are more likely to place a high value on attractiveness or popularity; more likely to engage in processes of selective attention, perception, and avoidance; more likely to be high in need for closure (a psychological trait indicating an aversion to ambiguity and uncertainty); and more likely to prefer order and predictability. People high in need for cognition tend to be more curious, more willing to dedicate long periods of time to a dedicated task, more open to new ideas, and more likely to see social and political issues as affecting them personally.

Based on the correlates just outlined, it will likely be unsurprising to learn that need for cognition is related to humor appreciation. People who enjoy thinking are more likely to appreciate humor than those who don't.[19] Given that joke comprehension is akin to a playful form of riddle-solving, the notion that people who enjoy thinking are more appreciative of jokes makes sense. Recent work by Mark Mayer, Plamen Peev, and Piyush Kumar, however, places an interesting condition on this relationship.[20] They found that the link between need for cognition and humor appreciation works when the humor is predominantly rooted in incongruity resolution (which, as I've discussed, is cognitively taxing). However, when a joke is disparagement-oriented (making fun of someone or something, as in the "Yo mama" jokes discussed earlier), the effects of need for cognition disappear. It seems that when incongruities are high, as they are in ironic texts, need for cognition is an important predictor of enjoyment.

Along with my colleague Ben Bagozzi and graduate students Shannon Poulsen, Abigail Goldring, and Erin Drouin, I conducted an experiment to understand the predictors of appreciation for ironic and exaggeration-based jokes. We attempted to isolate which psychological traits explain the types of jokes people generally find funny and which traits predict appreciation of humor overall. When responding to both ironic jokes and hyperbolic (or exaggeration-based) jokes, need for cognition was a significant, positive predictor. People who enjoy thinking are more likely to appreciate jokes than people who don't. The same was true of the generic "sense of humor" measure.[21] People who scored high in their appreciation for—and use of—humor in general were more likely to be high in need for cognition.[22] Given that humor is inherently complex and requires cognitive investment on the part of the audience, these findings are not surprising.

Where things get downright fascinating, though, is in the connections between humor appreciation and another category of psychological traits: tolerance for ambiguity and its converse traits, need for closure and need for order. In 1993, Willibald Ruch and Franz-Josel Hehl explored how the psychological trait of need for order relates to appreciation for various kinds of humor.[23] As defined in their study, need for order captures how concerned an individual is with keeping personal effects neat and organized, developing ways to keep materials organized, disliking clutter and confusion, and disliking a lack of organization. Ruch and Hehl hypothesize that "appreciation of the incongruity-resolution structure in humour is a manifestation of a broader need of individuals for contact with structured, stable, unambiguous forms of stimulation, whereas appreciation of the nonsense structure in humour reflects a generalized need for uncertain, unpredictable, and ambiguous stimuli."[24] In other words, Ruch and Hehl wanted to test their theory that people who like order in their lives also like order in the humor they consume. They proposed that people who needed order would be more likely to appreciate the incongruity-resolution jokes: jokes in which "a recipient first discovers an incongruity which is then fully resolvable upon consideration of information available elsewhere in the joke or cartoon."[25] In these kinds of jokes, the reconciliation of the incongruity doesn't require as much cognitive effort on the part of the listener, as the information necessary to solve the riddle is present in the joke text. In contrast, the nonsense jokes "1) provide no resolution at all, 2) provide a partial resolution (leaving an essential part of the incongruity unresolved), or 3) actually create new absurdities or incongruities." What I find most interesting about the Ruch and Hehl study is its effort to link audience psychology to the appreciation of humor—not based on what the joke is about or who it targets—but based on the structure of the humor in the joke. Ruch and Hehl write: "the tendency to keep personal surroundings and personal effects neat and organized extends to liking of punch lines in which the surprise induced by the incongruity can be overcome completely."[26]

Nonthreatening and Operating in a Playful Mode

Additional criteria Attardo proposes as necessary for humor appreciation are that the humor occurs in a playful mode (framed as humor) and that the joke resolution is nonthreatening. Humor, in general—and satire more specifically—won't work if the audience won't play along. For any form of humor to be appreciated and bring about mirth, it must be experienced in what psychologist Michael Apter refers to as the "paratelic" mode.[27] According to Apter's reversal theory, humans encounter the world through various motivational states. Apter suggests that people vacillate between states depending on their personalities, their psychological profiles, and cues in their environment. For example, sometimes people operate in a more serious, goal-driven, "telic" state and other times in a more playful, spontaneous, "paratelic" state. It is in the paratelic state that people are able to experience and appreciate humor. In order to enter the state of play, Attardo argues, the audience must perceive the environment and the joke itself as nonthreatening. Since people have different values and opinions, what they consider threatening will most certainly vary. In determining whether someone will consider a joke or joke topic non-threatening, it is key to understand the joke target and the audience's in-group/out-group alliances.[28]

First rule of comedy: know your audience.

Dozens of studies have examined how people will find humor that targets their own "in-group" to be less funny than humor that targets their "out-group." Democrats find jokes about Republicans funnier than Republicans do, and vice versa.[29] But jokes that contradict one's values or belief systems (regardless of in-group status) may be rejected as well. Caroline Thomas and Victoria Esses studied how men responded to sexist humor disparaging women.[30] "Results revealed that men who were higher in hostile sexism were especially likely to report that they would repeat the female-disparaging jokes, and rated these jokes as funnier than did men who were lower in hostile sexism."[31] Dolf Zillmann and Joanne Cantor's "disposition theory of humor" helps to account for humor appreciation that is shaped not only by one's own reference-group status, but by one's antipathies and sympathies toward various groups.[32] The theory posits that "humor appreciation is facilitated when the respondent feels antipathy or resentment towards disparaged protagonists and impaired when he feels sympathy or liking for these protagonists."[33] So, while I myself might not *be* Black, Latino, Muslim, LGBTQ, or Jewish, my feelings of empathy for, and liking of, members of these communities will most certainly shape how funny I will find jokes made at their expense.

I experienced this as an undergraduate at the University of New Hampshire, where I performed in an improvisational comedy group once a month. One night, while playing a game called Worst Movies That Were Never Made, I blurted out the line "Schindler's Pissed!" An acquaintance of mine at the time, who was president of our university's chapter of Hillel, was in the audience. He stood up in the middle of the show, angered by the fact that I had referred to a film about the Holocaust in the context of a comedy show. The joke didn't make any statements about the Holocaust. It didn't issue any judgment or identify any targets. It wasn't sophisticated. It wasn't even funny, to be honest. It was a play on words: rhyming "List" with "Pissed." But my classmate considered the mere activation of this construct in the context of a comedy show inappropriate and offensive. I had violated Attardo's criterion.

Obviously, most people are *unwilling* to entertain certain ideas in the state of play, but might there be ideas that are perceived to be so threatening or offensive that one might be psychologically *unable* to consider them in a playful way? On Friday, July 28, 2017, addressing an audience of police officers in Suffolk County, New York, Present Donald Trump joked about how law enforcement shouldn't be so careful about the physical comfort and safety of alleged criminals: "when you see these thugs being thrown into the back of a paddy wagon, you just see them thrown in, rough. I said, 'Please don't be too nice,' Like when you guys put somebody in the car and you're protecting their head, you know, the way you put their hand over? Like, don't hit their head and they've just killed somebody. Don't hit their head? I said, 'You can take the hand away, OK?'"[34] Following his address, various police departments publicly renounced Trump's sentiments, including the Suffolk County Police Department, who had hosted the address: "as a department, we do not and will not tolerate 'rough(ing)' up prisoners.... The Suffolk County Police Department has strict rules and procedures relating to the handling of prisoners, and violations of those rules and procedures are treated extremely seriously."[35] When asked about Trump's comments during a White House press briefing the following week, Press Secretary Sarah Huckabee Sanders replied: "I believe he was making a joke at the time." But for members of the public wary of police brutality aimed at people of color and for members of law enforcement trying to earn the trust of various minority communities, this "joke" posed an actual threat—in large part because it was made by the president of the United States. For many, the fear and anger ignited by this statement precluded any possibility of humor appreciation. And this might not be a result of people not *wanting* to see the joke as nonthreatening. This might stem from certain people not being *able* to see it in that light. In retrospect, perhaps my classmate's reaction to the "Schindler's Pissed" joke was about ability, too. For a person whose identity or safety is threatened by the activation of a certain construct in memory, maybe it really is about not being able to consider a certain topic in the state of play at all.

Not only must a person be willing and able to consider an idea in a paratelic or playful mode, but she must be able to recognize the humorous intent of the speaker. Recognizing that someone is operating in a playful mode is especially important when dealing with irony. Recall that irony is a two-step process that requires a listener to first access the joke's literal meaning. Irony comprehension requires the listener to recognize the speaker's ironic intent, in order to know that they must invert the valence of the speaker's statement. The literal meaning is what is processed first in the brain, before the ironic inversion.[36] The complexity of this processing task is illustrated by the fact that ironic texts take longer to process in the brain than do literal ones.[37]

Based on Available Scripts/Knowledge

Since jokes require that people activate two incompatible schemas, or mental networks of information, people must have those networks available somewhere in long-term memory to get a joke at all. Without the requisite knowledge structures, a joke will remain incongruous and unfunny. In a classroom exercise with my university students, I ask them to map out the psychological process of joke comprehension and appreciation for various political jokes. In 2016, I gave them this joke by Seth Meyers: "Hillary Clinton campaigned in Florida today with Al Gore. You're making Al Gore go back to Florida? That's so cruel. That's like making Joe Frazier go back to Manila." Many students understood the relevance of Florida to Al Gore (the unresolved 2000 election, which he ultimately lost to George W. Bush after the Supreme Court decision on vote tabulation). However, the second frame of reference activated by this joke, Joe Frazier and Manila, might as well have been delivered in another language. First, who is Joe Frazier? Second, where is Manila? Third, what is the relationship between Joe Frazier and Manila? Other than the one or two boxing fans in the room, the rest of the students had to Google the punchline, where they learned that Joe Frazier was a famous boxer who lost to Mohammed Ali in the 1975 heavyweight championship, held in Manila (the "Thrilla in Manila"). Needless to say, the students who had to Google the punchline didn't find the joke funny.

The availability of scripts and knowledge structures also explains the difficulty in getting jokes to translate across cultures. Without shared cultural understandings, popular culture references, or stereotypes, the appropriate knowledge structures simply do not exist. During my junior year studying abroad in France, I found myself at a loss when French people made jokes. I quickly learned that there was one kind of joke that I had to get on board with relatively quickly: "stupid Belgian" jokes. In France, Belgians are the source of endless comedy for their supposed stupidity. I don't know why. I never tried to figure it out. But I quickly learned that if I wanted to get the jokes that my host family often made at the dinner table, I had better recognize the French cultural rule: Belgians are stupid. To make this easy for myself, I simply took my existing American knowledge structure labeled "dumb blondes" and superimposed "Belgians" on it. As a blonde myself, I am exceptionally familiar with this particular stereotyped knowledge structure.

A fitting example of a Belgians-are-stupid joke comes from author Romain Seignovert:

> Two Belgians are driving a truck and arrive at a bridge with a warning sign: maximum height 4 meters. They get off and measure their truck. It's 6 meters high.
> —What shall we do? asks the one.
> —I don't see any police, says the other one, so let's drive on.[38]

For French people who are familiar with the stupid Belgian stereotype, the mere mention of "two Belgians" in the lead-in to the joke triggers an entire mental network related to the stereotypes of Belgians as stupid. Without that requisite knowledge structure, the listener is instead activating information related to bridges, and perhaps math. Four meters. Six meters. Four minus six equals negative two. By the punchline, the non-French listener might conclude through implication that the drivers weren't very bright, but it wouldn't result in the same kind of "Aha!" moment as it might for people who already have that stupid Belgian schema readily available in memory.

When appreciating a political joke, having requisite knowledge structures available depends heavily on the cognitive habits of the audience. Knowledge structures that are rarely used are buried (difficult to access) and disorganized. Knowledge structures that are used frequently are salient (easy to access) and well-organized. For instance, critics of President Trump are frequently activating aspects of his administration and presidency that are less than flattering. Their mental models associated with Trump include many well-rehearsed negative traits, unflattering quotations, and problematic policy positions. Partisans tend to bask in the comfort of homogenous social networks in which their opinion is the majority opinion.[39] This leads to the reactivation of belief-confirming ideas through conversation, creating an interpersonal "echo chamber" effect. Partisans also tend to self-select into partisan media audiences where like-minded programming constantly reminds them of all the things they hate about the other side and all the things they love about their own side.[40] This, too, creates an echo chamber, but in a mediated context instead of an interpersonal one. These behavior patterns, and their chronic reactivation of partisan ideas, mean that the kinds of knowledge structures

Republicans have about Democrats are entirely different from the ones Democrats have about Democrats. So, not only might my willingness to appreciate a joke at my own political party's expense be diminished due to my allegiances; I might literally not have the right ideas readily available in my mind to get the joke. Think: Democrat trying to access the "Hillary Clinton responsible for deaths at Benghazi" proposition. Or Republican trying to access the "Republicans want to strip healthcare from millions of Americans" proposition. They're just not as easy to get to.

Can You *Ever* Appreciate a Joke without Comprehending It?

The Strange Case of Irony

Earlier I alluded to the fact that people must comprehend a joke in order to appreciate it. However, comprehension doesn't necessarily mean comprehension in a manner consistent with what the speaker or writer intended. People often make sense of jokes on their own, based on whatever information or knowledge structures they have available—and based on their own motivations. It's possible that this process could result in a person "getting" a joke but not "getting it right." So yes, I can still find something funny even if I comprehend it in a way that is inconsistent with what the speaker intended.

Perhaps the most well-known academic example of this comes from a study of how audiences interpreted and appreciated Norman Lear's popular 1970s sitcom *All in the Family*. "Lovable bigot" Archie Bunker (played by Carroll O'Connor), an aging patriarch, was reluctant to adapt to the increasingly progressive era of the early 1970s. The foil to Archie's character was his live-in son-in-law, Mike Stivic (portrayed by a young Rob Reiner), a liberal Democrat who was especially liberal on social issues related to race and gender. While patriarch Archie was portrayed in a sympathetic light, as *personally* morally decent, his bigotry, prejudices, and fear of social and political change were the target of the show's jokes, often revealed through exchanges with Mike and Mike's wife, Archie's daughter, Gloria.

Archie referred to England as a "fag country." He lamented increasing racial integration, declaring: "the coons are comin'" and "equality is unfair!" Lear wrote the character Archie as an opportunity to poke fun at such a provincial belief system. As Lear stated in a 2012 interview with journalist Roger Rosenblatt: "Archie was afraid of tomorrow. He was afraid of progress. Things had been moving too fast for him. Having grown up in communities where he never saw a black person, a black family moving in next door was anathema to him. The world was falling apart. So, he came at that out of fear more than…hatred."[41] Perhaps aware of the risks inherent in satirizing bigotry in such an implicit form, CBS sought to distance itself from the controversial nature of the programming through a disclaimer. Before the first episode, the following text scrolled up the screen: "The program you are about to see is ALL IN THE FAMILY. It seeks to throw a humorous spotlight on our frailties, prejudices and concerns. By making them a source of laughter, we hope to show—in a mature fashion—just how absurd they are." As stodgy as the disclaimer may have seemed, the folks at CBS were smart to include it. As it turns out, concerns over how viewers might comprehend and appreciate *All in the Family* were well founded. In 1974, social psychologists Neil Vidmar and Milton Rokeach studied perceptions of *All in the Family* among American teenagers and Canadian adults.[42] While only 10 percent of the Canadian sample believed that the liberal son-in-law, Mike, was the most mocked character in the show (instead seeing Archie and his wife as the main target of the jokes), among the teenage American respondents, almost *half* saw Mike as the main target of the jokes. When the samples were split into "low-" and "high-prejudiced" respondents, the phenomenon of selective perception was clear. Among those high in prejudice, 38 percent reported admiring Archie, compared to only 24 percent of those low in prejudice. Among those high in prejudice, 29 percent believed that Archie won the most arguments in the show, compared to only 13 percent of those lower in prejudice.

Vidmar and Rokeach concluded: "we found that many persons did not see the program as satire on bigotry and that these persons were more likely to be viewers who scored high on measures of prejudice.…All such findings seem to suggest that the program is more likely reinforcing prejudice and racism than combating it."[43] People across the samples enjoyed the show, but those on the left saw the show as supporting their own worldview, and those on the right also saw it as supporting their worldview. Vidmar and Rokeach describe this process in terms of the audience's motivation to avoid cognitive dissonance. People in general do not want to feel challenged in their belief systems, especially when in the context of play and entertainment. But I would suggest that audiences' selective readings of the show also stem from their ability to engage certain constructs in memory. Understanding and appreciating *All in the Family* in the spirit Lear intended would have required that viewers have certain beliefs accessible in their mental models related to politics and society. These beliefs included: "racial equality is good and natural"; "racial segregation is bad"; "women are equal to men"; "diversity is good." And "people who reject these belief systems are backward and worthy of derision."

Without those beliefs already accessible in memory, a viewer would not be able to make the appropriate cognitive contributions to reconcile the incongruity between Mike's view of the world and Archie's. Notice my term "appropriate cognitive contribution." Viewers who did not have these liberal tenets accessible in their memories would still be able to access other information that would help them get the joke. For these folks, the scenarios intended to reveal and mock Archie's bigotry would instead serve to activate in their minds the race- and gender-based stereotypes central to the insults and epithets that Archie casually throws around: "England is a fag country." "The coons are comin.'" "Equality is unfair!" "Men are worth more than women." As a result of these differences, liberals saw Archie as the butt of the joke and Mike as the hero. Conservatives saw Mike as the butt of the joke and Archie as the hero. Yet they all found it funny.

More recently, in 2009, Heather LaMarre, Kristen Landreville, and Michael Beam documented a very similar phenomenon in the context of ironic political satire.[44] They studied how college undergraduates perceived the humor and intent of Colbert's performance as a conservative, blowhard political pundit on *The Colbert Report*. After watching the segment, students in the study were asked to what extent they believed Colbert was himself a social conservative or a Republican. They were also asked if they thought Colbert really meant what he said in his ironic interview of Amy Goodman, the host of *Democracy Now*.

The first thing I should note here is that the students who reported having watched Colbert's show in the past were more likely to identify the irony in the show. So, at least for those people with a history of watching it, they were most likely getting it right. But, controlling for prior viewing and other factors, conservative students assigned to watch the Colbert clip in the study were "significantly more likely to get it wrong." That is, conservative students believed that Colbert really meant what he was saying in the segment with Goodman and that he personally didn't like liberals. These students were also more likely to believe that Colbert himself was socially conservative.

Most important, though, is the place where conservative and liberal students agreed—and that is in how funny they found the clip. Liberal and conservative students, in spite of their significantly different interpretations of Colbert, all found him funny. Perhaps the students had a vested interest in the meaning of the humor coming from an affable, confident comic. They wanted

Colbert to be on their side, and so their self-serving biases served as a filter through which they processed the joke. And without clear irony markers to denote that Colbert didn't mean what he was literally saying, those students who were unfamiliar with the show or the comic would be left to their own devices to determine what he really meant. And one's own devices usually operate to make one feel good and right.

While this is certainly true, I would argue that how we interpret ironic humor is about more than just "seeing what we want to see" (as LaMarre and her colleagues explain it). It's also about "seeing what we are most able to see." The availability of certain constructs or ideas in working memory will determine how people interpret ironic information. In the clip used in the study, Goodman discussed how many of the soldiers fighting in Iraq saw the war as unnecessary. She argued that embedding journalists with soldiers was preventing journalists from being critical and independent in their war coverage. She pointed to the story of an army medic who went to Iraq, applied for conscientious objector status, was denied, and turned himself in. Colbert interrupted, "He broke the law. We have laws for that. That's settled. What he did is against the law. You accept that. He disobeyed an order. We're not fighting for guys to not fight. We're fighting so guys will fight."

Just as viewers' ability to see Archie Bunker as the butt of the jokes depended on the presence of certain constructs in their working memories, viewers' ability to see Colbert's statements as ironic was contingent on the accessibility of certain assumptions and constructs in the mind of the audience. Without having these—markedly liberal—arguments and assumptions accessible in memory, the audience would go with other accessible information to make sense of the joke. Conservatives, equipped with networked information in memory that contains the same arguments and assumptions that Colbert is literally stating, will read Colbert as mocking the left, not the right. After all, he is saying these things aggressively and hyperbolically, and these words map directly onto the very things they believe to be true and often think about. So, liberals saw Colbert as mocking conservatives. Conservatives saw Colbert as mocking liberals. Yet they all found him funny.

As a postscript, it's worthwhile to reflect on Colbert's own admission that he had grown nervous about the possible influence of his ironic character. In 2016, about two years after leaving *The Colbert Report*, he explained his departure to *Fresh Air*'s Terry Gross. "It wasn't because I didn't like it anymore—I still liked it—but I just thought 'I'm not sure if I can actually keep this up without hurting someone.'"[45]

Gross pushed him on this phrasing and asked for clarification: "*hurting* someone? What do you mean?"

Colbert replied slowly and deliberately: "I don't know. It's a feeling. I thought maybe I would make some big mistake with the character. Because he says—he would say—*terrible* things. And I got away with some of the terrible things he would say or do because it was all filtered through his mask, but if I didn't maintain the mask, it would just be me being terrible and he would say hateful things or hurtful things. And I thought if I don't play this tightly…If I didn't maintain this discipline…I would simply slide into being *like* the thing I was mocking."[46] Based on the research, I would say that Colbert's fears were well founded.

Satire is most likely to be appreciated by people who—due to personality, psychology, and aspects of the environment—can get it and are willing to get it. These are people who possess the requisite knowledge to reconcile the incongruity. Their openness to and enjoyment of thinking increase their motivation to try to get the joke. And they are willing and able to entertain the topic in the state of play. As I'll show in chapter 6, regardless of the topic or target of the humor, many of these general criteria for humor comprehension and appreciation are indirectly related to political ideology. In other words, satire and irony as modes of political expression might actually have an inherent liberal bias.

6

The Psychology of the Left and the Right

The Psychology of Aesthetic Preferences

When it comes to artwork, my friend Amy enjoys abstract designs with blended colors and blurred lines. Annie on the other hand likes paintings that look like photographs: realistic and true to life. People like to think of such preferences as stemming from a highly personal, almost spiritual place. ("This painting just speaks to me.") Yet research indicates that these preferences reflect deep psychological characteristics. Psychologists and philosophers have tackled the question of aesthetic preferences for centuries, dating back to Gustav Fechner in the late 1800s.[1] These scholars sought to understand how people's preferences for images, shapes, and artwork reflect their underlying psychological traits, which make some aesthetic forms more appealing than others to them. As Stephen Palmer, Karen Schloss, and Jonathan Sammartino summarize it: "aesthetics is the study of those mental processes that underlie disinterested evaluative experiences that are anchored at the positive end by feelings that would accompany verbal expressions such as "Oh wow! That's wonderful! I love it!" and at the negative end by "Oh yuck! That's awful! I hate it!"[2] But people's preferences for art are not the only preferences these underlying mental processes shape. In fact, aesthetic preferences "occur anywhere in response to seeing any sort of object, scene, or event."[3]

Could this mean that these aesthetic preferences shape how we respond to humorous incongruities? Political satire? Or even in response to the genre known as outrage?

Yes.

And might these preferences be driven by "underlying mental processes" that derive from people's psychological—even physiological, biological, or genetic—predispositions?

Indeed.

Recall the psychological trait need for cognition—how much some people enjoy thinking—and how it contributes to their appreciation for complex jokes. People high in need for cognition are more appreciative of humor in general, likely because it requires cognitive work to reconcile the incongruity.[4] Need for cognition also shapes how people process different forms of information and hence what kinds of information or aesthetic forms they appreciate, seek out, and enjoy. When consumers respond to advertisements, for example, people who enjoy thinking (that is, are high in need for cognition) tend to evaluate the arguments in the ads more extensively than people who don't. Among people high in need for cognition, the strength of the arguments made in an advertisement tends to be a stronger determinant of their overall opinion of the ad and of the product it is advertising than it is among those who are lower in need for cognition. Meanwhile, among those lower in need for cognition, their opinion of the ad and its product will be determined more by surface-level characteristics, like the attractiveness of the message source, music, and visual cues.[5] This means that different kinds of people end up liking—and being persuaded by—very different kinds of ads.

Need for cognition also shapes aesthetic preferences captured through people's recreational habits—like reading. It turns out that how much people enjoy thinking plays a role in influencing the kinds of books they read. Those higher in need for cognition are more likely to report reading complex works of fiction than those lower in need for cognition.[6] Mia Stokmans, a professor at Tilburg University, found that the participants who were lowest in need for cognition reported the highest proportion of pleasure reading in the genres of romance (least complex) and mystery (moderately complex), while those high in need for cognition were the most likely to report the highest proportion of pleasure reading in the genre of complex works of literature. These relationships are undoubtedly shaped and reinforced by social cues and context. People who think of themselves as intellectually curious and thoughtful will gravitate toward the kinds of books they think people like them ought to be reading. But at least some of these patterns stem from psychological characteristics.

Need for cognition also tends to be high among people who are tolerant of ambiguity. Tolerance for ambiguity is another key trait that contributes to artistic and aesthetic preferences. Tolerance for ambiguity, also known in association with its converse, need for closure, refers to how comfortable an individual is with novelty and uncertainty.[7] People who are high in tolerance for ambiguity adapt easily to new situations, are open to new experiences, and tend to reject structure, order, and predictability. Those low in tolerance for ambiguity, who are high in need for closure, are less comfortable with new experiences and tend to *prefer* routines, order, structure, and predictability.

The psychological battery of questions used to measure need for closure includes 47 items relating to one's comfort with and preference for certain kinds of experiences over others.[8] Developed by Arie Kruglanski and his colleagues, the measure involves asking respondents to what extent they agree or disagree with statements such as these: *I don't like situations that are uncertain. I dislike questions which could be answered in many different ways. I find that a well-ordered life with regular hours suits my temperament. I usually make important decisions quickly and confidently.* The measure also includes agreement with items which denotes lower need for closure: *I tend to struggle with most decisions. When considering most conflict situations, I can usually see how both sides could be right.*[9]

As is clear from the items listed here, the need for closure scale includes several different underlying dimensions, including need for order, need for predictability, need for decisiveness, intolerance for ambiguity, and closed-mindedness. In spite of these unique underlying dimensions, people who score high in one tend to also score higher in the others. This means that need for order, predictability, decisiveness, and intolerance for ambiguity tend to work together. They coexist. Which explains how and why this trait—which seems mostly about one's comfort with social situations and life routines—also shapes people's preferences for certain kinds of information and art.

In studies of people's artistic preferences, people low in tolerance for ambiguity have been found to reject abstract art in favor of more realistic work.[10] Justin Ostrofsky and Elizabeth Shobe, for example, found that when it came to highly realistic paintings, people with varying levels of need for closure showed little variance in how much they understood them or liked them.[11] But in the case of nonrealistic paintings (more abstract work), people high in tolerance for ambiguity liked them more than people lower in tolerance for ambiguity. Ostrofsky and Shobe explain that participants who were less tolerant of ambiguity didn't want to look at the nonrealistic paintings for very long, so they cut their time short compared to people without such need for closure. In a massive study of artistic preferences using over 91,000 participants from the United Kingdom, Tomas Chamorro-Premuzic and his colleagues found that openness to experience (a dimension of tolerance for ambiguity) was "the strongest and only consistent personality correlate of artistic preferences, affecting both overall and specific preferences, as well as visits to galleries, and artistic (rather than scientific) self-perception."[12]

Tolerance for ambiguity shapes preferences for the performing arts as well. Daphne Weirsema and her colleagues at the University of Amsterdam examined the link between need for closure and aesthetic preferences in the context of abstract paintings and theatrical productions featuring plots that remain unresolved at the end.[13] Appreciation for both the abstract paintings and the open-ended plays was highest among those who scored highest in tolerance for ambiguity. The people who needed cognitive closure preferred realistic art and plays that resolved all of their plot points at the end. Again, these findings support the idea that those high in need for closure have less appreciation of ideas that do not provide explicit conclusions. As the authors write, "individuals high in need for closure are less attracted to art forms that do not satisfy their need for clarity, meaning, and quick answers."[14]

For Some People, an Ellipsis Is *Not OK*

In 2004, I sat in a Philadelphia movie theater to watch the romantic indie movie *Garden State* with my husband. In the film, Andrew (portrayed by Zach Braff) returns from his life as an aspiring actor in Los Angeles to his hometown in New Jersey to attend his mother's funeral. For two hours, we watch a traumatized and neurotic Zach Braff and a quirky and beautiful Natalie Portman spend four strange, intense, and oddly romantic days together. Against the backdrop of a familiar and angst-inducing suburbia, and set to the melancholy music of The Shins and Coldplay, the film is a portrait of two flawed people, Braff and Portman, falling in love.

Spoiler alert (although if you haven't seen a 2004 film by now, chances are, you're safe). In the final scene of the film, Braff is scheduled to return to his life in Los Angeles. Portman escorts him to the airport to see him off.

So, will they stay together? Are they breaking up?

They sit at the bottom of a stairway, and Portman asks Braff pointedly, "You're not coming back are you?"

He then delivers the most frustrating line in the history of movie lines:

"Look, this isn't a conversation about this being over. It's . . . I'm not, like, putting a period at the end of this, you know? I'm putting, like, an ellipsis on it . . ."

An ellipsis?

I remember turning to my husband at this very moment in the theater, tears streaming down my face, and angrily whispering,

"An ellipsis is *not OK.*"

As Braff leaves Portman and runs away to his gate, audiences fully expect him to turn around and run back to her. After all, that's what happens in romantic movies. But he keeps running. He gets on the plane. We see him sitting on the plane. And then we see Portman sobbing in a phone booth in the airport.

At this point, I was ready to demand a refund. Because not only am I already someone who is relatively high in need for closure...I was also six months pregnant with our son. I didn't go to the theater to get jerked around and left not knowing what was going to happen next as I was about to bring a child into the world and was especially high in need for order, closure, certainty, and predictability.

But then...all of a sudden...Braff barges into the phone booth where Portman is sobbing! He came back!

He pulls Portman out of the phone booth. "You remember that idea I had about working stuff out on my own and then finding you once I figured that stuff out?" he breathlessly asks her.

"The ellipsis?" she wipes her tears away.

"Yeah, the ellipsis. It's dumb. It's dumb. It's an awful idea, I'm not going to do it, OK? And like you said, this is it. This is life. And I'm in love with you, Samantha."

Need for closure, indeed.

The Psychology of Political Ideology

Where all of this is heading, of course, is to a discussion of the unique psychological profiles of liberals and conservatives—unique psychological profiles that contribute to people's aesthetic preferences and so might help explain the abundance of satire on the left and the lack of it on the right. Dating back to Theodor Adorno and others' work on *The Authoritarian Personality*,[15] written in the wake of World War II, political psychologists have explored how psychological and personality traits are correlated with political attitudes. More recent work in neuroscience and cognitive psychology has helped to establish these important links, explaining how and why people's psychological profiles relate to their political preferences.

Before getting too deep into the psychological correlates of political ideology, let me first be clear that these correlations are about *probabilities*, not deterministic relationships. Research on the "psychology of the left and right" does not assert that "conservatives are always this way" and "liberals are always that way." Rather, it explores the probability that people will have certain traits given their political preferences and, conversely, the probability that people will have certain political preferences given their psychological traits. Social science never involves propositions in the form "If this is true then that is necessarily also true." If it did, then studying social science would be a lot easier that it actually is. Instead, that pesky phenomenon known as "free will" gets in the way. People can choose to believe whatever they want, do whatever they want, and respond to external stimuli however they want.

People *can* choose to do any of these things.... However, people *tend to* organize their beliefs, attitudes, and behaviors in patterns, making them somewhat predictable.

And this is the underlying logic of social science.

So, what are some of the psychological traits that correlate with political ideology? Conveniently, for the purposes of the argument I'm crafting here, they are the exact same traits that shape information processing and aesthetic preferences: chief among them being need for cognition and tolerance for ambiguity (and its converse, need for closure). A number of surveys and experiments have demonstrated that need for cognition (enjoyment of thinking) tends to be higher among political liberals than among political conservatives.[16] These studies show that individuals who enjoy thinking also tend to be more politically liberal, both when measured as self-described political ideology and when measured in terms of policy preferences. Several studies have sought to understand how this link between ideology and psychology plays out in the context of specific political judgments. For example, Michael Sargent explored people's opinions on the use of harsh responses to criminal acts and confirmed that people high in need for cognition "were less supportive of punitive measures."[17] This phenomenon can be attributed to the fact that low need for cognition contributes to judgments that are made based on gut reactions and heuristics: cues that do not involve as much effortful processing and hence lead to quick, reflexive, and often emotional responses.[18] Another study, by Chadly Stern and his colleagues, used gender cues to assess how liberals and conservatives determined someone's sexual orientation— that is, how do people decide if they think a person is gay or straight?[19] Conservatives were more likely than liberals to make determinations of strangers' sexual orientations based on existing stereotypes about gays and lesbians.[20] Such findings are consistent with a model in which conservatives' lower need for cognition drives a reliance on heuristic cues that lead to quick, emotional responses.

Second, across numerous studies and various methodologies, conservatives have been found to be higher in need for closure than liberals.[21] This association is especially pronounced when examining the link between need for closure and social/cultural conservatism, in contrast to economic conservatism.[22] Strong cultural conservatives demonstrate lower tolerance for aspects of social change that may present uncertainty or pose a threat to the existing social order.[23] A recent study I conducted with my colleagues at the University of Delaware examined the link between need for closure and opinions about transgender people and transgender rights.[24] Our results confirmed our suspicions that need for closure would predict more negative feelings toward transgender people and rights. Thus, we argued that "individuals with a high need for cognitive closure [will] be uncomfortable with the ambiguity inherent in the concept of a gender identity that does not match the sex assigned at birth."[25] Indeed, this lack of comfort with ambiguity correlated with more negative opinions of transgender people and lower support for transgender rights.

John Jost and his colleagues at New York University completed a meta-analysis of 88 unique samples that explored this link between political conservatism and various dimensions of need for closure.[26] This mammoth "study of other studies" included over 22,000 respondents in data sets from 12 countries. All told, the analyses confirmed a strong consistent relationship between political conservatism and measures of tolerance for ambiguity. The authors conclude: "conservative ideologies, like virtually all other belief systems, are adopted in part because they satisfy various psychological needs.... We regard political conservatism as an ideological belief system that is significantly (but not completely) related to motivational concerns having to do with the psychological management of uncertainty and fear. Specifically, the avoidance of uncertainty (and the striving for certainty) may be particularly tied to one core dimension of conservative thought, resistance to change."[27] In recent years, some political psychologists have been publicly critical of this so-called rigidity-of-the-right literature, arguing that some of the studies have methodological and conceptual flaws.[28] Of concern to scholars like Ariel Malka and Yphtach Lelkes is the fact that the questions sometimes included in the need for closure scales may contain subtle political themes, hence making it all but certain that researchers will find that these "psychological traits" correlate with political conservatism. Another critique is that scholars in this area have not gone far enough to highlight how these linkages are less pronounced in the context of economic or fiscal conservatism. While the link between need for closure and social and cultural conservatism (immigration attitudes, beliefs about gay marriage and abortion) are robust and consistent, the connections between need for closure and attitudes toward taxation and regulation, for example, are less clear. I highlight these critiques simply to say that the literature is not without its critics. For my purposes, though, the consistent finding that the psychological profile of social/cultural conservatives is distinct from that of social/cultural liberals is most important. And while individual studies may have used psychological items that conflate political ideology with need for closure or openness, I remain convinced that, taken as a whole, the unique psychological profiles of the left and the right are not wholly attributable to an artifact of measurement.

Mounting evidence suggests that these psychological differences are real and that they stem from distinct physiological characteristics. Studies conducted in the emerging field of political neuroscience point to differences in brain structures between liberals and conservatives—differences that map onto their unique psychological traits and orientations to the world. For instance, studies of the neurological structures of conservatives' brains indicate that conservative individuals have larger amygdalas—the region of the brain that responds to threat.[29] The size and activity in your amygdala predicts your likeliness to react in a more emotionally charged way when responding to threatening situations.[30] This evidence from brain science fits with the finding that conservatives report high "mortality salience," that is, they are significantly more cognizant of their own deaths. They also report greater fear of threat and loss than liberals do.[31]

In contrast, liberals have bigger anterior cingulates—the region of the brain involved in conflict monitoring.[32] Conflict monitoring is the process through which you determine whether your automatic response matches with the response that would be most appropriate for the situation at hand.[33] Hence, with a larger anterior cingulate, liberals are more likely to change how they react to certain events, as they tend to devote cognitive resources to choosing the most suitable responses to various situations.[34] Whereas conservatives are commonly monitoring their environments for threats, liberals are evaluating information and verifying that the data coming in matches their attitudes and judgments. Jost and Amodio conclude: "given that the ACC [anterior cingulate] is associated with conflict monitoring and the amygdala is centrally involved in physiological and behavioral responses to threat, this neuroanatomical evidence appears to lend further support to the notion that political ideology is linked to basic neurocognitive orientations toward uncertainty and threat."[35] Over the past decade, Jost has worked to develop a thorough account of the cognitive psychology and neuropsychology behind political ideology. His work is rooted in the premise that people are guided by social cognitive motives—socially related motivations that are shaped by people's psychological traits.[36] In other words, people are motivated to engage with the world and the people in it in ways that are shaped by their own psychological profiles. These motivations then affect the kinds of things they see as correct, appropriate, or desirable in their society and around the globe. By thinking of political ideology as motivated social cognition, Jost suggests, political preferences can be viewed as just an outcome of people's underlying psychological tendencies.

According to this logic, we humans have innate psychological traits—maybe we are open to new experiences and enjoy thinking, or maybe we prefer certainty and structure and do not enjoy thinking—and these traits inform the ways we approach the world around us. People who prefer to rely on heuristics (mental shortcuts), rather than cognitively investing in the processing of new information, will be more likely to resist change and will continue to support existing policies and social practices. Indeed, the two traits of need for cognition and tolerance for ambiguity are very closely related. People who enjoy thinking are, on average, more likely to be open to new experiences, particularly in the realm of aesthetics, actions, ideas, and values.[37] And these people, based on their underlying orientations to the world, tend to be politically liberal.

In *Prius or Pickup*, political scientists Marc Hetherington and Jonathan Weiler summarize the distinct psychological profiles of the right and left as "fixed" (signaling a high need for closure and order) and "fluid" (signaling a high tolerance for ambiguity), respectively. Using four parenting-related questions, Hetherington and Weiler measure "how people impose order on a dangerous and potentially chaotic world."[38] The questions are framed as follows.

> Although there are a number of qualities that people feel children should have, every person thinks that some are more important than others. I am going to read you pairs of desirable qualities. Please tell me which one you think is more important for a child to have.
> 1. Independence versus respect for elders
> 2. Obedience versus self-reliance
> 3. Curiosity versus good manners
> 4. Being considerate versus being well-behaved.[39]

Hetherington and Weiler present a detailed empirical case that the two different worldviews captured by these items relate not only to political ideology, party, attitudes, and beliefs but also to seemingly apolitical aspects of lifestyle and consumer behavior. Everything from people's choice of occupation and where to raise a family to brand allegiance and the types of cars they drive are related to whether they fall into a "fixed" or "fluid" worldview.

And these tendencies go deeper than people's value systems and even deeper than their cognitive motivations. Research from political psychology points to the existence of a "behavioral immune system"[40] that guides people's interactions with the world through the lens of disease-avoidance and hygiene. Laboratory research shows stronger and more visceral physiological reactions from conservatives (compared to liberals) in the face of threatening nonpolitical stimuli.[41] In a controlled experiment, Douglas Oxley and his colleagues prescreened people via telephone to identify 46 adults who held particularly strong political attitudes.[42] These participants completed questionnaires about their attitudes and beliefs on a range of political issues. Two months later, the same people were brought into a laboratory where they were hooked up to physiological equipment to measure their heart rates, blink rates, and skin conductance (sweating) in response to various images and sounds. Participants were exposed to nonpolitical pictures and sounds of varying threat potential—that is, some were deliberately peaceful and pleasant and some were deliberately threatening (e.g., an image of a large spider sitting on a frightened person's face; an image of an injured individual with a bloody face; an image of an open wound with maggots in it; unexpected unpleasant loud noises). The researchers found that those participants who supported capital punishment, patriotism, defense spending, and the Iraq War (conservative positions) were significantly more physiologically aroused (sweating and blinking) by the threatening stimuli than those who favored liberal policies (e.g., liberal immigration policies, foreign aid, pacifism, and gun control). In addition to these experimental studies, large-scale survey research has also confirmed the link between disgust sensitivity and conservatism.[43]

Disgust captures one's physical and emotional aversion to potentially harmful substances, environments, and people.[44] People experience it in response to rotting foods and human excrement, but also in response to perceived violations of social and moral contracts.[45] Conservatives are significantly more easily disgusted than liberals and significantly more concerned about pathogens and communicable disease than are liberals. Lest you think these linkages are isolated or spurious, Yoel Inbar, David Pizarro, and Ravi Iyer looked at the link between conservatism and disgust in a sample that included participants from 121 countries.[46] Their work, and the work of others, confirms that people who report the highest concern with pathogens and communicable diseases tend to be socially and culturally conservative.[47] This

 **Donald J. Trump** ✓
@realDonaldTrump

The U.S. cannot allow EBOLA infected people back. People that go to far away places to help out are great-but must suffer the consequences!

6:22 PM - 1 Aug 2014

FIGURE 6.1 Donald Trump, tweet, August 1, 2014 (two years before he was elected president).

certainly sheds new light on the classic conservative insult "dirty hippy," doesn't it? Or Trump's 2014 tweet (fig. 6.1) insisting that Americans who had contracted Ebola abroad should not be allowed to return to the United States?

In an effort to isolate the causal mechanism linking conservatism and disgust, scholars have even sought to artificially manipulate disgust to understand how it shapes subsequent political beliefs, and how this link can be altered. The results are startling. Researchers can manipulate disgust by introducing a small (but disgusting) informational prompt. Once people experience the feeling of disgust, more conservative political beliefs follow—among those who were more politically conservative from the start. In other words, if you expose people to something disgusting, the conservative people in the group will become more conservative in their social and cultural beliefs (hence the term "disgust sensitivity").

In a study of attitudes toward gays and lesbians, for example, John Terrizzi, Jr., and his colleagues manipulated disgust by randomly assigning participants to write essays about one of two hypothetical experiences, either "eating lettuce" or "eating maggots."[48] After writing the essay, participants were asked questions about political and social beliefs, including their attitudes toward gays and lesbians. Results showed that writing the "eating maggots" essay didn't cause all of those participants to become more conservative in their beliefs compared to the "eating lettuce" assignment. Rather, the results varied with the political ideology of the participant. The authors write: "inducing disgust in more conservative participants led to more prejudice compared to the control."[49] It seems that conservatives who experienced the disgust prime (writing the maggot essay), due to their higher disgust sensitivity, were more affected in their political beliefs than liberals who experienced the same prime.

A recent experiment by Lene Aarøe, Michael Petersen, and Kevin Arceneaux sought to introduce a disease protection prime prior to asking about attitudes toward immigration.[50] Here, the researchers wanted to see if providing disease protection information would lessen the effects of conservatives' physiological disgust response, thereby reducing hostile attitudes toward immigrants. Here again, participants experienced a (really) gross "disgust" prime—in this case they read a hospital orderly's first-person description of the process of cleaning up vomit. The story included graphic details such as "I had to get on my knees and clean it up with my hands. I do not think I will ever get used to feeling bile, half-digested food, and, in this case, a bit of blood cover my fingers as I remove everything from the floor. It is absolutely revolting." In the more disgusting version, participants stopped here. In the "disease protection" version, respondents read about how the orderly was then relieved to enter a "freshly cleaned" washroom, use "heavy-duty soap," and "finish by putting on a refreshing disinfecting lotion."[51] After reading the essay, the participants completed a questionnaire about their attitudes toward immigration. Again, the findings revealed that just with the introduction of this small handwashing cue, people's antiimmigration attitudes were 47 percent lower than those who read the "just cleaning vomit without washing hands" version. The authors conclude that disgust sensitivity "plays a causal role in the formation of immigration attitudes. . . . Because hand washing is not logically connected with immigration attitudes, it ostensibly does so outside of one's conscious awareness."[52]

Similarly, studies of the role of certain "safety and security" informational cues indicate that inducing feelings of safety and creating the illusion of the absence of physical threats minimizes the influence of people's core psychological traits on their political attitudes.[53] Researchers at Yale asked participants to imagine themselves as superheroes who were invulnerable to physical harm (versus the control group, who were told to imagine having the ability to fly). Participants in the "invulnerability" group felt significantly safer than those in the "flight" group. Following this manipulation, the participants were asked about various political beliefs. Among conservative participants who had experienced the "invulnerability" visualization exercise, socially conservative beliefs decreased more than they did among the conservatives who had experienced the flight condition.[54] Imagining that they were invulnerable superheroes caused conservative participants to become more liberal on policy issues and less resistant to social change.

Central to this conversation about how such proclivities might shape political beliefs is the concept of "epistemic motivation." The term "epistemology" simply refers to how we come to know what we know. Underlying people's epistemological orientations to the world are different kinds of motivations that might lead to different styles of sense-making.[55] If I am someone who is naturally high in need for closure, for example, I will tend to be motivated by efficiency and heuristics when I process information. This will guide how I form judgments when watching the news or even when meeting a new person at a party. If I am someone who is tolerant of ambiguity and high in need for cognition, I will be especially interested in getting to the truth of a given situation with little interest in efficiency. I will also be less likely to rely on heuristics and more likely to exhaustively search the information environment to be sure that I am correct in my judgment. If I am someone who is especially conscious of infectious pathogens in my environment, I will operate from a place of self-protection, processing information in a way that privileges the survival (and isolation) of myself and my in-group.

Genes: The Big Elephant (or Donkey) in the Room

Increasingly, political scientists are acknowledging the role of genetics in shaping people's political ideologies and their individual political beliefs.[56] In a recent study of the link between political ideology, need for cognition, and need for closure, Aleksander Ksiazkiewicz and his colleagues at the University of Illinois looked at these tendencies through the lens of genetics.[57] These researchers studied the genetic basis for both need for cognition and need for closure and found that both traits are linked directly to political ideology (measured three different ways) through genetic factors. The results of this research suggest that while environmental factors certainly contribute to people's political identities and outlooks, biology—basic genetic predispositions—play a role as well. The authors conclude simply: "genes link political ideology to cognitive style."[58]

Drawing on traditional genetic research methodologies, John Alford, Carolyn Funk, and John Hibbing completed an enormous study of "twin pairs" to try to understand to what extent political attitudes are heritable.[59] Given that monozygotic (identical) twins and dizygotic (fraternal) twins vary in the extent of the genetic material they share, examining various monozygotic and dizygotic twins' attitudinal and behavioral similarities helps to explain the extent to which such attitudes and beliefs stem from one's inherited genetic material. The twin participants in these studies completed an extensive questionnaire about their thoughts on everything from pajama parties, nudist camps, and horoscopes to disarmament, patriotism, and the death penalty.

Results indicated that the monozygotic twins (sharing 100 percent of their DNA) were significantly closer in their beliefs on political and social issues than were the dizygotic twins (sharing only 50 percent of their DNA). In other words, among twin siblings raised in the same environments, genes predict political, social, and cultural beliefs. As the authors describe it, "the substantive findings we present here offer a direct challenge to common assumptions and interpretations that political attitudes and behavioral tendencies are shaped primarily or even exclusively by environmental, especially familial, factors."[60]

Of course, as Alford and his colleagues concede, humans' genetic makeup also contributes to what environment they choose for themselves, what friends they have, and what information they seek, all of which then go on to shape political beliefs. So the way people's genes interact with their environment and their culture is crucial to understanding how they come to believe what they believe. And in an effort to quell fears that these findings should be read as evidence that our politics are "completely determined from birth," the authors offer this primer in probabilistic relationships: "it is not biological determinism to posit the existence of complex collections of genes that increase the probability that certain people will display heightened or deadened response patterns to given environmental cues."[61] Remember, in the studies of how conservatives and liberals responded differently to cues like writing about "eating maggots" or imagining they were "invincible," certain kinds of people displayed "heightened" or "deadened" response patterns to "given environmental cues."

So what is the mechanism through which genes shape political beliefs? Scholars at the University of Nebraska at Lincoln have offered a theoretical account of how and why genes shape political attitudes.[62] Their work explores political ideology as a translation of our "dispositional preferences for mass-scale social rules, order, and conduct."[63] The way that I think of my place as an individual organism within a system (like my society or community) is affected by my genetic predispositions. In this model, proposed by Kevin B. Smith and his colleagues, genetics determine humans' biology and physiology, which then naturally contributes to their emotional and cognitive processes.[64] These processes then shape how you interact with your environment, hence shaping your personality and values. Your personality and values then make up your ideology and resulting political issue positions.

Smith and his colleagues argue that at the fifth stage of this model, where personality and values shape ideology, multiple dimensions are at play. Personality and values contribute not only to your political ideology, but also to your religious preferences, educational preferences, occupational preferences, child-rearing preferences, recreational preferences, and finally... your musical, artistic, and even *humor* preferences.

And there it is.

When you start talking about genes and biology, there's an assumption that this means that these are innate traits or are characteristics determined from birth. But none of this research says that these relationships are immutable, nor does it imply that they are deterministic. In fact, you can actually *change* people's epistemic motivations (their informational and processing goals) by introducing a simple instruction; for instance, a prompt emphasizing accuracy over efficiency.[65] In one study exploring how people judged others, researchers artificially reduced the participants' need for closure by instructing them: "I want you to form the most accurate impression of [this person] that you can because after you have given your impression of them, I will ask you to *justify* it to me and a clinical psychologist who is also involved in this project."[66] When instructed to perform the task with this an emphasis on accuracy over efficiency, the study participants based their judgments far less on the primed features of the person in question and more on other available information. The authors conclude: "to avoid forming a hasty impression, [participants] considered other interpretations of [the person's] behavior and were, therefore, less likely to characterize him in terms of the primed trait construct."[67]

What seems essential, then, is that despite the deep linkages between political ideology, psychology, physiology, and biology, the relationships between these characteristics are complex, affected by social and environmental context, and thus, still somewhat malleable. To explore this a bit, I give you my most readily available and overanalyzed human subject: me. I am relatively high in need for closure, as illustrated by my feeling of frustration when I thought Zach Braff was going to end the film *Garden State* with an ellipsis instead of a period. Left to my own devices, I am prone to efficient, heuristic judgments. I tend to judge people quickly on first meeting them.[68] My default response is to take some action—any action—rather than to explore the pros and cons of every possible avenue. I also like routine and order in my schedule and in my work, although my office and bedroom are always messy—with papers and clothing strewn about. So I am high in need for predictability but not necessarily in my need for order. I am also relatively low in tolerance of ambiguity and high in need for decisiveness.

Some of my tendencies have changed over time, which the research suggests is, in fact, possible. Need for closure can be altered by exposure to new experiences and information.[69] Rich and diverse life experiences as well as education can reduce your need for closure and render you more tolerant of ambiguity. Studying abroad, in particular, is associated with increased openness and tolerance for ambiguity.[70] One long-standing goal of a liberal arts education is to promote tolerance for ambiguity in order to foster a sense of openness, adaptability, and a willingness to change one's point of view.[71] Perhaps it shouldn't be that surprising that after almost 22 years of liberal arts education and a year studying and living in France, I've become slightly more tolerant of ambiguity (though apparently not in my preferences for movie endings).

In spite of my high need for closure, and contrary to the work of Aleksander Ksiazkiewicz, I am also high in need for cognition and have been since I was a kid. I love puzzles, logic problems, and finding solutions to complex issues. When I think about the world, I want to know why things are the way they are—from the most minute observation (why is there heavy traffic on Route 70 at 2 p.m. on a Tuesday) to the most complex problem (why is there such abject poverty in Camden, New Jersey, and what can be done to fix it). I enjoy coming up with hypotheses that might account for things I observe and testing them against available information. (It's probably good that I am in this line of work, or I would be even more insufferable than I already am.) So where do these traits put me in terms of my political ideology? Well, I'm liberal on social and cultural issues, but I'm slightly more conservative on issues related to crime. I'm liberal in my economic politics, yet I recognize the limits and dangers of overzealous entitlement programs. So, like my psychological profile, I'm sort of a mixed bag—but a mixed bag that leans to the left.

Also highlighting the fact that these linkages between personality, psychology, and ideology are tendencies and not necessarily fixed, I give you my dear friend Patrick (name changed to protect the innocent). Patrick is so routinized and averse to new situations that he eats the same foods almost every day, goes to the same restaurants, orders the same meal whenever he's there, has the most tidy and spare home I've ever seen, and rotates through about four of his favorite T-shirts that are all various shades of heather gray. Once Patrick went to buy new glasses, since his lenses were scratched from three years of wear. He raved about the new frames he had picked out and swore that we would all love them for their novelty. Unbeknownst to Patrick, he had purchased the *exact* same frames he had been wearing for three years. Same name brand and everything. And he did the same with a "brand new" rain jacket he purchased to replace his "old" rain jacket the following month. It was the *same damn jacket.*

So Patrick is extremely high in need for predictability and order. He has low tolerance for ambiguity, and yet... Pat is a progressive vegan who drives a hybrid and supports LGBTQ rights. When you talk to him about the roots of his more progressive political belief system, you start to realize that his high need for cognition causes him to read. A lot. Like the books that most people only read if they are assigned for a class. And even then, they don't read them. But Pat does. Meanwhile, he grew up with a relatively strict Catholic upbringing and with a vocal and opinionated father, whose conservative views were the source of many household debates throughout Pat's oppositional and defiant teenage years. As Pat's cousin said, "if your dad had been a Democrat, you would probably be a right-wing conservative right now." Pat's cousin may be right. When I talked to Pat about the hilarity of the "dirty hippy" insult in light of conservatives' high disgust sensitivity, he replied: "come to think of it, maybe I actually *am* conservative... because when I see a Grateful Dead fan with dirty dreadlocks, I just want to tell them to trim that hair and take a shower."

So the link between psychology and ideology is flexible when examined on a case-by-case basis. However, the underlying trend—and logic—holds up. Conservatives (especially social or cultural ones) tend to be less tolerant of ambiguity and lower in need for cognition than liberals. This makes conservatives especially good at quick, efficient decision-making tasks and well-suited to certain leadership roles where taking quick action is needed. This also makes them not so good at changing their minds in light of new information and less than stellar at thinking about issues in terms of complex, systemic causes. Liberals, though, tend to be more tolerant of ambiguity and lower in need for closure, with a higher need for cognition. This makes them less efficient decision-makers, more likely to make use of various forms of information when making up their minds, and less likely to "go with their gut." This makes liberals especially good at analytical thinking, scientific inquiry, and higher education, where thinking for the sake of thinking is an advantage, not a hindrance. It also makes them not as great at quick decisive judgments.

So if you're looking for someone to diagnose your complicated medical condition, you probably want a liberal doctor. But if you get your arm cut off in an elevator door, you probably want a conservative.

A Note from Dear Ol' Dad

After reading the above section detailing the psychological traits that map onto political ideology, my 78-year-old father suggested that my liberal bias was showing through: "you don't make a strong enough case for the potential advantages of a conservative mind and the potential disadvantages of a liberal one," he argued.

While I have acknowledged that there are situations, occupations, and contexts in which a high need for closure and low need for cognition lead to desirable outcomes, Dad thought I had not gone far enough in highlighting how both the conservative and the liberal minds have particular strengths and weaknesses. He was right. This book originated as an exploration of how and why satire leans to the left. As such, tolerance for ambiguity and need for cognition—which are related to successful humor production and appreciation—emerge as unequivocally positive traits.

But they are not unequivocally positive.

Dad's critical eye stems in part from the fact that he is admittedly high in need for closure and driven to heuristic thinking. As a boy he had strict conservative inclinations, from belief in a strong military to "Don't challenge those in positions of authority." Following four years at the University of Massachusetts, he was drafted and spent three years in the US Army, from 1962 to 1964. In basic training he was a platoon leader, in charge of about 30 men. He scored at the top of his 120-man company, earning the highest marksmanship honor and the award for top soldier of the company. Military life—its order, structure, and hierarchies—played to Dad's inherent strengths.

After the army, he worked for the US Fish and Wildlife Service as a manager of several fish hatcheries across the country. My parents moved to a small Appalachian town with poverty unlike anything they had ever seen. On arriving, they both had clear notions of how the government should handle the largely uneducated, unemployed people of this town.

"We thought we knew everything," Dad admits. "It only took about a month to realize that we didn't know much. We just didn't understand the complexity of the situations these families were in."

As Mom and Dad moved into new communities and made new friends with new cultural norms, they found themselves becoming increasingly tolerant of ambiguity and increasingly cognizant of the need to stifle their impulses toward heuristic-driven first impressions. They did so not necessarily because they wanted to change but simply because they had to if they were going to find happiness and community in these new places.

Dad's inherent needs for order, closure, and heuristic-based judgments were still there. But he came to see these as skills that he could employ strategically rather than as dominant traits that ruled his world. As he read my earlier draft's description of tolerance for ambiguity and need for cognition, he reminded me of the tale of one of his professors at the University of

Massachusetts. This professor of fishery science had worked for over a decade reorganizing all the genera and species of fish into a new typology based on new classification criteria. Dissatisfied with his first attempt, he undertook the project a second time.

Dissatisfied with his second attempt, he started over yet again.

Dissatisfied a third time, he gave up.

I have a distinct recollection of my dad telling me this story over the years as a sort of cautionary tale of the perils of endless tolerance for ambiguity and need for cognition. Of course Dad didn't call it that, but that's exactly what it was. It was a story about how too much thinking and not enough closure can be paralyzing.

"If you're going to write a book that speaks to both the left and right," Dad said, "You'll need to be more honest about the advantages of a conservative mind, and the ways in which a high tolerance for ambiguity and a need for cognition can be problematic."

I thought for a moment.... "Like how when you get twenty liberal university faculty members in a room for a meeting and everyone evaluates and ruminates and no decisions get made?"

"Exactly."

In sum, people's psychological and physiological traits interact with their environments and social contexts in ways that influence their political attitudes and beliefs. In the next chapter, I'll begin to integrate this understanding of the psychological profiles of the left and right with a consideration of aesthetic preferences. If people's political beliefs are shaped (directly and indirectly) by psychological traits, and those same traits inform people's preferences for art, music, and even genres of political information, then of course researchers should find differences in the preferred aesthetics of the left and the right—and indeed they do.

The Psychological Roots of Humor's Liberal Bias

COMEDIAN MARC MARON, in an episode of his podcast *WTF with Marc Maron*, interviewed television producer George Schlatter, known for his role as cocreator of NBC's 1970s comedy variety show *Rowan & Martin's Laugh-In*.[1] Maron asked Schlatter about the eccentric 1950s television comic Ernie Kovacs, with whom Schlatter's wife had performed in the 1950s. "What was [Ernie Kovacs] like?" Maron asked Schlatter. "'Cause he was such a, like, abstract thinker..."

"We used to argue all the time," Schlatter replied, "because my whole life was punchlines. He never did a punchline. I would say 'Ernie, you're so close to a joke....Just one more thing at the end. A punchline.' He'd say 'I don't want to do punchlines.'"

Maron replied, "Yeah, who needs closure?"

As I'll show in this chapter, these questions—of whether jokes need punchlines and whether audience members need closure—are answered differently by liberals and conservatives.

Aesthetic Preferences of the Left and Right

Given that psychological traits shape people's aesthetic preferences and those same traits correlate with people's political ideologies, it shouldn't be surprising to learn that liberals and conservatives like different works of art. Studies of how liberals and conservatives interact with various apolitical stimuli, such as artwork, paintings, and plays, indicate that the psychological characteristics of the left and right inform their distinct aesthetic preferences. A study by Glenn Wilson and his colleagues linked liberals' higher need for cognition and higher tolerance for ambiguity to their greater appreciation for complex abstract art.[2] Meanwhile, the conservatives in the study preferred simple, representational art. Using a sample of college students, Gregory Feist and Tara Brady studied the link between different art forms, such as representational and abstract, and political orientation. They found the same pattern: conservative students in their sample reported significantly less appreciation than did liberal students did for abstract art.[3] In the same study, respondents high in "openness" (a dimension of tolerance for ambiguity) appreciated the abstract art more than the realistic art. The authors conclude: "those with attitudes more tolerant of political liberalism and drug use preferred abstract art the most."[4]

Those pot-smoking, hippy Picasso-lovers.

The notion that psychological traits, aesthetic preferences, and political orientations come together as a package is an observation that political psychologists increasingly embrace. Political psychologists John Hibbing, Kevin Smith, and John Alford write: "bedrock political orientations just naturally mesh with a broader set of orientations, tastes, and preferences because they are all part of the same biologically rooted inner self."[5] In their book *Predisposed*, Hibbing, Smith, and Alford make the case that innate biological and physiological differences between conservatives and liberals contribute to distinct lifestyle and aesthetic preferences.[6] Based on years of research conducted at the University of Nebraska, these authors outline the many differences between liberals and conservatives, most of which seem to have nothing to do with politics at all. For example, conservatives are more able to smell certain odors than are liberals. They keep their living spaces tidier than liberals do. They are less likely to try new foods than liberals. Summarizing their extensive survey research of hundreds of participants, the authors conclude that

> across a range of topics, the mean responses of liberals consistently favored the new experience, the abstract, and the nonconforming. Conservatives just as consistently favored traditional experiences that were closer to reality and predictable patterns. Conservatives, for example, preferred their poems to rhyme and fiction that ended with a clear resolution. Liberals were more likely to write fiction and paint, or attend a music concert. Experimental arrhythmic verse, amorphous story lines, and ambiguous endings just do not trip the triggers of many conservatives and, perhaps relatedly, they are less likely to be performers, a fact that is all too apparent from the announced political affiliations of comedians, rock stars, and Hollywood actors.[7]

Remember my extreme dissatisfaction with the scene in *Garden State* when Braff tells Portman "I'm putting, like, an ellipsis on it"? As it turns out, I'm not the only person high in need for closure to feel frustrated by a story with an ambiguous ending. Studies confirm that in general, conservatives' low tolerance for ambiguity contributes to their experiencing more dissatisfaction with ambiguous story endings than liberals do.[8]

Conservative media critic Kyle Smith illustrated this very sentiment in a review of another Natalie Portman film, the 2018 sci-fi thriller *Annihilation*. In his assessment of it for the conservative *National Review*, Smith wrote: "*Annihilation* is one of those mystery-cloaked movies in which so much depends on the final resolution that you can't really assess it until the end. But there is no final resolution: Questions simply remain unanswered, or only partially answered, and after spending much of the movie enthralled I walked out of the theater deflated."[9] The *plot* of the film was not altogether off-putting to Smith. Rather, it was the vague ending, which left the audience unsure about the identity and fate of Portman's character that he found troubling. As he put it, he didn't just experience dissatisfaction at the lack of plot resolution but actually felt that the filmmakers did not "finish their job."[10] This kind of assessment extends beyond mere comfort with ambiguity to inform the way one comes to define successful storytelling. "In the end, the viewer is left to judge for himself exactly what has happened and what it means. Making movies steeped in vagueness these days is proving to be an excellent way to earn critical praise, but being artfully ambiguous strikes me as a way to cover for not being able to finish the job."[11] Compare Smith's opinion of the film's ending to that of *Nerdist* columnist Lindsey Romain, who wrote: "the film is intentionally ambiguous about the real answer here—but in a way that makes it everlasting, the sort of sci-fi possibility we'll be questioning forevermore."[12]

Boundaries in Conservatives' Minds (and on Their Borders)

A creative contribution to this body of research on aesthetic preferences and political ideology comes to us from Belgian psychologists Alain Van Hiel and Ivan Mervielde, who looked at correlations between "openness to experience" and political ideology.[13] They integrated into their models a novel construct that psychiatrist Ernest Hartmann called "boundaries in the mind."[14] For years, Hartmann had studied the characteristics of people who suffered from recurring nightmares. According to his work, nightmare sufferers are different from the rest of us in terms of their psychological traits, personalities, and habits. Van Hiel and Mervielde describe Hartmann's main findings regarding the unique traits of these nightmare sufferers:

> their jobs were mostly in artistic and creative fields; they were unusually open and tended to share their problems with other people; they failed to isolate thought from feeling, letting themselves get too emotionally involved; and some were reported to be unusually sensitive to perceptual stimuli and were easily upset by bright lights or noise. In short, when we tried to describe these people globally, [these were] some of the words [that] kept coming up: "unguarded," "undefended," "fluid," "artistic," "vulnerable," "open." The term that seemed best to encompass all this was that they had thin boundaries in many different senses.[15]

Inspired by Hartmann's creation and measurement of this construct, Van Hiel and Mervielde incorporated the trait "boundaries in the mind" into their work on the psychological correlates of political conservatism.[16] Working with a large sample of participants from Flanders—the northern, Dutch-speaking region of Belgium—the researchers sought to understand how these characteristics might correlate. Given the intuitive parallels between boundaries in the mind and tolerance for ambiguity, Van Hiel and Mervielde suggested, perhaps incorporating "boundaries in the mind" into analyses of political psychology would offer unique insights that existing measures had not yet captured. As they put it, "to date, not a single study or theory about conservative ideology documents or predicts a preference of conservatives for solid frames, straight lines, and particular clothing styles.... Hence, the study of the relationship between [boundaries in the mind] and conservative beliefs could bring us novel insights in the psychology of the conservative mind and offer us unexpected and less obtrusive indicators of conservatism."[17]

Van Hiel and Mervielde's measure included a total of 103 items, divided into 12 subscales or dimensions of boundaries in the mind. Below are the twelve subscales and an example of the type of items used to measure each. Participants were asked to what extent each statement described them.

Sleep, wake, dream: "I have daymares."
Unusual experiences: "I have had deja vu experiences."
Thoughts, feelings, moods: "My thoughts blend into one another."
Childhood, adolescence, adulthood: "I am very close to my childhood feelings."

Interpersonal: "When I get involved with someone, we sometimes get too close."

Sensitivity: "I am very sensitive to other people's feelings."

Neat, exact, precise: "I keep my desk or worktable neat and well organized"—reversed.

Edges, lines, clothing: "I like paintings or drawings with soft and blurred edges."

Opinions about children and others: "I think that a good teacher must remain in part a child."

Opinions about organizations and relationships: "In an organization, everyone should have a definite place and a specific role"—reversed.

Opinions about peoples, nations, groups: "People of different nations are basically very much alike."

Opinions about beauty, truth: "All important thought involves feelings, too."[18]

Van Hiel and Mervielde were also careful to use multiple measures of conservatism to capture political ideology—measures including self-reported ideology, right-wing authoritarianism, and political party preferences. The researchers also explored cultural conservatism versus economic conservatism as they related to different dimensions of boundaries in the mind.

The results are startling in their strength and consistency. Conservatism, measured all different ways, is negatively associated with "blurred boundaries" of all kinds. Conservatives tended to reject the notion that people from different countries were basically the same (opinions about peoples, nations, groups) and were more likely to believe that people in organizations should operate within specific fixed roles (opinions about organizations and relationships). Conservatives rejected the blurring of emotions and cognition in matters related to "beauty and truth" (e.g., "All important thought involves feelings, too") and, perhaps most centrally related to the conversation here, showed a reduced preference for blurred edges, lines, and clothing patterns (e.g., "I like paintings or drawings with soft and blurred edges").

The more conservative the participants, the higher the likelihood that they would prefer solid edges and lines—and pictures in frames. Conservatives were literally more likely than liberals to agree with the sentiment "Good solid frames are very important for a picture or a painting." To extrapolate to today's political reality, it seems that the same people who support the building of a physical boundary (a literal wall) along the United States' southern border to keep out illegal immigrants probably also want a physical boundary (a frame) to visually separate their artwork from the drywall around it.

In a related area of research, a decade earlier two humor scholars were beginning to think about how traits like need for closure related to appreciation for various forms of humor. In 1993, Willibald Ruch and Franz-Josef Hehl looked at how need for order (part of the need for closure scale) affects appreciation for different kinds of jokes.[19] By considering how humor structure, rather than targets or subject matter, affected humor appreciation, Ruch and Hehl were opening the door for scholars to think of humor structure as a kind of aesthetic preference. Ruch and Hehl found that people who were high in need for order were more likely to appreciate jokes with simple incongruity resolution, while those who were low in need for order were more appreciative of the jokes that required the listener to draw information from outside the joke text in order to make sense of it.

Using a sample of Italian respondents, Giovannantonio Forabosco and Willibald Ruch completed a related study, also exploring appreciation for jokes that reconciled incongruity and jokes that did not.[20] Here, though, they examined sociodemographic factors as predictors of humor appreciation—things like age, political ideology, and even specific policy positions. Consistent with everything that I have shown thus far, older, conservative respondents preferred the jokes with readily reconciled incongruity (e.g., jokes with easy-to-get punchlines). This finding was replicated when conservatism was operationalized through specific policy positions and with self-reported ideology. That is, people who opposed mixed marriage, euthanasia, abortion, and smoking pot showed a preference for readily reconciled jokes over the more incongruous, complex ones.

So if you vote Republican, you not only want frames for your artwork; apparently, you also want your jokes to have really clear punchlines.

Irony Is *Extremely* Ambiguous

Inspired by this work on psychology, political ideology, and aesthetic preference, I decided to explore appreciation for *satire* as an aesthetic preference. My goal was to determine whether the liberal roots of satire rested in the fact that appreciation of irony (a preferred vehicle for satire) requires a tolerance for ambiguity and need for cognition that are simply greater on the left than the right.

I identified and defined two different kinds of humor: one relying on ironic inversion and the other relying on a simple heightening of the comic's actual point of view. The former is simply the concept of "irony" as described in chapter 6. The second is "hyperbole" or "exaggeration." Hyperbole is "a description of the state of affairs in obviously exaggerated terms."[21] Whereas irony requires that the listener invert the literal valence of the speaker to infer what the speaker actually means, in hyperbole/exaggeration, the listener has much less cognitive work to do. The assumption underlying this work, which has been confirmed in various studies from neuroscience, is that irony as a form of communication is inherently ambiguous and, as such, is cognitively taxing. Given that, and given conservatives' lower tolerance for ambiguity and need for cognition than liberals', I thought that perhaps the unique complexity and ambiguity of irony make it less likely that conservatives would enjoy it.

In my first attempt to study this in 2012, my research assistant Nicole van de Vliet and I found preexisting clips of stand-up comics who used either irony or exaggeration. On the irony side were Louis C.K., Sarah Silverman, and Dave Chappelle.[22] On the exaggeration side were Dane Cook, Kathleen Madigan, and Mike Marino. Using a sample of undergraduate respondents and a second more diverse sample of Americans, we used an online survey to randomly assign respondents to view various clips and asked them their perceptions of each (e.g., was the clip funny, interesting, boring, offensive, enjoyable). They were then asked an open-ended question about what they thought the comic's main point was in the clip: "What do you think was this comic's intended argument or point (if any)?" Participants were also asked to complete various political and psychological scales, including the right-wing authoritarianism scale and assessments of postmodern values, traditional values, need for cognition, and tolerance for ambiguity.

As we began analyzing the data, we found that many of our hypotheses were confirmed. Liberals appreciated the ironic clips from Louis C.K., Dave Chappelle, and Sarah Silverman significantly more than conservatives did, and so did those who scored highest in postmodern values and lowest in traditional values. And people higher in tolerance for ambiguity and need for cognition reported significantly greater appreciation of the ironic clips than people lower in those traits, a pattern that was not true for the exaggeration-based humor.

But there was a huge problem.

The ironic clips used in the study all made liberal arguments in an ironic way. So of course the liberal participants appreciated them more. The problem was that irony and liberalism are such a natural pairing that we actually could not find any ironic clips that made conservative—or even ideologically neutral—arguments. As a result, we had created a systematic confound between irony and liberal argumentation.

Take, for example, this clip (from our experiment) of Louis C.K.:

I'm a lucky guy I got a lot going for me.... I'm *white*, which... thank god for that shit. That is a huge leg up, are you kiddin' me? Oh god I love being white.... Seriously if you're not white you are missing out because this shit is *thoroughly* good. Let me be clear by the way, I'm not saying white people are better. I'm saying that *being* white is *clearly* better. Who could even argue?... Here's how great it is to be white. I can get into a time machine and go to any time and it would be fucking awesome when I get there. That is exclusively a white privilege. Black people can't fuck with time machines, a black guy in a time machine would be like "Hey anything before 1980 no thank you." But I can go to any time, the year 2. I don't even know what was happening then but I know when I get there, "Welcome we have a table right here for you, sir." ... I can go to *any* time... in the *past*. I don't want to go to the future and find out what happens to white people because we're gonna pay hard for this shit, you gotta know that. We're not gonna just fall from number 1 to 2. They're gonna hold us down and fuck us in the ass forever... and we totally deserve it. But for now... "wheeeeee!"

This is a difficult one to unpack, as Louie literally states that it is *great* to be white. He also literally states: "I'm not saying white people are better. I'm saying that *being* white is *clearly* better." But, by offering his example of the time machine, he is illustrating Bergson's contrast between "what is and what ought to be."[23] What Louie is stating literally is what actually is: "it is better to be white than not." What the audience derives from his bit, though, is what ought to be: "it shouldn't be 'great' to be white. Life's goodness should be the same for everyone regardless of skin color."

Now consider this ironic clip from Dave Chappelle that we used in our experiment:

I was in Mississippi doing a show and I go to a restaurant to order some food and I say to the guy, I say "I would like to have..." and before I even finished my sentence he says "the chicken!" I said "What the fuck?" I could not believe it, could not believe that shit. This man was absolutely right. I said "how did he know that I was gonna get some chicken?" I asked him I said, "How did you know that? How'd you know I was gonna get some chicken?" He looked at me like I was crazy, "Come on, come on buddy, everybody knew soon as you walked through the goddamn door you were gonna get some chicken. It is no secret down here that blacks and chickens are quite fond of one another…Then I finally understood what he was saying and I got upset. I wasn't mad. I was just upset. I wasn't ready to hear that shit. All these years, I thought I liked chicken because it was delicious. Turns out I am genetically predisposed to liking chicken. I got no say in the matter.

Irony is defined by saying the opposite of what the speaker literally means. Or to remind you of my definition from earlier chapters: "irony is a relevant, context-specific form of judgment, aimed at a target; and its literal and intended meanings are at odds with one another." Chappelle literally states that up until that moment, he thought that he liked chicken because it was delicious. Were it not for that restaurant employee, he would never have learned the "truth": that he only likes it because of the color of his skin. What Chappelle is offering here is a wonderful example of irony, in that he is issuing a subtle inverted judgment. While his literal expression targets his own naiveté, the inverted meaning tells the audience that the actual target of the joke is the absurdity of the race-based stereotype itself.

By the way, if you think the point of Louie's bit is that it is great to be white and there is nothing wrong with that fact, then I fear that this book is not really for you. Similarly, if you think the point of Chappelle's bit is that he actually thinks black people like chicken because they are black, this book is not really for you, either. Unfortunately, by the looks of our open-ended responses to these clips, it seems that lots of people do misinterpret the intended meaning of these ironic jokes. Remember LaMarre and her colleagues' study about "Seeing what you want to see in Colbert," in which conservative students interpreted the show as though Colbert were actually targeting liberals?[24] And remember the famous 1974 Vidmar and Rokeach study that showed that people with racially prejudiced views enjoyed *All in the Family* and saw Archie as the hero of the show?[25] It turns out that people "see what they want to see" all over the place. Like a 24-year-old participant in our 2012 study, a self-described "conservative independent" with a high school diploma who wrote in response to Louie's time machine bit: "I think the comic's point was that being white is awesome." Or the 36-year-old self-described "conservative Republican" with some college experience who wrote that Louie's main argument was that "being white is awesome, compared to being black."

There were some who did understand Louie's bit as intended but used it as an opportunity to disagree with the ironic premise and reveal their controversial attitudes in the process, like the 52-year-old "independent moderate" with a bachelor's degree who wrote: "Louis C.K. doesn't need a time machine.

He should just get in a plane and go to Africa to find a place where white people are not number 1. Maybe he is confusing the number 1 race with the number 1 country, which is America. It is very nice to live in America, for everyone, compared to living in Africa. How many Americans migrate to Africa, or anywhere else?" Other respondents interpreted Louie's irony as intended. A 35-year-old "very liberal independent" with a master's degree wrote: "he's saying that being white is, and has been for a long time, an institutional and social advantage. He's saying that even if there is no overt individual racism, institutional racism has created a society where being white is a personal advantage." A 34-year-old "somewhat liberal-leaning Democrat" with a bachelor's degree wrote that Louie's argument was that "white people really have it good and need to realize how lucky they are compared to the oppression and negative histories of other races."

Now, before I get charged with cherry-picking self-described conservative respondents to illustrate ironic comprehension gone wrong, let me highlight two misinterpretations of Dave Chappelle's sketch (about "blacks liking chicken") that come from liberal respondents. First is the 21-year-old "somewhat liberal Democrat" in our sample who wrote that Chappelle's main argument was that "blacks are fond of chicken." Or the "very liberal Democrat" who wrote: "I think he was trying to say that stereotypes are sometimes true and it's best just to laugh at them." Of course, some respondents identified the ironic meaning in Chappelle's bit, too. A "very liberal, strong Democrat" with a bachelor's degree wrote that Chappelle's intended argument was that "racism can show in ways that are so blatant and in-your-face that it's almost EASY to dismiss them and not see them for what they really are. But we should fight and acknowledge this racism just as much as any other kind."

Side note here for comedy geeks. When Dave Chappelle infamously walked away from a $50 million contract at Comedy Central for his popular sketch show *Chappelle Show*, people said he went "crazy"; that he "ran away to Africa"; that he had a nervous breakdown. But in interviews with Oprah and with *Time*'s Christopher Farley, Chappelle explained that what influenced his decision to leave his sketch show was primarily a concern about how his humor was being received and interpreted—especially by white audiences.[26] He was worried that his metaracist humor was being used by whites to confirm their racist beliefs. As defined by Katie Brown and William Youmans, "meta-disparagement humor adds a layer of irony to create the multi-level targets of ironic satire."[27] In metaracist humor, the comic adopts a racist view ironically in an effort to highlight the hypocrisy or illogic of racist beliefs. The problem is that such "meta-disparagement" humor, if misinterpreted, can serve to undermine the comic's point and reinforce the problematic beliefs it sets out to critique. Chappelle discussed this fear in the context of a particular metaracist sketch from his show. In it, he played a tiny pixie in blackface. The pixie appeared as a figment of life-sized Dave Chappelle's imagination, teasing him to behave in ways that were "stereotypically black." Appearing to Chappelle on an airplane, the pixie goaded him to "order the fried chicken." The sketch is similar in ironic premise to that of the stand-up act we tested in our experiment. Farley writes: "Chappelle thought the sketch was funny, the kind of thing his friends would laugh at. But at the taping, one spectator, a white man, laughed particularly loud and long. His laughter struck Chappelle as wrong, and he wondered if the new season of his show had gone from sending up stereotypes to merely reinforcing them. 'When he laughed, it made me uncomfortable,' says Chappelle. 'As a matter of fact, that was the last thing I shot before I told myself I gotta take f—— time out after this. Because my head almost exploded.'"[28] As indicated by the responses we saw in our experiment, Chappelle's fears were well-founded. Irony is a complex rhetorical form and, if misinterpreted, has the potential to reinforce the very societal ills and stereotypes it sets out to challenge.

I mentioned that even though my 2012 experiment benefited from the use of real-world comics and stand-up acts, it had a fatal flaw. Since the ironic clips were more liberal in argumentation than the exaggerated clips, we had to go back to the drawing board to find a way to separate the ideological argument from the type of humor being used. To isolate the humor structures (irony versus exaggeration) from the underlying ideological bias of a joke (liberal versus conservative), we realized we had to actually create custom "stimuli." In other words, we had to write jokes. Working with a professional comedy writer and performer, Don Montrey, my coauthors and I identified nonpolitical news headlines we could use as fodder for joke scripts. The goal was to write a set of jokes that advanced a particular point of view—that made an argument aimed at a target—through irony on the one hand and exaggeration on the other. However, the point of view advanced through the joke had to be as nonpartisan and ideologically neutral as possible. We needed the jokes to make the same argument but through two different kinds of humor. If ironic satire leans to the left in part because of how tolerance for ambiguity and need for cognition relate to political ideology, we should be able to create jokes that have no political content whatsoever, and just by virtue of the varying complexity and ambiguity of irony versus exaggeration, we should find different levels of joke appreciation from people on the left and on the right.

Take for instance the following jokes we crafted based on a news article about a US Forest Service announcement from 2014:

Ironic: The US Forest Service issued an advisory to park goers warning them to stop taking selfies with bears. Well, excuse *me*, US Forest Service! *How* am I supposed to enjoy my vacation if I can't document *every moment* leading up to my own mauling?

Exaggerated: The US Forest Service issued an advisory to park goers warning them to stop taking selfies with bears. This would be a helpful advisory to the .001% of the population who would actually *want* to take a photo of themselves with a *bear*. If only those people could *read*.

Both jokes make the argument that taking a selfie with a bear is a dumb thing to do. It's unsafe, and the people who do it are unwise. However, the first one makes the argument in a Colbertesque ironic persona—requiring that the audience recognize the ironic intent of the speaker. The speaker feigns outrage that the Forest Service is prohibiting him from taking a selfie with a bear. Once he acknowledges that he would want to livestream his own death, it cues the listener to realize that this statement is in jest. The second uses hyperbole to suggest that (1) very few people would want to do this, and (2) those who would are not smart—not even smart enough to read.

After pretesting the jokes using a group of trained coders who rated how "ironic" and "exaggerated" they found the jokes, we were left with eight pairs of jokes to test. We obtained a national sample of 305 participants through Qualtrics, a national survey company that recruits study participants with consumer rewards like gift cards and coupons. We specified that we needed a sample with 45 percent self-reporting a conservative ideology and 45 percent a liberal ideology (and 10 percent moderates). The participants watched the eight short joke videos, each of which was randomized to show each participant either the ironic or exaggerated version. If our baseline assumptions were correct, we would find that the conservative participants were lower in tolerance for ambiguity and in need for cognition than liberals. If our hypotheses were correct, we would find that conservative participants appreciated the ironic jokes less than liberals and that this relationship was explained in part (statistically speaking) by the lower tolerance for ambiguity and need for cognition among the conservative respondents. We also believed that the converse would be true of the exaggerated jokes; that conservatives would appreciate them more than liberals, and this result would again be explained by lower tolerance for ambiguity and need for cognition.

After analyzing the data with my colleague Ben Bagozzi, I learned that we were half right (or half wrong, depending on your mood—and ideology). The conservatives in our study were indeed significantly lower in tolerance for ambiguity and need for cognition than the liberals; and the conservatives were significantly less appreciative of irony than the liberals. But the conservatives were *also* less appreciative of the exaggerated jokes than the liberals.

The mechanism we hypothesized wasn't quite right either. Conservatives' lower need for cognition helped account for some of their lower humor appreciation, but tolerance for ambiguity was not a significant factor. Unfortunately, the measure of tolerance for ambiguity we used didn't have great statistical reliability, so we may have underestimated the role of that construct. Yet one additional finding was important. In addition to measuring how funny participants found the specific jokes they watched, we also measured the general psychological trait "sense of humor" using a nine-item scale adapted from the work of James Thorson and F. C. Powell.[29]

What we found was that conservatism was a strong and significant negative predictor of the general trait "sense of humor." Conservatives scored significantly lower on "sense of humor" than liberals—even when controlling for tolerance for ambiguity and need for cognition. And this measure of "sense of humor" helped explain the lower joke appreciation we found among conservatives in our study. Before you get angry at me for saying that Republicans have no sense of humor, let me be specific about what this scale is actually measuring. I like to think of this scale as a measure of *the extent to which people value the production and reception of humor in their lives.* The scale requires people to say how much they agree with the following statements: "Other people tell me that I say funny things." "I use humor to entertain my friends." "I can ease a tense situation by saying something funny." "Humor helps me cope." "I like a good joke." The scale also asked questions that were coded as indicating a low sense of humor: "Calling someone a 'comedian' is a real insult." "I dislike comics." "People who tell jokes are a pain in the neck." "I'm uncomfortable when everyone is cracking jokes." And yes, some people do actually "strongly agree" with these last three items. And these people are more likely to be conservative than liberal.

Our results indicated that the role of your political ideology in shaping how funny you find a joke might have very little to do with the explicit political content in that joke. Our jokes were designed to avoid explicitly political issues, people, or events. Yet conservatives still found the jokes (both ironic and exaggerated) less funny than did liberals—due in part to the conservatives' lower scores than their liberal counterparts on both need for cognition and "sense of humor." In addition, need for cognition and the general sense of humor scale were found to be strongly correlated with one another. This says that enjoyment of thinking is central to appreciation of humor and that this may be putting liberals at a "laugh advantage" when it comes to finding jokes funny. It also suggests that sense of humor and need for cognition are fundamentally related and help account for appreciation of specific humorous stimuli, such as jokes.

Considering the extensive research on conservatives' high mortality salience, active monitoring for threat, and high need for certainty and closure, the negative correlation between conservatism and "sense of humor" makes sense. But I don't see this as particularly insulting to conservatives, though Fox News might frame it as such. Humor is a deliberately inefficient form of communication. Rather than explicitly communicating information with the goal of being clear and understood, humor transforms the act of communication into a game—a riddle. The fact that the people who appreciate this rhetorical form the most are those least likely to be monitoring the environment for threats could be interpreted as a sign of their own naiveté rather than enlightenment. As conservatives might say, "of course you liberals can joke around all the time. You've got us conservatives doing the hard work to keep society safe and free from harm. This gives you the luxury of creating and enjoying abstract art, ambiguous sci-fi films, and ironic TV shows. So, sure...go have fun with your silly jokes."

Could Humor Production Be Political Even If the Joke Is Not?

So far, the bulk of this discussion has centered on humor comprehension and appreciation by the audience. While this might explain differences in humor appreciation between liberals and conservatives, it doesn't explain ideological differences among the kinds of people who *produce* humor. Research has shown that the personality traits that predict appreciation of jokes do overlap with the traits that predict production of jokes. People who enjoy receiving humor and people who enjoy making humor share some traits. However, they are not identical.

Daniel Howrigan at the University of Colorado at Boulder sought to understand the relationship between general intelligence, personality traits, and humor production: What kinds of people are funny?[30] To a sample of undergraduate participants from two colleges in California, Howrigan and his colleague Kevin MacDonald administered questionnaires that measured various personality traits, including extravertedness and openness. The researchers also used a complex measure—Raven's Progressive Matrices Test—to capture general intelligence.[31] To measure participants' "humor production," Howrigan and MacDonald created three separate humor production tasks. These tasks—which look really fun to do, quite frankly—allowed students to fill in the punchlines to illustrate their humor production abilities. Participants were told that the goal of the tasks was to be funny in their responses, and that these responses would be judged by anonymous raters.

One task, for example, provided participants with a picture of a person and asked the participants to come up with the person's name, occupation, hobbies, and a typical day in that person's life. The anonymous raters of the students' responses included 28 undergraduate and graduate students who worked independently to rate how funny they found each participant's contributions. These scores were then used as the measure of "humor production" for each participant. The results showed that general intelligence is a strong predictor of humor production. Smart people are funnier than not-smart people. In view of the complexity of humor as a form of implicit and incongruous communication, this makes a lot of sense. The findings also point to an important social dimension that factors into humor production: extraversion. Extraverts are more adept at the production of funny jokes. Finally, and consistent with other work in this area, Howrigan and MacDonald did find support for the idea that openness (a dimension of tolerance for ambiguity) is related to humor production as well.

While "general intelligence" is about ability rather than motivation, it would seem that in order to craft and create humorous juxtapositions, comics probably also "enjoy thinking" more than the average person—that is, they are higher in need for cognition than other people. In my conversations with comedy writer David Misch, he put it this way: "there is no question there is one thing that is distinctive about comedians. They think about things a little more. You see a napkin on a table—Jerry Seinfeld can do a 10-minute routine about it. They think about things and what they could mean; they look at them askew, from different vantage points." He then emphasized: "but that's true of every artist: painting, music, dance…."[32]

While the study by Howrigan and MacDonald helps explain the kinds of people that are funny,[33] it doesn't necessarily shed light on the kinds of people who are professional comedians and comedy writers. There are other factors that determine the kind of profession one seeks out, aside from one's own raw talent. For goodness' sake, *I* could be the funniest person in the city of Philadelphia (I'm not, by the way), but if I have a desire for financial stability or predictability in my life (which I do), becoming a professional stand-up comic is probably not going to be my first choice. Political scientist Alison Dagnes writes: "the poverty-paved road to thespianism is riddled with tricky potholes that serve as obstacles from continuing in a profession with wildly uneven work schedules and paychecks."[34]

In her book *A Conservative Walks into a Bar*, Dagnes explores the political and psychological characteristics of political satirists through qualitative interviews with comedians and comedy writers. Her sense throughout the book is that the liberal nature of satire is a function of the personality of the satirist as "unconventional," "artsy," "freethinking," and "unpredictable," traits that are more prevalent among liberals than conservatives. "It is not fixed that these people are liberals," Dagnes suggests, "but given their education and training, it is likely that they are."[35] After dozens of interviews with professional political comics and writers, Dagnes found that none of them had majored in political science in college—instead they steered toward artistic majors like theater and the humanities. They also had a certain expectation of unemployment and financial hardship early in their careers—and while they certainly weren't "OK with that," they tolerated it well enough for that lifestyle to sustain them for a while. Dagnes writes: "all put together, the profession itself may attract a certain type of individual: someone with a predilection for free thought, a desire to explore a variety of viewpoints, and a willingness to work odd hours with unpredictable schedules alongside people whose lifestyles Pat Robertson thinks were the real reason for the September 11 attacks. Performers and writers are used to the unpredictability of their careers while others in different professions are not."[36]

Echoing Dagnes's observation, David Misch posits that the lifestyle of the professional comics and comedy writers is consistent with the ethos of comedy itself. "Being a comic," he argues, is about "comfort with ambiguity and chaos."[37] Ashley Black, a writer for *Full Frontal with Samantha Bee*,[38] agrees with the underlying premise: "in order to get good at [comedy] you have to be part of a community. And that community is very much centered on hanging out and drinking, and *not* having children. Having children is a huge barrier to entry. A lot of things conservatives want to do like get married early, have kids, show up early, go to church on Sundays...there's none of that [in comedy]." Instead it's "get a shitty job that you know is shitty and beneath you so that you can devote every working hour to your jokes, staying up until 3 in the morning." She pauses for emphasis—"Your actual job ends at 3 a.m."[39]

I'm reminded of a scene from Lenny Bruce's autobiography, *How to Talk Dirty and Influence People*. Bruce describes being on the road, performing a show in Milwaukee. After his set, a couple, about 50 years old, invites him over to their table to chat and then invites him to their house for dinner the very next day.

> That night I go to my hotel—I'm staying at the local show-business hotel; the other show people consist of two people, the guy who runs the movie projector and another guy who sells Capezio shoes—and I read a little, write a little. I finally get to sleep about seven o'clock in the morning.
>
> The phone rings at nine o'clock.
>
> "Hello, hello, hello, this is the Sheckners—the people from last night. We didn't wake you up, did we?"
>
> "No, I always get up at nine in the morning. I like to get up about ten hours before work so I can brush my teeth and get some coffee. It's good you got me up. I probably would have overslept otherwise."[40]

But the lifestyle of the comic is not the only aspect of the work that requires comfort with ambiguity. "I think certainly in the doing of it, the only way to do comedy is to get comfortable in ambiguity," says Black, "and that is extremely difficult to do."[41] Black's background, before being hired as a writer at *Full Frontal*, was in improvisation, working for many years at The Second City in Chicago. In improvisation, Black points out, ambiguity and uncertainty are central. And while there are "rehearsals," you're not rehearsing specific lines or scenes. "You're rehearsing being open. You're rehearsing being OK with not knowing. In improv, the goal is to step out in front of however many people with your scene partner and figure out what the scene is together. It's just a level of openness to ambiguity that is insane…and that your body physically fights against."[42]

As Ashley said this to me, I felt like a light went on. While I have never earned a living through comedy, I have been doing improv for 25 years. I started performing in TheatreSports at the University of New Hampshire in 1994. Since 1999 I have been performing regularly with ComedySportz Philadelphia in a short-form structure in which two teams "compete" against each other by playing iterations of Viola Spolin's theater games. When I started performing in ComedySportz, my relatively high need for closure was most certainly limiting my performance. When Black described improv as "figuring out what the scene is *together*," I reflected on my tendency, in my early days of improv, to "declare" things rather than "discover" them collaboratively with my scene-mate. My own desire for certainty caused me to push against the not knowing. Instead my inclination was to declare who we were, where we were, and what we were doing and find some kind of trouble to drive the scene ahead. It took years of training and practice to unlearn these habits, to just listen to the last offer made by my scene-mate and build only on that offer. My default setting was to feel uncomfortable with the ambiguity and to try to fix it. But with practice and experience, I came to embrace that "not knowing" as the place where remarkable truths would have room to reveal themselves.

Dating back to the early writings of improvisational theater guru Spolin, comfort with ambiguity has been central to improvisation. Spolin's theater exercises and philosophies (including the still central concept "yes, and...") require performers to listen, accept their scene-partner's offer (be it verbal, emotional, or physical), and then (without hesitation or planning) build on that offer. This practice requires a degree of psychological and emotional openness—and a tacit assumption of equality between performers.

Interestingly, Spolin's writings make frequent mention of the need to discourage the spirit of authoritarianism from entering into improvisational techniques and teaching. In the preface to the second edition of her book *Improvisation for the Theater*, Spolin writes: "my years of working with the games have shown that this living, organic, non-authoritarian climate can inform the learning process and, in fact, is the only way in which artistic and intuitive freedom can grow."[43] Later she states: "the language and attitudes of authoritarianism must be constantly scourged if the total personality is to emerge as a working unit."[44]

For Spolin, the climate of nonjudgment and equality is what enables artists and improvisers to thrive. In her view, the codified roles of teacher and student should be reconsidered in order to discourage students from actively seeking "approval" and from trying to avoid doing something "wrong." "Eliminating the roles of teacher and student helps players get beyond the need for approval or disapproval, which distracts them from experiencing themselves and solving the problem," she writes. "There is no right or wrong way to solve a problem; there is only one way—the seeking—in which one learns by going through the process itself."[45] And in perhaps the most explicit reference to the essential role of tolerance for ambiguity in improvisational theater, Spolin urges her readers to remember that "the teacher cannot truly judge good or bad for another, for *there is no absolutely right or wrong way to solve a problem.*"[46]

These observations open up an empirical question that can be addressed through social science: what are the links between psychological traits, political traits, and the lifestyle of the comic? Gil Greengross and Geoffrey Miller, an anthropologist and psychologist, respectively, from the University of New Mexico, sought to answer this question in 2009.[47] They surveyed 31 professional stand-up comics, 9 amateur comics, and 10 comedy writers, along with 400 undergraduate college students at the University of New Mexico. Using the well-documented "Big Five" personality measure, the researchers looked at how *openness to experience, conscientiousness, extraversion, agreeableness,* and *neuroticism* differed between professional and amateur comics and their graduate student sample.

In contrast to the work of Howrigan and MacDonald showing that funny people tended to be more extraverted, Greengross and Miller found that comics are not. Instead, the professional and amateur comics were significantly more introverted than the general student sample. Of most relevance to my line of inquiry here, it seems that openness to experience, just as it is a predictor of humor appreciation, is key for successful humor production as well. Comics (professionals, amateurs, and writers) are significantly more open to experience (tolerant of ambiguity) than noncomics. This relationship was particularly noteworthy among comedy writers, among whom openness was the highest of all the participants in the study.

In sum, professional comics and comedy writers are more open to new experiences than noncomics. The process of creating humor itself involves complex cognitive processing. As discussed earlier, tolerance for ambiguity, openness to experience, and need for cognition are all correlated with a more liberal ideology (particularly on social and cultural issues). So, just as appreciation of complex humor—like satire and irony—ought to be greater among political liberals than among political conservatives, successful humor production ought to be greater among political liberals than political conservatives.

Trump: A Case Study in the Noncomic

In writing this chapter, I keep coming back to the trouble President Trump seems to have with jokes: saying that statements are jokes when they are offensive or simply not funny (like suggesting that police *not* protect people's heads when tossing them in the back of a "paddy wagon"); delivering jabs (meant to be jokes) constructed without capitalizing on the implicit nature of incongruity to get the audience on his side ("Hillary Clinton is *so* corrupt"). Journalists have also commented on the infrequency with which Trump laughs, pointing to a lack of appreciation of humor in addition to the trouble he seems to have with humor production.

Referencing Trump's behavior in the contentious September 26, 2016 general election debate against Hillary Clinton, the *Atlantic*'s Alex Wagner writes: "among the many remarkable exhibitions of abnormal behavior on stage Monday night, one of the most peculiar was that Donald Trump never once displayed a sense of humor."[48] Chuck Todd, host of NBC's *Meet the Press*, has noted this same phenomenon after having interviewed Trump several times over the years. "[It] drives me crazy," he told *Politico*'s Glenn Thrush. "Do you know what? I've never seen him laugh, I challenge somebody to find him laughing, and that person has yet to find an example, in my opinion. . . . Watch him at the Al Smith dinner [discussed in chapter 4]. He doesn't really laugh. He looks for others to laugh. It is just weird."[49]

In the *Atlantic*, Wagner goes on to describe Trump's unique angle when trying to make jokes: "this isn't to say that Trump can't get laughs," Wagner writes. "It's simply that when he gets them, he's humiliating people—whether 'Low Energy' Jeb Bush, 'Lyin'' Ted Cruz or 'Little' Marco Rubio. Humor borne out of cruelty happens to be the easiest and therefore lowest form of comedy."[50] Given what I have already reviewed here about the way "Yo mama" jokes—scalar humor—are processed in the brain, I can't say that I disagree.

One fascinating glimpse into Trump's relationship with humor comes from comedians' accounts of Comedy Central's *Roast of Donald Trump* in 2011. Comedy Central's roasts, which premiered on the network in 2003, are held annually. The subject of the vicious, humorous insults is often a celebrity or musician (think: James Franco, Rob Lowe, or Pamela Anderson). In 2011, after some negotiations, the network actually got Trump to agree to be roasted on national television.

According to an account by the *Huffington Post*'s Daniel Libit, the Trump team prohibited any jokes about Trump's bankruptcies and forbade "any suggestion that he was not as wealthy as he claimed to be."[51] In addition to outlining the kinds of jokes comics weren't allowed to make about him, Trump engaged in extensive edits of the comedians' drafts of his "rebuttal," the part of the program in which the roastee gets to roast the comics in return. His edits were fascinating. He deleted entire sections from the script and added new jokes in the margins, including this comment aimed at the comedians (the roasters) on stage: "Their [sic] all losers and I like associating with loser [sic] because it makes me feel even better about myself."[52] Perhaps most intriguing, though, is an observation Jesse Joyce, one of the writers, made to Libit. Libit writes: "After the writers went through numerous drafts of Trump's rebuttal, they forwarded a version to him in early March. He responded a week later with his first set of edits, handwritten in black Sharpie. 'I have done this a long time and nobody blacks out punchlines,' said Jesse Joyce.... Scrapping punchlines represents 'a classic lack of an understanding of how a joke works.'"[53] Just as psychologists and psychiatrists abide by the 1973 Goldwater Rule, which prohibits them from diagnosing a public figure without having examined that person, I'm pretty sure I can't say whether someone is high in need for closure or low in need for cognition if I've never actually measured where he or she falls on those scales. However, let me itemize several observations that are interesting in light of the argument I've advanced throughout this chapter: (1) Trump campaigned on a promise to ban people from predominantly Muslim countries "until we figure out what the hell is going on." (2) Five months into his first term in office he issued a directive to prohibit transgender people from serving in the military. And (3) he campaigned on a promise of building a wall—a physical boundary—between Mexico and the United States in an effort to keep out illegal immigrants. This is one individual for whom "closure" and "boundaries" seem to play a central role in both his aesthetic preferences and his political policies.

Ideology as an Aesthetic

The psychological account in this chapter of political satire's ideological "bias"—on both the side of the audience and the side of the creators—has important implications for how scholars, journalists, and citizens think about the genres and rhetoric used by the left and the right. In contrast to explanations that are tied to the targets and content of satire—for example, the notion that humor is poking fun at the status quo or people in positions of power—this psychological and epistemological approach suggests that political genres and rhetorical styles should be thought of as aesthetic forms.

Consider the possibility that in the context of political information and messaging, liberals and conservatives are naturally inclined to respond to distinct aspects of content. Given the vast differences in the psychological profiles of the left and right and given the unique internal logic of humor, it stands to reason that the left and the right should be asymmetrical in their preferences for humor as a mode of expression in the realm of politics. And it seems that, even outside the world of televised political information, they are. In an examination of the most successful political posts on Facebook, scholars at the Hebrew University of Jerusalem analyzed how various aspects of the content of Facebook posts (the presence of emotions, anger-evoking cues, first-person point of view, in-group and out-group references, humor, visuals) might predict a post's success (likes and shares). When looking at the overall sample, the most successful posts were those that included implied emotional content. But the researchers also looked to see if the most successful posts of right-wing and left-wing political actors were substantively different. And they were. The most successful left-wing posts were those that used humor. The most successful right-wing posts were those that made reference to an explicit out-group. The scholars conclude: "these findings therefore suggest that these features of humor and out-group reference are distinctive to left-wing and right-wing settings, respectively."[54]

It stands to reason that the aesthetic forms most appreciated and produced by liberals—high in tolerance for ambiguity and need for cognition—ought to be complex, ambiguous, and nuanced. One should expect liberals to gravitate toward—and produce—political information and political genres that invite multiple layers of processing by audiences; are ambiguous by design; and have unclear intent and varied meanings. In other words: ironic satire. If the intent is too clear, the argumentation too strident and explicit, liberals might be less likely to enjoy it. In fact, not only might they enjoy it less but they might be more likely to actively resist it. In addition, need for cognition predicts how thoughtfully and critically people engage with information. Armed with higher need for cognition, liberals should be actively scrutinizing claims and offering counterarguments when claims are weak. Obviously, one wouldn't expect liberals to actively resist all messages of this kind (after all, ideologically motivated reasoning is a powerful thing), but they might roll their eyes at claims they feel are weakly argued or rooted too heavily in emotional appeals rather than evidence. Particularly when faced with explicit, didactic, emotion-based efforts at persuasion ("Think *this* way, not *that* way!"), liberals might prove to be a particularly tough crowd.

8

The Aesthetics of Outrage

I ENDED CHAPTER 7 with the proposition that one should expect liberals to be drawn to "political information and political genres that invite multiple layers of processing by audiences; are ambiguous by design; and have unclear intent and varied meanings." But what about conservatives? What should one expect conservatives to be drawn to? Based on the research covered thus far, the aesthetics conservatives most appreciate should have hard lines—both literally and figuratively. One should expect conservative political commentary to say what it means and mean what it says. It should offer clear, explicit, descriptive, and prescriptive arguments about the way the world is and the way the world should be. And it should do this not through ironic implication or subtlety but through direct, unambiguous, emotionally charged argumentation. This would satisfy conservatives' high need for closure and tendency toward heuristic (instinct-based) processing. Think: Clarence Manion, Dan Smoot, H. L. Hunt in the 1950s and 1960s, or...Rush Limbaugh, Sean Hannity, or Bill O'Reilly today.

In *The Outrage Industry*, political scientist Jeffrey Berry and sociologist Sarah Sobieraj identify and describe what constitutes "outrage" programming.[1] They identify outrage as a function of such programming's tone, content, and tactics. The tone of outrage is emotional, angry, and fearful. The content is "personality centered, with a given program, column, or blog defined by a dominant charismatic voice."[2] And the tactics? Simultaneously engaging and ruthless. The specific tactics of outrage include hyperbole, sensationalism, ad hominem attacks, ridicule, extreme language, and "proving" that an opponent is a hypocrite. Writing in 2014, Berry and Sobieraj proposed that the outrage genre was exemplified by partisan hosts such as Sean Hannity and Bill O'Reilly at Fox, Rush Limbaugh on talk radio, and Rachel Maddow and Keith Olbermann, then at MSNBC.

Drawing from the literature on the psychology of conservatism reviewed in the previous chapters, it's easy to make the case that the central characteristics of this outrage genre ought to appeal to the psychological profile of conservatives more than liberals. Outrage as a genre is focused on "unveiling enemies."[3] It does this explicitly by pointing out institutions (media), individuals (Hillary Clinton), and policies (Obamacare) that are threatening. Since conservatives have a higher threat and mortality salience than liberals, one should expect them to be drawn to information that monitors for threats. Outrage typically identifies and constructs enemies and threats symbolically, through juxtaposition. "So that the audience is perfectly clear who the villains are," Berry and Sobieraj write; "hosts and bloggers use semiotic shortcuts, attempting to symbolically pollute their enemies by linking them to the groups most reviled by American audiences."[4] Some of the most popular references used to create these linkages? Communists, socialists, Nazis, and of course, Adolf Hitler. Constructing and demonizing enemies through symbolic association is an efficient way to capitalize on conservatives' efficient heuristic processing. It is known that conservatives are more likely to make use of such cognitive shortcuts in memory. Among viewers high in need for closure and low in need for cognition, one should expect that decisions driven by gut instinct, implicit associations, and emotions will dominate.

Outrage appeals to people not because of the information it delivers but because of the experience it provides. Outrage helps viewers feel validated in their opinions and allows them to avoid belief-disconfirming points of view. It seems reasonable to assume that for people who are low in tolerance for ambiguity, it would be far more comfortable to swim in a sea of like-minded opinion than to have to entertain the possibility (that exists when viewing mainstream news) that occasionally your side may be incorrect. Outrage also helps audience members feel like they are part of a clear like-minded in-group. "Whereas political conversation generates fears of social exclusion," Berry and Sobieraj write; "outrage programs incorporate and include viewers and listeners. The host presents as a kindred spirit who 'gets you' even when other folks don't."[5] Outrage hosts make viewers feel smart—especially compared to all those dupes out there—as though their "fans are more intelligent than the idiotic others who don't 'get it.'"[6]

These shows purport to give the "real" story, the one that has been hidden by the other side or by mainstream media, typically in a way that assigns blame and responsibility to certain individuals or entities. These strategic appeals would seem to speak to a mind inclined toward closure and certainty, as they reduce complex situations and processes to readily understandable narratives with easily identifiable antagonists. It seems somewhat ironic that in reality, these shows don't provide the "real story" at all. What they often provide are stories constructed through deliberate misrepresentative exaggeration, designed to give viewers a strong valenced impression of a policy, person, or institution. These evaluative presentations help people make even more efficient use of their heuristic-dominant inclinations and minimize the need for internal debate or scrutiny. All told, it would seem that fans of outrage programming would probably agree with statements like "It's annoying to listen to someone who cannot seem to make up his or her mind" and "I feel uncomfortable when someone's meaning or intention is unclear to me" (two of the items used to measure need for closure). They would also be the same kind of people who would likely *disagree* with statements like "when considering most conflict situations, I can usually see how both sides could be right" or "I prefer interacting with people whose opinions are very different from my own" (two items used to measure tolerance for ambiguity).

As Berry and Sobieraj outline, both liberals and conservatives produce and consume outrage, with hosts like Maddow occupying the space on the left and hosts like Hannity and Limbaugh the space on the right. Berry and Sobieraj do not describe outrage as an exclusively conservative genre. However, they do provide empirical evidence that conservative outrage programming is "more outrageous" than liberal outrage programming. Even within the genre of outrage, Berry and Sobieraj found that conservative outrage shows included more "incidents of outrage" than liberal outrage shows including more insulting language, name-calling, emotional displays, emotional language, misrepresentative exaggeration, and ideologically extremizing language. The authors conclude: "those shows with the highest levels of outrage are far more likely to be conservative than liberal."[7,8]

This means that MSNBC programs like *The Rachel Maddow Show*, *All In with Chris Hayes*, and *The Last Word with Lawrence O'Donnell* all constitute outrage programming according to the definitional criteria, but based on their actual content, the "outrage" on MSNBC doesn't run quite as deep as it does on Fox. Maddow, the most successful of the liberal outrage hosts, typically uses long drawn-out segments to explain boring and convoluted events and details underlying political stories. *Forbes*'s Mark Joyella described a 27-minute segment in which Maddow "slowly and methodically tied together thread after thread in the messy confusing and complicated story of Donald Trump and Russia.[9] So, while Maddow's show is "personality centered...defined by a dominant charismatic voice,"[10] and while it is working to expose perceived hypocrisy and wrongdoing of the other side, she performs it in the spirit and tone of an engaging but incredulous college professor rather than with the fire and brimstone of an evangelical minister.

In her 2015 book *In-Your-Face Politics: The Consequences of Uncivil Media*, Professor Diana Mutz of the University of Pennsylvania presents the results of dozens of experiments exploring the audience and impact of the kind of emotionally charged debate common in outrage shows. Assessing the levels of negative arousal that result from exposure to this "in-your-face" media, Mutz found significantly higher negative arousal among Republicans than Democrats, regardless of a show's content. She also found a greater preference for this kind of programming among conservatives and Republicans than among liberals and Democrats. She concludes that "conservatives and Republicans are particularly likely to expose themselves to in-your-face programs" and "are especially likely to react once exposed."[11]

Given that conservatives are more negatively aroused by the kinds of content that defines the outrage genre, it makes sense that Berry and Sobieraj found conservative outrage programming to be more "outrageous" than liberal outrage programming. If outrage is a genre that disproportionately appeals to the right (which is the case I am trying to make here, just in case that's still not clear), one should also find that the ideological leaning of conservative outrage audiences is more extreme than that of liberal outrage audiences. To explore this, I analyzed 2010 data from Pew that included respondents' political ideologies and what specific programs they reported watching (table 8.1). The results show that conservative outrage audiences (of Beck, Hannity, O'Reilly, and Limbaugh) self-identify as more conservative than liberal outrage audiences (of Olbermann and Maddow) self-identify as liberal.

So conservative outrage audiences are far more conservative than liberal outrage audiences are liberal. Yet, as illustrated by Berry and Sobieraj, the

Table 8.1 **Average political ideology among regular viewers of outrage programs.**

Show host	Mean ideology of "regular" viewers/listeners
Olbermann	0.42
Maddow	0.22
Beck	−.94
O'Reilly	−.88
Hannity	−1.04
Limbaugh	−1.06

N = 3,006. Range: −2 = very conservative; 0 = moderate; 2 = very liberal.

Source: Pew Research Center, Media Consumption Survey, 2010.

genre—defined by its tone and tactics—exists on both sides. Even so, Berry and Sobieraj concede that conservatives especially dominate the talk radio landscape of outrage, referencing the work of Marc Hetherington and Jonathan Weiler on the psychology of authoritarianism.[12] They propose that the conservative dominance of outrage media could stem from the "authoritarian divide" between personalities of the left and right. In fact, they conclude, "individuals who embrace [an authoritarian personality style] are more attracted to aggressive rhetoric in political commentary, which narrates the world in black and white."[13]

Irony and Outrage: Left and Right

Before starting to test how tolerance for ambiguity or need for cognition relate to consumption of satire and outrage, it would be worthwhile to test the major assumption underlying this book's argument thus far: that satire is watched by liberals and outrage is watched by conservatives. Data from the Pew Research Center's 2014 American Trends Panel (March 19–April 29, 2014; N = 2,901), clearly show that Limbaugh's, Hannity's, and O'Reilly's audiences skew more conservative and Republican, while Colbert's and Stewart's audiences skew more liberal and Democratic (see figs. 8.1 and 8.2).[14] The audience

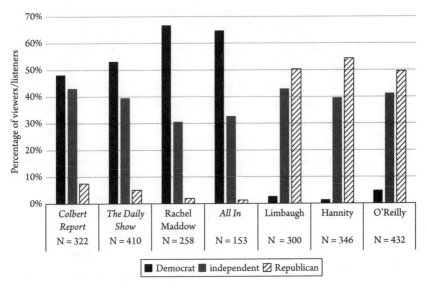

FIGURE 8.1 Party identification of people who report "getting news" from each source in the past week.

Data source: Pew Research Center, American Trends Panel, 2014.

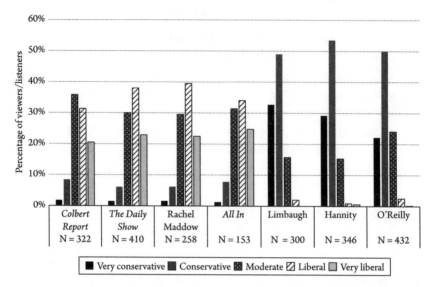

FIGURE 8.2 Political ideology of people who report "getting news" from each source in the past week.

Data source: Pew Research Center, American Trends Panel, 2014.

of the liberal outrage shows, *The Rachel Maddow Show* and *All In with Chris Hayes*, looks an awful lot like the audience of Stewart and Colbert in terms of party and ideology. The major difference between the audiences of liberal outrage and those of liberal satire, at least from 2010 to 2015, was audience size. Notably, in 2012–2013 Maddow's ratings hit all-time lows, with less than 750,000 nightly viewers,[15] at the same time that *The Daily Show* with Jon Stewart and the *Colbert Report* were scoring all-time highs,[16] averaging 2.5 million and 1.9 million nightly viewers, respectively. Pew data dating back to 2010 show this same trend (table 8.2): Democrats making up the majority of the audiences of satire shows on Comedy Central and Republicans making up the majority of audiences of Beck, O'Reilly, Hannity (on Fox), and Limbaugh (on the radio). And while Democrats have also made up the majority of the audiences of Olbermann and Maddow (liberal outrage hosts on MSNBC), their regular viewers were consistently fewer in number than those of Stewart and Colbert.[17]

More recently (March 2018), I ran a similar analysis on a national online sample.[18] The same pattern in audience ideology and partisanship emerged. The audiences of *The Daily Show with Trevor Noah* and the *Late Show with Stephen Colbert* were significantly more liberal and Democratic than the average American; the audiences of Hannity and Limbaugh were significantly more conservative and Republican than the average American. Again,

Table 8.2 Party identification and political ideology of "regular viewers" of satire and outrage programs.

	Percent of total respondents who are "regular" viewers/listeners	Percent of "regular" viewers/ listeners who are Republicans or Democrats		Mean ideology of "regular" viewers/ listeners*
		Republican	Democrat	
Olbermann	2.8	3.1	60.0	0.42
Maddow	2.9	12.2	50.0	0.22
Daily Show with Jon Stewart	7.3	14.4	41.3	0.24
Colbert Report	5.6	13.8	38.7	0.23
Beck	6.8	52.9	9.2	–.94
O'Reilly	9.7	54.4	9.9	–.88
Hannity	6.2	61.6	5.9	–1.04
Limbaugh	5.2	63.1	9.6	–1.06

N = 3,006.

* Range: −2 = very conservative; 0 = moderate; 2 = very liberal.

Source: Pew Research Center, Media Consumption Survey, 2010.

Maddow's audience on MSNBC mirrored the ideological and party leanings of Colbert and Noah (see figs. 8.3 and 8.4). However, according to 2018 Nielsen viewing data, the ratings for Maddow's show under the Trump administration rose up from the lows experienced in 2012–2013. Following Trump's inauguration, and fueled by the investigation into possible collusion between the Trump campaign and Russia, Maddow's ratings increased steadily through 2017 and 2018.[19]

These data confirm the notion that satire audiences are liberal and Hannity's and Limbaugh's audiences are conservative (shocking, I know), but what about the proposition that these differences in viewing preferences stem from the unique psychological characteristics of the audiences? This proposition is complicated by the fact that outrage is clearly not exclusively a conservative enterprise. Maddow, Olbermann, and Hayes have been able to create success-

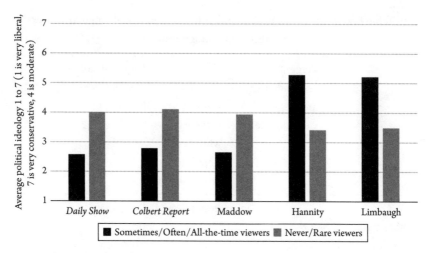

FIGURE 8.3 Average political ideology of program viewers (on scale from 1 to 7 where 1 is very liberal and 7 is very conservative).

Source: University of Delaware's Center for Political Communication, 2018 (N = 601).

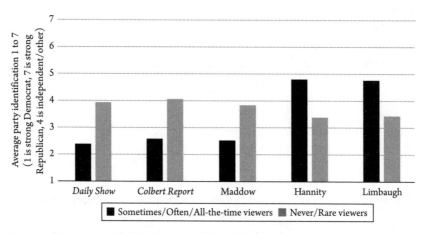

FIGURE 8.4 Average political party affiliation of program viewers (where 1 is strong Democrat and 7 is strong Republican).

Source: University of Delaware's Center for Political Communication, 2018 (N = 601).

ful careers out of the liberal outrage genre, even if their audiences have tended to be smaller than those of their conservative counterparts. So how does tolerance for ambiguity relate to consumption of outrage and satire?

To understand this relationship, I examined two national data sets from 2015 and 2018.[20] In the 2015 data set, viewers of satire programs scored significantly higher in tolerance for ambiguity than nonviewers of these shows.[21] The same was true in 2018.[22] (See figs. 8.5 and 8.6.) In fact, in the 2015 data,

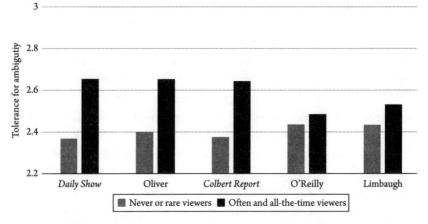

FIGURE 8.5 Mean tolerance for ambiguity among audiences of satire and outrage programming (coded from

Source: Qualtrics, March 2015 (N = 305).

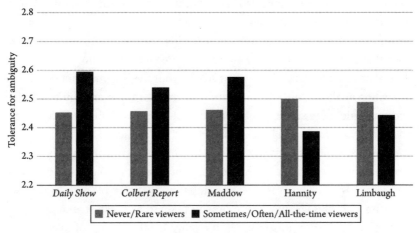

FIGURE 8.6 Mean tolerance for ambiguity among audiences of satire and outrage programming.

Source: University of Delaware's Center for Political Communication, 2018 (N = 601).

people who reported watching *The Daily Show* with Jon Stewart or the *Colbert Report* on Comedy Central scored significantly higher in tolerance for ambiguity, even when controlling for party, ideology, age, education, political interest, gender, need for cognition, and sense of humor.[23] While tolerance for ambiguity was not associated with exposure to O'Reilly or Limbaugh in 2015, both genres were viewed most by those with high levels of political interest and education.

To account for the possibility that tolerance for ambiguity only relates to viewing preferences because of its relationship with "sense of humor" (measured with nine items that capture "appreciation for production and consumption of humor"), I added "sense of humor" to the models predicting exposure. Surprisingly, "sense of humor" did not correlate with satire viewing at all. Instead, tolerance for ambiguity remained the strongest predictor of viewing Stewart, Colbert, and Oliver. However, sense of humor *did* correlate— *in a negative direction*—with viewing O'Reilly and Limbaugh. This means that those who scored highest in sense of humor were significantly less likely to report watching O'Reilly or Limbaugh—even when controlling for the factors mentioned above.[24]

Thus far there is empirical evidence that viewing satire is associated with being liberal, Democratic, younger, and politically interested and having high tolerance for ambiguity. There is also empirical evidence that viewing conservative outrage programming is associated with being conservative, Republican, politically interested, and educated and scoring lower in sense of humor. But to what extent does a psychological trait like tolerance for ambiguity shape program preferences through its effects on political ideology?[25] How does this psychological trait relate to your broader orientation to the world (liberal or conservative) in a way that shapes your media consumption habits? Mediation analyses suggest that those who are tolerant of ambiguity lean left and consume more satire. Those who are not tolerant of ambiguity lean right and consume more outrage. That finding is a solid place to start.

The next logical step is to unpack whether satire consumption is highest among those liberals who are highest in tolerance for ambiguity. If tolerance for ambiguity contributes to liberals being more comfortable with (and drawn to) satire, data should show satire consumption to be greatest among liberals who score highest on this trait. On the other hand, if a lack of tolerance for ambiguity contributes to conservatives being more comfortable with (and drawn to) conservative outrage programming, data should show that consumption of conservative outrage is greatest among conservatives who score the lowest on this trait.

I explored these relationships in a March 2018 poll conducted by the University of Delaware's Center for Political Communication (N = 608). The data show that the relationship between tolerance for ambiguity and viewing satire is significantly different for liberals and conservatives. Similarly, the relationship between tolerance for ambiguity and viewing outrage is significantly different for liberals and conservatives.[26] Among liberals, as tolerance for ambiguity increased, so too did exposure to *The Daily Show with Trevor Noah* (see fig. 8.8). For conservatives, this relationship was the opposite—which makes sense given the ideological leaning of the show. If you're a conservative with little tolerance for ambiguity, you're definitely not watching *The Daily Show*. The same is true of liberals low in tolerance for ambiguity in their consumption of Hannity or Limbaugh. If you are liberal and not tolerant of ambiguity, you are not watching conservative outrage programming that challenges your worldview.

What is intriguing about these relationships, though, is what the data show among those partisans who are *highest* in tolerance for ambiguity. Among conservatives, as tolerance for ambiguity increases, exposure to belief-confirming Hannity and Limbaugh decreases. Limbaugh and Hannity are consumed most by conservatives with the lowest tolerance for ambiguity (see fig. 8.7 for the Limbaugh findings). But *The Daily Show with Trevor Noah* is consumed most by liberals with the *highest* tolerance for ambiguity (see fig. 8.8). These findings are consistent with the proposition that liberals' and conservatives' unique underlying psychological predispositions—especially tolerance for ambiguity—lead them to consume distinct forms of political information, and it seems that irony and outrage (respectively) fit the bill.

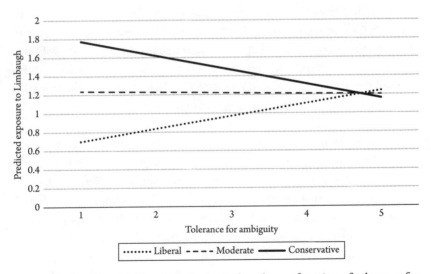

FIGURE 8.7 Predicted exposure to Rush Limbaugh as a function of tolerance for ambiguity and political ideology.

Source: University of Delaware's Center for Political Communication, 2018 (N = 601).

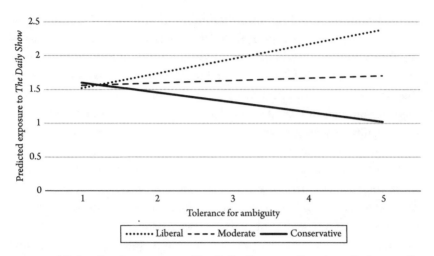

FIGURE 8.8 Predicted exposure to *The Daily Show* as a function of tolerance for ambiguity and political ideology.

Source: University of Delaware's Center for Political Communication, 2018 (N = 601).

But Isn't Satire "Outrageous-ish?"

While Berry and Sobieraj characterize outrage as a genre of both the left and the right, they wrestle with how to fit "political satire" into the outrage landscape. In their final chapter, they dedicate several pages to "the satire circuit" in which they acknowledge that satire shares some characteristics with outrage. Satire is personality-driven, emotional, and engaging. But they explicitly rejected the notion that satire shows like *The Daily Show with Jon Stewart* or *The Colbert Report* constitute "outrage" in their own right.

> Some might argue that the satire shows are themselves outrageous— mockery, belittling, and the use of insulting language are the mainstay of both programs.…We see them as fundamentally different. These are programs that are deeply engaged with the [outrage] genre, but not themselves a part of it. They draw on the material produced in the outrage industry to unmask it. What's more, *The Daily Show* and *Colbert Report* are on *Comedy Central*, not a news network, and don't purport to be journalism. As Jon Stewart reminded Tucker Carlson, "You're on *CNN*. The show that leads into me is puppets making crank phone calls."[27]

I certainly understand not wanting to toss Stewart and Colbert into a stew with Hannity, Limbaugh, and O'Reilly. They are clearly different animals. But I reject the notion that satire programs are different from outrage programs because of the label they place on themselves (comedy, not news), where they appear (Comedy Central), or what programming leads into their show (puppets making crank phone calls). Michael Delli Carpini and Bruce Williams address these artificial distinctions in their discussion of the obsolete boundaries between "entertainment" and "public affairs programming":[28] "[these] traditional categories fail as a way of making such distinctions.... They are social constructions that tell us more about the distribution of political power than about the political relevance of different genres. Further... these categories are rapidly losing what power they once had to privilege certain gatekeepers and genres in the process of constructing political reality."[29] What a particular program is called, how it categorizes itself, and where it airs do not determine whether or not it facilitates political meaning-making. Perhaps, in drawing substantive distinctions between these genres, one could instead think about criteria such as (1) what the programming does, and (2) why people seek it out (both of which are coming up in the next chapter). Fortunately, I have gotten to know Sarah Sobieraj through our mutual work with the National Institute for Civil Discourse at the University of Arizona. I started digging into Sobieraj's work with Berry on *The Outrage Industry*, and the more I did so, the more questions I realized I had for her.

Moral "Un-certainty" and Genre Hybridity

On the night before Thanksgiving 2017, Sobieraj joined me to sit at a cozy bar in a suburb of Boston. She acknowledged to me that there are similarities in the features and functions of both outrage and satire. She also agreed that it is useful to define a genre not by what it feels or smells like but by what it does. She also held firm in her contention that to put satire in the same category as outrage simply did not feel right. In her estimation, satire has enough differences in its spirit, aesthetics, and position in the media landscape that it merits a separate category. "In terms of use and information outcomes, I'm not sure [outrage and satire] are different, but I'm also pretty sure they're not the same," she said, smiling. She then elaborated on how she sees these genres as distinct:

> The networks treat [outrage programs] as serious—everything from the staging to where [these programs] are in the lineup and the timing

of the programs. The networks are positioning it as serious even though they are not saying it is news. They're saying it's analysis, but I'm not sure that the average person at home knows what "analysis" is. And, it's not just that the networks are positioning it as serious based on when they schedule it, based on the staging, or based on the clothing. It's also that the hosts are saying "We have the truth and conventional news can't be trusted." These two different things [the way the networks position and stage the shows and the way the hosts approach their own importance] say "we are real and credible." I don't think that is present in the same way [in satire].[30]

At the heart of this distinction is not just the fact that outrage is serious and satire is funny. It is not just the positioning of outrage as news and of satire as entertainment. It is about the moral certainty and authority with which these hosts speak. Hannity, O'Reilly, and Limbaugh present their criticisms and claims as the truth that they are dutifully illuminating for the audience. They place themselves in a higher position—above the audience and above other media—and in possession of information that only they have. It is this assumed status and moral certainty inherent in outrage that is consistent with a conservative psychological framework. Recall that conservatives prefer art that is realistic in its representation of the world, narratives that are clear and resolved at the end, and borders that are strong. Given all that, conservatives should be drawn to a political information genre that is explicit in its political, ideological, and information goals; for example, O'Reilly's catchphrase "You are about to enter the No-Spin Zone," Hannity's guest segment unironically titled "The Great American Panel," or perhaps Tucker Carlson's show on Fox, which bills itself as "the sworn enemy of lying, pomposity, smugness, and groupthink."[31]

Consider, in contrast, the spirit and positioning of the comic: self-deprecating, unimportant, and outside the political world. This is how comics think of—or at least portray—themselves and their impact. In a denial of suggestions that his show, Last Week Tonight, had shaped the FCC's position on net neutrality in 2015, John Oliver stated: "I would argue that we have very little to do with any of those [political] things."[32] Stewart once said: "I am a tiny, neurotic man, standing in the back of the room throwing tomatoes at the chalkboard."[33] In 2004, he told Newsday: "We have no power. I would say influence implies results and influence implies we have a platform. We don't. No platform. No agenda. No reason for being, other than to entertain ourselves.[34] Samantha Bee, host of Full Frontal on TBS, shares this "we're not that important" ethos.

Margaret Sullivan of the *Washington Post* writes: "Bee rejects the notion that late-night comedy…seems to have an outsize influence on informing Americans about politics. 'I think the key word is 'seems,' Bee said. 'We may seem to have influence, but we really don't. We love to put our white-hot laser on things but that can't be the point of what we're doing."[35]

I suppose that is the key distinction right there: "*that* [putting a white-hot laser on things] can't be the point of what [comics are] doing." Political satire prioritizes the humor over the politics. Yes, in satire the politics "come first" in the sense that the political world shapes what comics choose to talk about and how they talk about it. But even so, it is the successful production of *humor* that is the main goal of the satirist. In an interview on NPR's *Fresh Air* in March 2018, Terry Gross asked John Oliver about the process involved in writing his show.[36] She articulated what she imagined the show's development process was like, that maybe the staff was a combination of journalists and comics, and "[they might] have this group of journalists who do this deep dive into a story, and then a group of comedy writers who turn that story into a comedic take. Using all the investigative stuff that the journalists have come up with, then the comics would transform that into a comic take on this really important story."[37]

"That's a pretty good guess, Terry," Oliver replied. "You've just revealed our secret sauce live on air. You've just 'Colonel Sanders-ed' our process."[38]

So the politics "come first," but the humor is the goal. The process of writing satire is a bit like writing for two entirely different shows at the same time: one news/opinion and one comedy. When I asked *Full Frontal's* Ashley Black what she thought was the biggest distinction between satire and outrage, she responded: "I can't speak to how people experience [these genres], but as far as making it, I would say satire is *a lot* harder to do. That's why that comparison [to outrage programs] is offensive," she joked. "Every story that comes across my desk, my initial response is like [Sean] Hannity's would be; like 'F**k these people! This is terrible!' And then I spend eight hours getting past that to the point of making jokes—doing something smarter, different, and more surprising."[39]

"We call it 'third thought,'" Black said, alluding to her Second City training. "Del Close said when you are responding to something on stage, your first thought is the thing that everyone in the audience would have said. Your second thought is the thing that a bad comedian would have said. Go with your third thought." She concluded: "A dude just going on TV and saying 'I hate this person. I hate that person?' That seems easy." She smiled. "I could write that very easily."[40]

Satire is an explicitly hybrid genre, one that intentionally and explicitly blurs lines: between fact and fiction, between entertainment and news, and between what is serious and what is playful. Geoffrey Baym explains that the concept of "hybridity" refers to a "blending...a loss of distinction, a process of de-differentiation. What were once seen as essentialized categories...have become replaced by unstable mixtures and uncertain assemblages."[41] If you are someone who prefers distinct categories, how comfortable will you be deriving political meaning from something that is an "unstable mixture" or an "uncertain assemblage?" Would you really want to get political news from something that is political in content but bills itself as "just for fun?" And sure, academics will point to the theatrical and entertainment-driven features of outrage programming, which render it, too, a "hybrid" genre. But the "hybridity" of Hannity and Limbaugh is something they work very hard to push from audiences' minds. They bill themselves as news. They bill themselves as truth. And yes, when it is convenient, Hannity will claim that he is "not a journalist" but "a talk show host" (see fig. 8.9), but in his next breath he'll seek the credibility and authority that come with being a "news" host.

After Fox News (actual) news program host Shep Smith referred to Fox's opinion shows—like Hannity's—as "strictly entertainment,"[42] Hannity clearly got his knickers in a twist, tweeting that Smith "is clueless about what we do every day. Hannity breaks news daily" (see fig. 8.10).

It is in their different levels of moral certainty that the genres of irony and outrage are especially distinct. Recall Sobieraj's observation that the hosts of outrage programming "are saying 'we have the truth and conventional news can't be trusted.'" In her view, people like Hannity and Limbaugh are operating

Sean Hannity ✔
@seanhannity

(Follow) ⌄

I'm not a journalist jackass. I'm a talk host.

Michael Cohen @speechboy71
Guys got a point ... after all Sean Hannity has a job in journalism
twitter.com/seanhannity/st...

9:22 PM - 25 Oct 2016

FIGURE 8.9 Sean Hannity, tweet, October 25, 2016.

Sean Hannity ✓
@seanhannity

Following ∨

While Shep is a friend with political views I do not share, and great at breaking news, he is clueless about what we do every day. Hannity breaks news daily-Warrant on a Trump assoc, the unmasking scandal, leaking intel, Fisa abuse, HRC lawbreaking, dossier and more REAL NEWS! 9p

The Hill ✓ @thehill
Shep Smith: Fox News opinion programs are strictly entertainment
hill.cm/m7upZl1

9:44 AM - 16 Mar 2018

FIGURE 8.10 Sean Hannity, tweet, March 16, 2016.

from a position that "'we are real and credible.'" But in satire programs, she suggests, this statement of truth and credibility "is not present in the same way."[43] This is the very aspect of satire that Black believes allows viewers to trust the satirist; as she put it,

> it's clear that [what we are doing] is performance in a way that news actively works against. That is why people trust comedians. For many years the idea of news was that "This is the objective truth. This white guy sitting behind a desk is telling you the truth and that's all it is." And then people got savvy and found out that that was not the case and that there *is* bias. No comedian has ever purported to tell you that *this is true.* You are coming in to hear this person's bias because you think it's funny. There is an element of trust that comes from "I know you're not trying to lie to me. I can hear a laugh track."[44]

With satire, Black continued, "you always know that it is this individual person's opinion about the news. There's a trust that comes from knowing 'this person never lied to me about what this is.'"[45] Maybe Black is right. Maybe this is why liberals trust satire. And perhaps the fact that "it's clear that [satire] is performance" and that "no comedian has ever purported to tell you that this is true," explains why conservatives are less likely to be drawn to satire as a mode of political expression. Similarly, perhaps the fact that outrage hosts are saying "we have the truth and conventional news can't be trusted," explains why conservatives are more likely to be drawn to outrage. If conservatives' information-seeking habits are driven by a need to reduce uncertainty, then these two genres might represent the aesthetic forms that make conservatives most comfortable and trusting (outrage) and most uncomfortable and suspicious (satire).

Two Aesthetics Collide: The Rumble in the Air-Conditioned Auditorium

On October 6, 2012, the competing aesthetics of irony and outrage were on display side by side in the much-publicized "Rumble in the Air-Conditioned Auditorium," a debate between O'Reilly and Stewart that was held on the campus of George Washington University and made available online. The two hosts were each offered a few minutes to issue an opening statement.

The Fox News host began:

> OK. I'm gonna have a 3 minute opening and he [pointing to Stewart] will mock it....about 20% of us are slackers and it's a growing industry. And that's what the election is all about. That is what the country is facing right now. We are spending an enormous amount of money on 20% who for whatever reason are like [mocking] "We're not going to cut it. We're not gonna make a living. We're not gonna really do anything. We want our stuff." And so, we're spending a lot of money. [Holds up and reads from a placard]: "Debt Is Bad."

O'Reilly then shifted his ire to one of the favorite targets of conservative outrage hosts from 2012: Georgetown University law student Sandra Fluke. If you are lucky enough to not remember outrage hosts' fascination with Fluke, let me be the one to remind you. After Republicans in Congress barred her from testifying before the House Oversight Committee on whether religiously affiliated institutions, such as universities and hospitals, should be required to cover contraceptive medications through their government-mandated health-care plans, the House Democratic Steering and Policy Committee invited her to offer testimony at a meeting they convened. There she made the point that the women students and employees at such institutions should have such coverage because such medications are frequently used to treat reproductive health conditions.

Several days after her testimony, Limbaugh attacked Fluke on his radio show for asking the government to "pay her to have sex," saying: "What does that make her? It makes her a slut, right? It makes her a prostitute. She wants to be paid to have sex. She's having so much sex she can't afford con-traception. She wants you and me and the taxpayers to pay her to have sex." In the "Rumble," O'Reilly took the baton from his fellow outrage host and kept on running, even injecting a hint of hyperbolic humor into the mix: "the poster person for the entitlement society is Sandra Fluke. Do you know Sandra? I left two tickets for Sandra plus a month's supply of birth control pills at 'will call.' Is she here tonight? No, she's not. Sandra, Buy. Your. Own." said O'Reilly, holding up a placard that read: "Buy Your Own." "We shouldn't be paying for this or for a lot of other stuff. That's why we owe 60 tril-lion dollars."

O'Reilly closed his statement and yielded the floor to Stewart. But before Stewart began, standing behind the podium, the five-foot-seven comic sud-denly began to grow taller with the use of a hydraulic lift, until he was literally eye to eye with the six-foot-four O'Reilly. The bit served as a salient visual reminder that Stewart is just "a tiny, neurotic man, standing in the back of the room throwing tomatoes at the chalkboard."[46] After navigating the lift up and down and up again, and when the crowd finally stopped laughing and cheer-ing, Stewart spoke with a subtle politician-on-soapbox patter, complete with faux formal vocal inflections and extensive hand gestures:

> My friend Bill O'Reilly...is completely full of shit....What is wrong with this country is that we face a deficiency in our problem solving mechanisms. The reason we face difficulty in our problem solving mechanism is that a good portion of this country has created an "alter-nate universe" in which the issues that we face revolve around a woman from Georgetown who wanted birth control which is a health issue for women covered under her health insurance in the same way Viagra is covered. I call this "alternate universe" where these folks live: Bullshit Mountain.

Whereas O'Reilly's tone was unironically self-assured, didactic, and conde-scending, Stewart's tone, while also self-assured and didactic, was ironically performed as though wearing a mask. Throughout his pointed statement, Stewart peppered his criticisms with punchlines that allowed him to step out of character in short bursts, thereby diffusing the aggression inherent in his argument. In the end, Stewart offered a quite literal example of Edward Bloom and Lillian Bloom's definition of satire as "pleading with man for a return to his moral senses."[47] Stewart begged O'Reilly to abandon his ways, stop fueling partisan divides through emotional appeals, and rejoin the world of verifiable and falsifiable reality:

> I have come here tonight to plead to the mayor of Bullshit Mountain [gesturing to O'Reilly]: talk to your people. I know you don't live on Bullshit Mountain all year long. Obviously you have to leave for pro-visions and I believe you have a summer place. But, until we can agree on a reality that exists in this country, you and those denizens believe that we face a cataclysm, a societal cataclysm between free-dom and socialism. On Bullshit Mountain our problems are ampli-fied and our solutions simplified and that's why they won't work. We face a deficit crisis we've never faced before. We are merely weeks from being a failed state or even worse, Greece, and the way to solve it is to kill Big Bird.

Conservatives' Trouble with Hybridity

I find it difficult to escape the thought that central to the preferred liberal polit-ical aesthetic is this concept of explicit hybridity—in format, in intention, and in representation of truth. Recall Alan Myerson's allusions to the "cross-polli-nation" of the creative political endeavors of 1960s San Francisco: guerrilla theater, the Artist Liberation Front, activist musicians, all creating a community alongside the Diggers and the Red Guards and the Black Panthers. These explorations and combinations were a logical extension of the epistemology and aesthetic of the counterculture. Meanwhile, the efforts of conservative radio hosts Dan Smoot, H. L. Hunt, and Clarence Manion never deviated from the straight genre of political information. There were no efforts to become playful or to experiment with other forms of expression. The content and the goals were explicitly political, and the tone was self-righteous and didactic.

This discomfort with—and judgment of—hybrid forms of political expression is not limited to conservatives' perceptions of art or satire. Consider recent conservative calls for celebrities in the entertainment or sports industries to stop speaking out about politics. In February 2019, Fox News host Laura Ingraham criticized the political expressions of professional athletes like the Cleveland Cavaliers' LeBron James. "It's always unwise to seek political advice from someone who gets paid $100 million a year to bounce a ball," she said. "Keep the political comments to yourselves.... Shut up and dribble."[48] In an interview about the Academy Awards, Republican National Committee spokesman Steve Guest told *Variety* in February 2018: "Americans aren't interested in Hollywood liberals blabbing about politics to a room full of Hollywood liberals."[49]

Undoubtedly, much of this belief that celebrities ought to "stay in their lane" is a reaction to the fact that athletes, actors, and artists tend to come from the left.[50] But I would also argue that conservatives' discomfort with celebrity political expression is broader than that. It seems to reflect an aversion to hybridity that is consistent with a low tolerance for ambiguity. To operate in the world with a high need for certainty requires sharp distinctions between categories, between people, and between concepts. Are you an actor or are you an activist? Are you an athlete or are you a political figure?

Pick. A. Lane.

To test the proposition that attitudes toward celebrities' political expression are related to psychological traits, my colleagues and I asked several survey questions about this topic in 2018.[51] We asked respondents "How appropriate do you think it is for the following kinds of people to speak out about political issues or causes?" The series of prompts that followed this question included "late-night comedians," "Hollywood actors," and "professional athletes." The respondents could answer "Not at all appropriate," "Not very appropriate," "Somewhat appropriate," or "Very appropriate." We also asked the respondents about their political party identification and their political ideology, and we asked them a series of questions to measure tolerance for ambiguity and need for cognition.[52]

The results showed that Republicans and conservatives found political expression by celebrities to be significantly less appropriate than did Democrats and liberals. Most interesting, though, is that tolerance for ambiguity was significantly related to how appropriate people thought it was for celebrities to engage in this kind of speech—even when political party, ideology, and countless sociodemographic factors were accounted for. Those

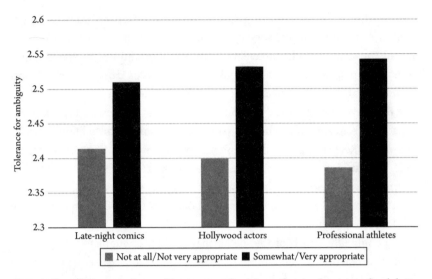

FIGURE 8.11 Tolerance for ambiguity as a function of attitudes toward celebrity political expression: "How appropriate do you think it is for the following kinds of people to speak out about political issues or causes?"

Source: University of Delaware's Center for Political Communication, 2018 (N = 608).

higher in tolerance for ambiguity found it more appropriate for celebrities of various kinds to speak out on political issues or causes than did respondents lower in tolerance for ambiguity (see fig. 8.11).

To begin to understand how tolerance for ambiguity relates to political ideology and how these two factors shape support for celebrity expression, I used the same statistical test for mediation described earlier.[53] The results suggest that tolerance for ambiguity shapes support for celebrity political expression—in part through its relationship with political ideology. People lower in tolerance for ambiguity tend to be conservative, and this political expression of their low tolerance for ambiguity (conservatism) predicts their views on hybrid political expression.

In a follow-up analysis, I wanted to visualize how political ideology and tolerance for ambiguity interact to shape public opinion on celebrities' political expression. The results, especially in the context of beliefs about political speech by professional athletes, highlight the unique role played by tolerance for ambiguity in shaping perceptions of appropriate speech, especially among liberals. As illustrated in figures 8.12 and 8.13, liberals were more supportive of professional athletes speaking out on political issues than conservatives, and this was in part a function of the high tolerance for ambiguity among

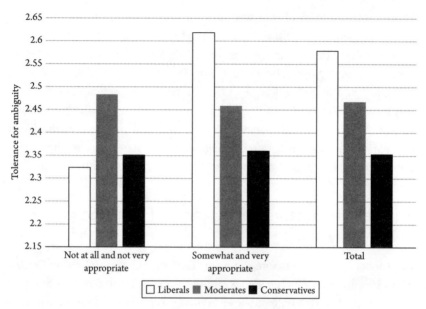

FIGURE 8.12 Tolerance for ambiguity, sorted by political ideology, as a function of attitudes toward celebrity political expression: "How appropriate is it for professional athletes to speak out about political issues or causes?"

Source: University of Delaware's Center for Political Communication, 2018 (N = 608).

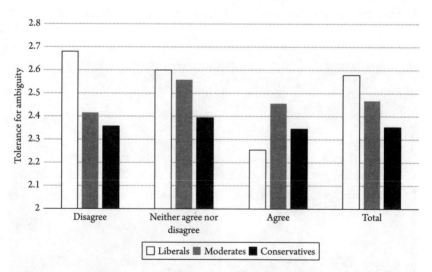

FIGURE 8.13 Tolerance for ambiguity, sorted by political ideology, as a function of attitudes toward celebrity political expression: "Agree/Disagree: Professional athletes are paid to play the game, not share their political opinions."

Source: University of Delaware's Center for Political Communication, 2018 (N = 608).

liberals. Among those liberals who opposed such speech, tolerance for ambiguity was down to (or below) the level found among conservatives.

I've realized through the process of writing this section that the argument I made earlier, regarding how satire or outrage are defined, is itself rooted in ambiguity and hybridity. I argued: "what a particular program is called, the way it categorizes itself, and where it airs do not determine whether or not it facilitates political meaning-making." But perhaps, if you are conservative, it does. Maybe the way a program is categorized and where it airs are the precise criteria conservatives use to demarcate "legitimate political information."

The Rally to Restore Sanity and/or Fear: A Study in Hybridity

In October 2010, days before the 2012 midterm elections, Comedy Central hosts Stewart and Colbert, along with their Comedy Central writers and producers, staged an elaborate public event that was part comedy show, part concert, and part nonpartisan (but definitely left-leaning) faux political rally. The event, playfully called the Rally to Restore Sanity and/or Fear, attracted hundreds of thousands of people of all ages, carrying signs about the media and politics and even ironic parody placards offering slogans like "THIS IS A GOOD SIGN" and "I fear my pants and so should you" (photo 8.1). The day featured comedy sketches, celebrity appearances, and performances by musical

PHOTO 8.1 Sign, Rally to Restore Sanity and/or Fear, October 30, 2010, Washington, DC. Courtesy of Angel Bourgoin.

guests like The Roots, Cat Stevens, and the O'Jays. The stage show was displayed on jumbotrons for 200,000-plus attendees to experience the event across the length of the mall.[54] At the end of this rally-spectacle-catharsis, Stewart spoke earnestly about his frustrations with the United States' polarized and sensationalized political media environment: "the country's 24-hour, political pundit perpetual panic conflictinator did not cause our problems, but its existence makes solving them that much harder. The press can hold its magnifying glass up to our problems, bringing them into focus, illuminating issues heretofore unseen. Or they can use that magnifying glass to light ants on fire, and then perhaps host a week of shows on the dangerous, unexpected flaming ants epidemic. If we amplify everything, we hear nothing."

But what was the Rally to Restore Sanity and/or Fear? Was it a political event? Performance art? An effort to increase turnout in the midterms among Democrats? Immediately following the rally, the two hosts responded to questions at a press conference held by the National Press Club. Journalists asked about the "purpose" of the rally and whether or not it was a "success." They asked about the boundaries of "fake pundits" like Stewart and Colbert and whether there were limits to what they could or should say and do. Stewart replied without hesitation: "the boundaries that we set for ourselves are based on our own sense of human decency. Not based on some preordained category of people who are allowed to speak seriously, people who must only speak in jokes or speak in rhyme. Our shows are just a reflection of our points of view. I'm not sure why there are 'lanes.'"[55]

Humor: Ambiguous and Inefficient

As I've already pointed out, the moral certainty with which outrage hosts speak is palpably different from the self-deprecation with which satire hosts speak. Outrage as a genre bills itself as important, as explicitly political, and as a vehicle for the dissemination of truth. Satire bills itself as playful, as designed to entertain, and as a vehicle for laughter. These distinct frames surrounding the two genres illustrate the two unique psychological profiles explored in chapters 6 and 7. And humor as a form of political discourse has another disadvantage for audiences who prefer clarity, closure, certainty, and efficiency. Humor is inherently inefficient.

I've explained the convoluted way humor is created through incongruous juxtapositions. I've chronicled the how the audience must go through a complex series of cognitive activities to access the first frame of reference, activate a second seemingly disconnected frame of reference, and then make a cognitive leap to put them together. I've also covered the fact that in satire, this cognitive leap is typically in the form of some argument or judgment that is implied through the joke but is never explicitly stated *in* the joke. To refresh your memory (and because it's fun), consider this bit from Seth Meyers from April 26, 2018: "The Senate today confirmed CIA director Mike Pompeo as secretary of state. Trump says he's excited, and looks forward to working with him for the next week or so." The first frame of reference you activate is the one associated with the Senate confirming CIA director Mike Pompeo as secretary of state. The second frame of reference (which introduces the incongruity) is the notion that Trump looks forward to "working with him for the next *week* or so." This forces you to draw on prior knowledge and consider why the secretary of state and the president would only work together for a week. Given the dozens of hirings and firings over the course of the Trump administration's tenure in office, you then come up with the argument that reconciles that incongruity: "Mike Pompeo will be fired soon just like everybody else in this administration."

As a lover of riddles and puns and all things comedy, I hear this and delight in the journey toward the joke's reconciliation. Meyers never says that Trump fires everybody in his administration. He never overtly insults Trump for these many staff changes. Those judgments all emerge from the contributions of the audience—assuming that the audience has the requisite knowledge to come to these conclusions. Jokes are playful and operate through implication. But that means they are also notoriously inefficient. The most basic function of communication is to convey information. And jokes are terrible at this.

In the context of serious topics or issues, if you are someone who values certainty and efficiency, perhaps jokes are perceived as undermining effective communication. Imagine someone for whom threat salience is high, someone who orients to the world in a way that prioritizes the reduction of uncertainty. When communicating information about important issues, jokes will probably frustrate this person: "Stop with the riddles and just say what you mean and mean what you say."

Compare Meyers's joke, which issues a judgment through humorous implication, to statements made by Hannity around the same time. On May 17, 2018, Hannity criticized Robert Mueller's investigation of the Trump administration: "the Special Counsel has been so abusive, so corrupt, they are so conflicted, that the president and his legal team are now rightly going on offense to combat the illicit 'deep state' scheme." Hannity continued: "Mueller already has everything that they have requested and the only point of a presidential interview is to set a perjury trap. This witch hunt is now a direct threat to this American republic. Mueller is causing irreparable damage to the rule of law in this country."[56]

Say what you will about Sean Hannity, a "riddler" he is not.

9

Satire and Outrage

PARALLEL FUNCTIONS AND IMPACT

THE LAST FEW chapters have focused on the fundamental differences between ironic satire and political outrage—in their logic, aesthetics, and epistemology. However, there are important parallels between the history, functions, and impact of these two genres have converged over the last several decades. In chapter 2, I discussed how political changes in the United States in the 1980s and 1990s contributed to political polarization and the commercialization of news, which contributed to sensationalism, the erosion of investigative journalism, and a reduction in trust in the media. Television satire and outrage both emerged as responses to these complex phenomena, and both genres were able to capitalize on technological developments through the 1990s—developments that created an increasingly fragmented and vast media landscape. Despite the divergent aesthetics and market positioning of satire and outrage as entertainment and news, respectively, both genres can be conceptualized as consequences of the same set of factors.

But this is not the only way these genres converge. Remember Berry and Sobieraj's justification for excluding satire from the outrage genre? They argued that satire is not the same as outrage because of its market positioning. I argued that the genres should be defined not by "their channel" but by the functions and outcomes of exposure to their content. And Sobieraj agreed. She explained that the main distinction between the two lies in the ways each conceptualizes and represents its own "moral certainty" and "truth," an observation that was particularly useful as I explained how the two genres relate to the psychology of the left and the right.

By arguing that these genres ought to be defined not by what they look like or where they air but, at least in part, by their functions and impact, I have introduced yet another question that can be explored empirically with social science data. If satire and outrage are serving similar roles for liberals and conservatives, respectively, one should be able to point to evidence illustrating parallel outcomes of exposure for both audiences. Such functions or outcomes might include political knowledge, trust in government and media, political efficacy (confidence in one's ability to understand and navigate the political world), and political participation, as well as distinct political attitudes or beliefs.

I use the terms "functions" and "outcomes" to highlight two different kinds of constructs. Functions are the reasons why audiences use the shows, explored both through self-reported viewing motivations (why people say they watch a certain program) and viewing orientations (whether audiences categorize that program as news, entertainment, or something else). Outcomes on the other hand are the effects of exposure: the consequences of viewing these shows.

Viewing outcomes can be studied through controlled experiments but are also frequently explored through correlational data obtained through cross-sectional survey research. While controlled experiments are especially good at isolating the causal effects of exposure (e.g., viewing this content *causes* this effect), their findings are sometimes difficult to generalize to the real world. In addition, experiments are a lot of work and are very expensive to conduct. Thus, much of the research on "outcomes of exposure" is based on cross-sectional survey data obtained at one point in time. That is, scholars have survey participants complete a questionnaire that asks how often they watch satire or outrage and asks questions to measure their political knowledge, attitudes, and behaviors. While nonexperimental studies like this can point to associations between viewing a program and having these other characteristics (knowledge, attitudes, and behaviors), they cannot definitively isolate causality between exposure and the proposed outcome. However, using statistical methods, researchers can control for the influences of other factors that might be responsible for correlations found in the data. While not ideal, these statistical methods at least provide researchers with a sense of the relationships between exposure and the proposed outcomes in a real-world context.

Functions: Who Watches and Why?

In the 1960s and 1970s, media scholars began studying the reasons why people consume certain media content. The subfield that emerged from these studies, dubbed the "uses and gratifications perspective,"[1] takes the view that media audiences are deliberate and thoughtful in their selection of media content. This approach characterizes the audience as active and discerning in their engagement with media. Viewers seek out media programming to satisfy certain needs or obtain certain gratifications, including diversion, information acquisition, or identify formation.

I'll admit that early in my career as a graduate student I found uses and gratifications literature neither interesting nor useful. People watch TV for different reasons. OK. So what? But more recently I've applied this theory to explain how different audience members might be differently affected by media content in different viewing contexts. For example, people who use media to attain certain goals or categorize programs a particular way (e.g., entertainment versus information) cognitively process that content differently as a result.[2] Therefore, if researchers are to understand whether irony and outrage serve similar functions for their audiences, researchers will need to understand why people tune in to these genres and how they categorize them.

In 2010, the Pew Research Center conducted a national survey that asked people why they turned to various information sources, including *The Daily Show*, *The Colbert Report*, and several outrage programs from the left and the right (see fig. 9.1).[3] Overwhelmingly, *Daily Show* and *Colbert* viewers reported watching for "entertainment." Meanwhile, audiences of the outrage programs

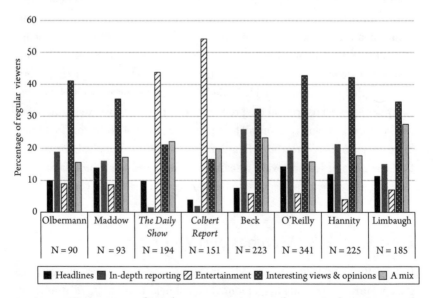

FIGURE 9.1 Percentages of regular program viewers who reported turning mostly to the eight information sources indicated, for the five reasons indicated.

Source: Pew Research Center, Media Consumption Survey, 2010 (N = 3,006).

rarely cited "entertainment" motivations, instead indicating that they watched these programs for "interesting views and opinions."

What these questions complicate, though, is that by asking "why do you turn to this source?" (e.g., *The Daily Show*, *Hannity*, or *Maddow*), viewers have likely already categorized these programs according to a particular genre. By virtue of the fact that they air on Comedy Central, *The Daily Show* and *Colbert* audiences likely categorize these shows as entertainment. Outrage shows, many of which are on MSNBC and Fox, are likely categorized as news(-ish). So, regardless of why people actually tune in, these preexisting categories likely inform viewers' responses to this question of why they watch.

Fortunately, Angela Lee studied why people watch these shows using a method that avoids some of the problems introduced by Pew's wording.[4] Lee asked respondents a series of general viewing motivation questions related to the reasons why they consume news programming in general.[5] She then ran statistical analyses to test how well these viewing motivations predicted exposure to specific shows (like *The Daily Show*, *Limbaugh*, or *Chris Matthews*). In other words, Lee's respondents were never asked to categorize a particular program as "entertainment" or "information." By separating the individual programs from viewers' categorization of them, Lee eliminated the problems posed by what people think the show is *supposed to be* and instead captured what shows are viewed by people with different viewing needs and goals.

First, Lee's results highlight an important distinction between motivations for the more entertainment-oriented network late-night comedy shows and the more pointed satire offered on Comedy Central. Whereas "entertainment motivations" most strongly predicted consumption of *The Tonight Show with Jay Leno*, *Saturday Night Live*, *Jimmy Kimmel Live!*, and *Conan with Conan O'Brian*,[6] it seems that *The Daily Show* and *The Colbert Report* behaved a bit more like *Maddow* or *Hardball with Chris Matthews*, driven slightly by entertainment motivations, but also by "opinion-motivations."[7] Meanwhile, entertainment motivations were least predictive of exposure to the top three conservative outrage shows discussed throughout this book: *The Rush Limbaugh Show*, *The Sean Hannity Show*, and *The O'Reilly Factor*. This finding, given the aesthetics of outrage, which are steeped in moral certainty and seriousness, shouldn't be too shocking. The fact that Lee's findings point to more "opinion-motivated" viewing of *The Daily Show* and *Colbert*, compared to what was found in the aforementioned Pew data, is important—and understandable, when you consider the distinct methods used in each study.

Next, I wanted to understand how ideology might affect the uses and gratifications liberals and conservatives reported seeking from various programs.

If liberals are more open to satire as a legitimate (yet hybrid) form of political commentary, one should find an increased willingness among liberals to report information-oriented viewing goals (as opposed to entertainment-oriented ones) in the context of satire. Using the same Pew data, I calculated the average ideological leanings of audience members who reported turning to each source for various reasons, including "entertainment," "interesting views/opinions," "in-depth reporting," and "headlines." If genre hybridity deters conservatives from conceptualizing satire as a form of legitimate political commentary, one should find ideological differences in people who consume the same content for different reasons.

As illustrated in figure 9.2, those who reported watching *The Daily Show* and *The Colbert Report* for interesting views and opinions, though small in number (17 and 21 percent of viewers, respectively), were *extremely* liberal. In fact, statistical tests revealed that those people who reported watching satire programming for "interesting views and opinions" were significantly more liberal than people who reported watching for other reasons.[8]

Now consider the ideological leaning of the conservative outrage audiences (see fig. 9.2). The audiences of conservative outrage programs were most likely to report watching them for interesting views and opinions. However, those viewers (30 percent) who reported tuning in to conservative

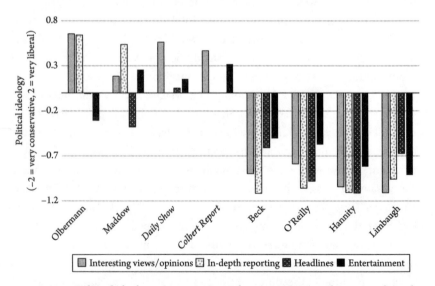

FIGURE 9.2 Political ideology among satire and outrage viewers who reported watching for the four reasons indicated; −2 = very conservative; 0 = moderate; 2 = liberal.
Source: Pew Research Center, Media Consumption Survey, 2010 (N = 3,006).

outrage for headlines or in-depth reporting (arguably the clearest informational viewing motivations captured in the study), were *extremely* conservative, more conservative than those who reported watching for other reasons. Similarly, for the smaller percentage (5 percent) of conservative outrage audiences who reported tuning in for "entertainment," their ideological leaning tended to be significantly *less conservative* than that of those who reported listening for other, more informational, reasons.[9]

These trends are consistent with the premise that the aesthetic of hybridity is more compatible with a liberal ideology, as strong liberals are comfortable both turning to comedy programming for political views and opinions and admitting that they do. Conservatives, meanwhile, were significantly less likely to label outrage programming a source of entertainment. They might enjoy watching these programs, and might even find the experience entertaining, but when asked why they turned to them, they overwhelmingly reported watching for "interesting views and opinions." Most important, the responses most in line with strict informational goals like "in-depth reporting" and "news and headlines" came from an even more conservative subset.[10] Together these findings suggest that satire's "entertainment" label and conservative outrage's "opinion" label might be so conflated with their audiences' psychological predispositions that the actual functions served by the genres are muddied. The next step is to move beyond why people say they tune in and figure out what happens to them when they do.

Satire, Outrage, and Political Knowledge

In 2004, as a graduate student at the Annenberg School I worked on the National Annenberg Election Survey to study Americans' political attitudes, knowledge, and behaviors. One of the questions we researchers wanted to answer was to what extent viewers of late-night comedy and satire shows were informed about their political worlds, particularly compared to viewers of other news programming. The results showed that not only did viewers of late-night comedy know more about politics than people who didn't watch those shows, but viewers of *The Daily Show*, in particular, knew more about politics than regular newspaper readers or network news viewers.[11] In 2012, Farleigh Dickinson University ran a similar study, assessing people's knowledge of both domestic and international issues.[12] Once again, viewers of *The Daily Show* ranked high in political knowledge, second only to regular listeners of NPR.[13]

Over the past five years, numerous studies have explored political knowledge as a function of the kinds of political programs people watch. The results are rather consistent: viewers of *The Daily Show, The Colbert Report,* and now *Last Week Tonight with John Oliver* have tended to be more knowledgeable about most political issues. And, importantly, these findings hold in the face of statistical controls. Viewers of political satire programs are, on average, more educated and politically interested than the general population,[14] so the link between viewing satire and scoring high on political knowledge isn't that surprising. To test whether satire viewers know more about politics because they are higher in political interest and education from the start, one can statistically control for these underlying characteristics.[15] In general, studies like this find that viewing satire programming contributes to political knowledge above and beyond the baseline political interest and education of their audience members.[16]

In 2012, my colleagues at University of Delaware's Center for Political Communication and I wanted to understand public opinion on (and knowledge about) the Occupy Wall Street protests that were occurring around the country. We learned that in spite of Fox News viewers' strong negative opinions about the Occupy Wall Street protests, those same viewers were among the least informed citizens regarding what the movement was actually about. The protests, which were mainly a rejection of the highly skewed distribution of wealth in the United States, typically used the slogan "We are the 99%," a reference to the fact of the wealthiest 1 percent of Americans being in possession of a disproportionate percentage of the country's wealth.[17] To capture the extent of the public's understanding of the reasons for the protests, we asked: "Which do you think comes closest to the Occupy Wall Street protesters' main message? Is it that too few people control the majority of the nation's wealth and power OR that there is too much regulation on business and industry?" The results showed that only 56 percent of Fox News viewers answered this question correctly, compared to 89 percent of Colbert viewers and 80 percent of *Daily Show* viewers.[18]

Satire programs have proven particularly good at educating their viewers on complex matters of public policy. There is perhaps no policy debate more tedious and complicated than the nuances of campaign finance reform. Yet in 2011–2012, Colbert found a way to make the issue understandable, absurd, and hilarious. Over the course of several months, in the wake of the Supreme Court's 2010 *Citizens United* ruling, Colbert explored the issue of so-called political super PACs, independent political action committees that operate as political fundraising organizations. *Citizens United* opened the door for unlimited sums of money from unions, corporations, and individuals to flow into US elections through super PACs and their associated 501(c)(4) groups. Colbert explored the issue by establishing his *own* super PAC, "Americans for a Better Tomorrow, Tomorrow," which he then handed over to Jon Stewart, declaring that he was a candidate for "president of the United States of South Carolina." Colbert's super PAC raised actual funds and created political ads. Meanwhile, in interviews on his show he consulted with Trevor Potter, former chair of the Federal Election Commission, learning what he could and could not do with his new political action committee. What he—and viewers—learned over the course of these months was that there weren't many things that the super PAC could *not* do. And with the establishment of a 501(c)(4) group, Colbert's organization could filter money that would never be traced back to its donors.

Jeffrey Jones, Geoffrey Baym, and Amber Day write: "from the start, the most sustained part of [*The Colbert Report*'s] experiment has been the extended civics lessons offered on the program itself.... By interviewing his lawyer Trevor Potter, and other policy experts, Colbert has explored campaign finance in far more detail than even the wonkiest of news reports."[19] And the effects on the audience were clear. Experimental and survey-based research pointed to the educational impact of Colbert's super PAC segments.[20] Viewers not only felt more knowledgeable about the issue but actually demonstrated more knowledge about the issue than viewers of CNN, Fox News, or network news.[21]

A similar finding emerged more recently in the context of John Oliver's satirical coverage of the net neutrality issue. In 2014, the Federal Communications Commission considered allowing internet service providers to charge content providers additional fees to facilitate faster streaming speeds to their customers. At the time, Comcast was proposing a deal with Netflix by which Netflix would buy from Comcast a so-called fast lane to consumers. The language and technical details of the net neutrality debate are complicated and painfully dry. Yet Oliver dedicated a 13-minute segment of his show to the issue on June 1, 2014.

> "Yes, net neutrality. The only two words that promise more boredom in the English language are 'featuring Sting,' and hearing people talking about it is somehow even worse.... But here's the thing, net neutrality is actually hugely important. Essentially, it means that all data has to be treated equally, no matter who created it. It's why the Internet is a weirdly level playing field.... Ending net neutrality would allow big companies to buy their way into the fast lane, leaving everyone else in the slow lane."[22]

Oliver's viewers benefited from his deep dives. Experimental research by Amy Becker and Leticia Bode showed that viewers learned just as much from Oliver's comical treatment of the topic as they did from an ABC news segment.[23] Survey research I was involved with at the University of Delaware's Center for Political Communication showed that watching Oliver was one of the strongest predictors of whether or not a person had "heard about the net neutrality debate" at all.[24]

In sum, satire viewers are the most knowledgeable about some political issues, while Fox viewers are the least knowledgeable. But is this a fair assessment? Maybe political knowledge is domain-specific or party-specific. Maybe there are some issues that conservative outrage audiences are highly knowledgeable about and satire audiences know very little about.

Or maybe conservative outrage audiences hold high levels of "knowledge," but it just so happens that this "knowledge" is factually inaccurate. Can you call that knowledge? Or are you then just talking about "beliefs?"

Imagine that it's 2007 and you are ambivalent about Senator Barack Obama. You then "learn" from conspiracy theorists on the internet that he is a Muslim (he's not) who was *not* born in the United States (he actually *was*). You then use that false information to form a belief about Obama (Obama is a Muslim born outside the US), and then you use that belief to form an overall impression of Obama (probably negative). According to a 2015 CNN poll, 43 percent of Republicans and 15 percent of Democrats reported that Obama was Muslim.[25] Do these misinformed people "know" that "Obama is a Muslim"? or do they merely "believe" that "Obama is a Muslim"?

Can you call something "knowledge" if it's false?

First of all, in reality, that's almost certainly not how most so-called Obama birthers came to be. It is highly unlikely that these were folks who were thinking "I am pretty neutral about this Obama guy" and then sought out information to be able to form a global impression of him. What is more likely is that these were people who were responding in a negative emotional way to then-senator Obama, due to his class or race or personality or issue positions (OK…race). Then, due to selective exposure (seeking out information that comports with your worldview), these people encountered the false "information" that Obama was a Muslim who wasn't born in the United States. Since that "information" was consistent with these people's preexisting negative opinion of Obama, that "information" could then be characterized as their "reason for disliking Obama," even though the reason came *after* the attitude, and therefore could not possibly have caused it.

Much of this discussion is rooted in a very slippery distinction between knowledge and beliefs. People think of knowledge as factual information that they store in their networked memory. Meanwhile, beliefs are "specific and cognitive" but are also strongly rooted in emotions. Beliefs typically imply a positive or negative valence toward a given attitude object. But, although what people believe is *shaped* by what they know (a process we think of as rational), what they believe also *contributes* to what they come to "know" (a process typically thought of as irrational). This question of how to define knowledge has plagued philosophers for centuries. For a long time, philosophers conceptualized knowledge as "justified true beliefs": beliefs that are thought to be true and that are justified in some way. But, as Edmund Gettier pointed out, this flawed conceptualization of knowledge allows for something to be "known" even if it is justified by false premises.[26]

Today, in the context of political communication research on misinformation, Gettier's conundrum looms large. Whether people think of something as political knowledge (factual) or as a political belief (opinion) is largely determined by their partisan-motivated reasoning processes. The Pew Research Center recently found that "Republicans and Democrats were more likely to classify both factual and opinion statements as factual when they appealed most to their side." So people think that things that they agree with are "facts" but things they disagree with are merely "opinions." In this study, factual statements were defined as those that could be proven or disproven based on objective evidence, regardless of whether it was accurate or inaccurate. In the language of scientific reasoning, factual statements are defined as those that are "falsifiable"; that is, one can articulate a way to objectively test it against evidence that will reveal whether it is false. An example of a hypothetical falsifiable statement would be: "Chocolate chip ice cream is the most frequently sold ice cream flavor in the world." By measuring the frequency of sales of all ice cream flavors in the world, this statement can be tested and, if false, will be shown to be so. A nonfalsifiable statement would be "Chocolate chip ice cream is the most delicious ice cream flavor in the world." No amount of objective evidence can show this statement to be false (or true). The Pew study's results indicate that when people hear pieces of nonfalsifiable (aka opinion-based) information that happen to match their underlying belief systems, they are more likely to identify such pieces of information as "factual" even when they are more accurately described as opinions.[27]

Illustrative of this conundrum between facts and opinions (and hence between knowledge and beliefs) is a 2003 report from the Program on International Policy Attitudes. The report indicated that Fox News viewers held the highest rates of "misperceptions" about the Iraq War.[28] Fox viewers were the most likely (compared to all other news audiences) to believe that there was evidence linking Saddam Hussein, the president of Iraq, to al-Qaeda (there wasn't), that weapons of mass destruction had been found in Iraq (they hadn't), and that public opinion toward US involvement in the war was favorable (it wasn't). These misperceptions were greatest among those Fox News viewers who paid the most attention while watching. These significant differences remained once the researchers controlled for political and demographic factors.

So Fox viewers were the least knowledgeable about the Iraq War. But Fox viewers were also updating their knowledge structures with the information from the network that was belief-confirming yet false/misleading/distorted. The result was that they were "learning"—acquiring "justified true beliefs" that happened to be based on false premises. Throughout the early 2000s, the Bush administration's speeches and public addresses consistently and falsely connected Saddam Hussein to al-Qaeda and the 9/11 attacks.[29] For example, in his 2003 State of the Union address, President Bush famously reported: "the British government has learned that Saddam Hussein recently sought significant quantities of uranium from Africa."[30] Moreover, content analyses suggest that Fox News relied more heavily than all the other cable networks on official sources in their programming. With more administration officials appearing on Fox, Fox viewers were more likely to be exposed to arguments favorable to the Bush administration and the war effort, some of which included false claims about both the presence of weapons of mass destruction in Iraq and an unverified link between Iraqi president Saddam Hussein and al-Qaeda.[31] Research by Ashley Muddiman, Natalie Jomini Stroud, and Maxwell McCombs also shows that the arguments presented on CNN, MSNBC, and Fox News related to the Iraq War differed in predictable ways. Sixty-four percent of the arguments about the Iraq War that were made on CNN were consistent with Democratic arguments (e.g., the war was unnecessary, Iraq was not central to the war on terror), compared to 69 percent on MSBNC and only 32 percent on Fox.[32] So, if Fox viewers were being given information that would prove factually inaccurate, did they "misperceive" the false information they were being given? On the contrary: it seems as though they perceived the information correctly. But the information itself was wrong.

Jamieson and Cappella explain that exposure to information from partisan programming contributes to the formation of distinct knowledge bases: networks of information that are made up of distinct sets of "facts." Jamieson and Cappella describe this as evidence of "balkanization" through partisan programming.[33] Exposure to ideological political programming creates specialized (sometimes distorted) knowledge structures among viewers. In the context of Limbaugh's audiences, knowledge about issues that were heavily covered by the host (such as US troops in Bosnia and knowledge of the Unabomber, Ted Kaczynski) was significantly greater among his listeners than among heavy consumers of mainstream news.[34] Yet, when asked about campaign issues that had been heavily covered by mainstream news outlets (like candidates' issue positions), "Limbaugh listeners were *less* accurate than those listening to liberal and moderate political talk radio and [less accurate] than heavy consumers of mainstream media."[35] Elizabeth Schroeder and Daniel Stone found a similar phenomenon in the context of National Annenberg Election Survey data from 2000, 2004, and 2008.[36] They looked at knowledge questions relating to which candidate (Republican or Democratic) supported which policy position. They separated the questions into pro-Republican ones (the questions for which the correct Republican issue position was the one that over half of the non-Democrat respondents favored) and anti-Republican ones (those for which the correct Republican issue position was the one that over half of the non-Democrat respondents opposed). Their analyses indicate that watching Fox News was associated with knowledge increases, but only on the questions that were favorable to Republicans and were covered on the network.[37]

When dealing with actual public policies that are supported by a majority of Republican voters, conservative outrage audiences tend to know a lot. I imagine, for example, that Hannity's, O'Reilly's, and Limbaugh's audiences were probably exceptionally knowledgeable about the facts of the 2012 attack on the US embassy in Benghazi, Libya. Following the attack, the Obama administration, and Secretary of State Hillary Clinton in particular, were the objects of intense scrutiny for failing to provide additional security that the facility's staff had requested in the year before the attack. The question of Clinton's culpability was at the center of Fox News programming throughout 2014 and 2015. The attack was easily framed in a way that confirmed Fox's narrative of Obama as weak on terrorism and weak on foreign policy. With such extensive coverage, it would be reasonable to assume that viewers would come away with high rates of factual knowledge about that event.

However, when facts complicate the Republican agenda (e.g., whether or not the United States had found weapons of mass destruction in Iraq—it had not found any), conservative outrage audiences come away with distorted knowledge structures that are highly elaborate and consistent with the ideologically framed content of their preferred programming; in other words, knowledge that constitutes "justified true beliefs" that just happens to have been justified with "false premises." In the case of satire, though, what researchers find are high rates of knowledge on factual matters of public policy that are verifiable and falsifiable. Examples include: what the Occupy Wall Street movement had as its stated goal; what the principle of net neutrality states about the regulation of the internet; what kinds of campaign financing are legal under *Citizens United*. The factual content on which satire is most frequently based can be tested and falsified. And in moments when assertions are made that are unverified or demonstrably false,[38] satirists, unlike their outrage counterparts,[39] tend not to "double down" but instead to offer mea culpas and hope for forgiveness.[40] As Stewart has said, "I will defend what we do on the show and if it turns out to be something that we were wrong about, I will correct it and say we screwed up."[41]

How Satire and Outrage Programming Both Shape Public Opinion

In the 1970s, political scientists Max McCombs and Don Shaw observed that the news media set the agenda for the public.[42] As a result of the news media covering certain issues repeatedly, the audience comes to see those issues as the most important ones facing the country. This phenomenon of media "agenda-setting" was later confirmed in time series data. Soon afterward, Shanto Iyengar and Donald Kinder documented that the issues that were covered repeatedly, once on the public's radar, then became the criteria on which they judged public officials' performance.[43] It works like this: because the news talks a lot about the economy, I come to think that the economy is a really important issue facing the country. Somebody asks me if I like the president. I rely on whatever comes to mind—which happens to now be the economy—and judge the president on the basis of performance on that issue.

While these phenomena were originally conceptualized in a mass media "everybody's watching the big three networks" environment, the underlying psychological processes are still at play in today's hyperfragmented media world. When topics and concepts are frequently activated in working memory, they become more salient in people's minds. (For example, a person watches a lot of Fox News, and Fox News hosts talk a lot about immigration, so that person thinks that immigration is an important issue facing the country.) Once an issue becomes salient in this way, it comes to inform decision-making processes in which it is deemed relevant. (When called on to evaluate the president, I rely on the issue that readily comes to mind—immigration—and I evaluate him on his performance on that issue.)

In the 1980s, researchers were capturing large-scale trends in public opinion among heavy news consumers. The public at that time tended to have a homogeneous issue agenda, mainly because almost everyone was consuming the same information. But now, with people separated into distinct ideological enclaves, the issues and topics the partisan news media feed people each day vary greatly from outlet to outlet, leaving people with vastly different agendas, priorities, and evaluative criteria for their leaders.[44] Looking at today's fragmented news landscape, you see that both satire and outrage have unique agenda-setting and priming effects on their viewers. Natalie Jomini Stroud's work shows that individuals' assessments of what issues are most important align with the issues that are most heavily covered by their preferred media outlets.[45] Fox viewers, for example, were significantly more likely to cite terrorism as an important problem facing the country than were viewers of other outlets, in keeping with the relatively high amount of coverage dedicated to terrorism on Fox. Looking at agenda-setting in the context of the 2008 economic crisis, Kathleen Searles and Glen Smith found a similar pattern.[46] Fox News, more than other outlets, set the agenda for its viewers regarding the relative importance of that crisis. Turning to the agenda-setting and priming effects of satire, one finds similar processes at work. My own research has found that when asked what comes to mind when people think about political candidates, viewers of late-night comedy are more likely to cite issues and candidate traits that are most discussed in the content of late-night jokes.[47]

It's clear that both outrage and satire shape their audiences' agendas and the primary criteria audiences use to judge political leaders. But what about persuasion? Are these genres successful at telling viewers not just what to think about but actually what to think? In 1993, in a reconsideration of the agenda-setting hypothesis in a fragmented media world, McCombs and Shaw described the concept as having been "turned inside out." Media research, they wrote, indicated that "the media not only tell us what to think about, but also how to think about it, and, consequently, what to think."[48]

I'm going to go out on a fairly sturdy limb here and say that outrage programming and satire shows do not explore issues in a neutral or objective way. If Hannity or Oliver are going to tackle an issue, they do it through a particular lens, with a point of view. The writers, producers, and hosts make decisions about what sources to consult, what words to use, and what visuals to select to accompany the story. They do so with the goal of encouraging a particular understanding of the issue and facilitating a particular interpretation of the problem. Such strategic decisions constitute what scholar Bob

Entman describes as "media framing." To frame a story, according to Entman, is to "select some aspects of a perceived reality and make them more salient in a communicating text, in such a way as to promote a particular problem definition, causal interpretation, moral evaluation, and/or treatment recommendation for the item described."[49]

Both outrage and satire engage in strategic framing by design. Both genres are successful in promoting, to reiterate Entman's description, "a particular problem definition, causal interpretation, moral evaluation, and/or treatment recommendation." Take satire, for example. As discussed in chapter 3, *The Daily Show's* coverage of the wars in Iraq and Afghanistan was decidedly critical. Research shows that Stewart's coverage of the Iraq War was extensive, was unequivocally negative, and depicted the US government in a negative light.[50] Studies also show that satire's consistently critical coverage of specific policies or issues affects viewers' opinions. When Oliver covered the issue of net neutrality, he did so in a light favorable to net neutrality protections. He even went so far as to equate Comcast's "throttling" of Netflix streaming content with a mob shakedown.[51]

In the University of Delaware's Center for Political Communication study of how various forms of media use and demographic variables were associated with awareness of and opinion on net neutrality, Paul Brewer, Jennifer Lambe, Lindsay Hoffman, Justin Collier, and I found that viewing *Last Week Tonight* was the strongest predictor of support for net neutrality protections— stronger than any other political, demographic, or media use variables.[52] This finding held in the face of extensive statistical controls, leading us to conclude that in the net neutrality debate, Oliver constituted what Oscar Gandy terms an "information subsidizer," a source who "controls the availability and interpretation of information about issues."[53] Similarly, when Colbert engaged in ironic performance art in 2012, creating his own super PAC and exploring the (seemingly nonexistent) limits of campaign fundraising under *Citizens United*, he was deliberately framing the issue of *Citizens' United* and super PACs. And, like Oliver's effects on public opinion on net neutrality, Colbert's coverage of super PACs contributed to views that were more critical of *Citizens United*.[54]

By highlighting certain character traits, issue positions, and moral failings, satire hosts are able to shape how people think about their leaders as well.[55] Exposure to this consistently critical coverage has been found to increase negative sentiments about politicians.[56] In an analysis of panel data from the 2004 national party conventions, political scientist Jay Morris found that *The Daily Show's* coverage of Republicans was more critical of policy positions and character than their coverage of Democrats.[57] Morris's results showed that watching *The Daily Show* during the convention contributed to more negative opinions of President Bush and Vice President Dick Cheney.

On the outrage side, the issues are different from those featured in satire, but the framing processes are the same. Lauren Feldman and her colleagues have documented the unique ways various opinion programs (especially on Fox) characterize and frame the issue of climate change. Whereas coverage on MSNBC and CNN tends to highlight the scientific consensus regarding humanmade climate change, Fox News shows are "dismissive" of climate change and tend to give greater airtime to climate change deniers.[58] This research also shows that this deliberate framing is effective: Fox viewers come away with a reduced acceptance of the reality of climate change and a reduced level of concern about it.[59]

In the context of coverage of the Iraq War, Muddiman, Stroud, and McCombs sought to link their analysis of how cable news outlets framed the war with an analysis of the impact those frames had on public opinion.[60] Their content analysis showed that Fox News programs were significantly more positive in their descriptions of the war in Iraq than CNN or MSNBC. Their analysis of national public opinion data confirms that Fox's deliberate framing of the Iraq War led to Fox viewers having more positive assessments of the war, including the belief that the United States should not withdraw its troops and that the war was "worth it."[61]

In reviewing these studies, I found it noteworthy that when "Fox News viewing" and "satire viewing" were both included as factors in elaborate statistical models that predict attitudes toward political policies, these two factors were often the strongest predictors of public opinion. For example, in 2014 and 2015 studies of attitudes toward net neutrality that my colleagues and I conducted, only two media sources predicted support for net neutrality protections once sociodemographic and political variables were included: Fox News viewing and viewing satire.[62] Viewing Fox News was associated with significantly *less* support for net neutrality protections, while viewing *Last Week Tonight with John Oliver* was associated with more support for them. No other media use variable was even significant. Not network news use. Not CNN. Not online news. Not newspaper reading. And no . . . not MSNBC.

Only Fox and John Oliver.

In a 2012 study by the University of Delaware's Center for Political Communication, my colleagues Paul Brewer, Jennifer Lambe, and Phil Jones examined public opinion about campaign finance using national survey data.[63] Once again, of all the unique media exposure variables included in the model predicting support for *Citizens United* (consumption of daily newspapers, national network evening news, Fox News, CNN, MSNBC, *The Daily Show/The Colbert Report*, and online news), only two media use measures were significant predictors of public opinion: viewing Fox News and viewing political satire. Watching Fox News was associated with more support for *Citizens United* and super PACs. Watching *The Daily Show with Jon Stewart* and *The Colbert Report* was associated with less support. Once again, these relationships held up in the face of demographic and political controls. And once again, no other media outlet was a significant predictor; not even the often-cited liberal "outrage" network MSNBC.

Remember, this is the same trend we found when we looked at audiences' opinions (and knowledge) of the Occupy Wall Street movement in 2012. The audiences of Fox and satire programs were the most polarized in their views of the movement, compared to audiences of countless other news outlets (see fig. 9.3).

Satire and outrage programming contribute to political knowledge (in many cases, "balkanized" knowledge), help set their audiences' issue agendas, shape impressions of political leaders, and contribute to the polarization of public opinion on countless political issues. But what about political behaviors—things like voting, participating in politics, seeking information, and paying attention to news?

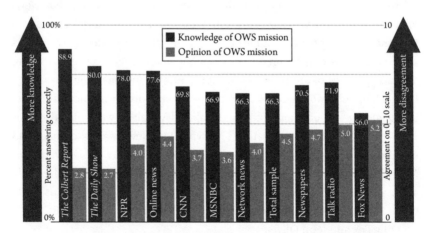

FIGURE 9.3 Media consumers' knowledge and opinion of Occupy Wall Street (OWS) protesters as a function of media use. The results shown are from those respondents who said they consumed the 11 media sources "regularly" and had heard of Occupy Wall Street.

Source: University of Delaware's Center for Political Communication, 2012.

Political Participation and Interest

The audiences of satire and outrage shows are among the country's most politically engaged and participatory citizens—across the board. They participate in politics more (attend rallies, donate money, volunteer, write to their elected officials). They talk about politics more (with friends, family, and coworkers and online). They follow politics more closely (by watching the news and seeking out information). All behaviors that are generally considered normatively healthy for maintaining a democratic society.

Dating back to 1993, scholars have recognized the potential of outrage programming to increase political participation. Barry Hollander's work showed significantly higher rates of political participation among regular talk radio listeners. Using data from 1996, Jamieson and Cappella confirmed this link between political participation (donating to a candidate, watching debates, volunteering with a campaign) and exposure to Limbaugh.[64] The notion that outrage fuels participation is both intuitive and theoretically sound. It is known from research on political advertising, for example, that emotionally evocative negative political ads fuel voter turnout.[65] It is also known that as much as people like to call for civility in elections, there is evidence that incivility (a popular trope of the outrage genre) can mobilize the electorate.[66] Paul Martin posits that negative ads fuel turnout by appealing to civic duty, articulating a threat, and increasing the perceived closeness of the election.[67]

Writing in 1962, French philosopher Jacques Ellul described hate as the "most profitable resource" in the successful creation of mobilizing agitation propaganda (agitprop).[68] Ellul writes: "it is extremely easy to launch a revolutionary movement based on hatred of a particular enemy. Hatred is probably the most spontaneous and common sentiment; it consists of attributing one's misfortunes and sins to 'another,' who must be killed in order to assure the disappearance of those misfortunes and sins."[69] Hate and anger are emotions that are oriented outward toward a target. Nicholas Valentino and his colleagues at the University of Michigan,[70] describe anger as the emotion that "arises when threats are attributable to a particular source and the individual feels that she has control over the situation."[71] Through a series of experiments and survey research, Valentino has found that anger mobilizes political participation. Political scientist David Ost argues that this mobilizing potential of anger is (and has always been) central to political life.[72] He also proposes that the extensive use of anger as a mobilizing tool on the right (more than on the left) stems from conservatives' skepticism of rationality. (Might he be referring—quite poetically—to conservatives' high reliance on heuristics and low need for cognition, perhaps?) Ost writes: "and so the political discourse of the Right has been filled with Others: the evil other country, nationality, race, religion, or morality."[73]

Berry and Sobieraj explain the mobilizing effect of outrage programming through the "signaling effect" it has on viewers. By highlighting issues like competitive electoral contests and other specific opportunities for policy change, outrage programming hones in on specific sources to which threat may be attributed and nudges local opinion leaders to take action aimed at these sources. This dynamic might explain the focused and raucous Tea Party activists who shouted down local Democratic officials in town hall meetings during the summer of 2009. I would argue that it also explains why CNN journalist Jim Acosta gets "accost-ed" by angry Trump supporters as he broadcasts from Trump's political rallies.[74] People can only listen to trusted sources (especially Trump himself) excoriate "the liberal media," "fake news," and "Crazy Jim Acosta of Fake News CNN" (see fig. 9.4) for so long before they feel compelled to take action.

Like outrage audiences, satire audiences are also highly participatory. The work of Xiaoxia Cao and Paul Brewer shows that people who watched political comedy programming were significantly more likely than other audiences to report having attended a political event or joined a political organization.[75] Jody Baumgartner and Brad Lockerbie found a similar relationship using 2012 data from the American National Election Studies.[76] Their analyses reveal that viewers of Comedy Central satire programming (*The Daily Show* and *The Colbert Report*) engage in more political behaviors like attending political rallies, discussing politics, contributing to a party, and even just wearing political buttons.

Donald J. Trump ✔
@realDonaldTrump

Follow ⌄

Even Crazy Jim Acosta of Fake News CNN agrees: "Trump World and WH sources dancing in end zone: Trump wins again...Schumer and Dems caved...gambled and lost." Thank you for your honesty Jim!

3:31 AM - 23 Jan 2018

FIGURE 9.4 President Donald Trump, tweet, January 23, 2018.

Some scholars suggest that viewing satire increases participation through interpersonal discussion, as satire viewing increases political conversations, which then go on to spur participation in politics.[77] My work with my colleague Lindsay Hoffman shows that for young audiences, watching satire increases "political efficacy," which may lead to more political participation.[78] "Political efficacy" refers to one's belief that one has the capacity to participate in political life (internal political efficacy) and the sense that the system will be responsive to one's voice (external political efficacy). In our study, viewing satire contributed to viewers' confidence in their ability to understand and participate in politics, which then increased the likelihood of their participating. Numerous studies have confirmed this link between viewing satire and being confident in one's ability to understand and participate in political life.[79] Given the vital role played by internal efficacy in helping citizens to translate knowledge and information into political action,[80] it seems apparent that satire can contribute to political engagement through this important characteristic.

Other democratically healthy political behaviors among satire viewers include talking about politics, following politics, and paying attention to current events in the news. Using data from the 2004 National Annenberg Election Survey, Sarah Esralew and I found significantly higher rates of political participation and political discussion (with friends and family, coworkers, and online) among viewers of *The Daily Show* than among just about any other group.[81] My work with Russ Tisinger has shown that viewers of *The Daily Show* are significantly more likely to report "following politics" than nonviewers. In a fascinating experimental study of the effects of satire viewing, Michael Xenos and Amy Becker documented how viewing *The Daily Show* contributed to "information-seeking" behaviors among viewers.[82] Viewers of *Daily Show* clips were more likely to seek out additional information on the topics covered in the show. My work with Lauren Feldman in the context of the 2004 political primaries mirrors these findings.[83] We found that late-night comedy viewers experience increases in news attention following their exposure to late-night programming.

Most of this work in the realm of satire fostering "information-seeking" behaviors is rooted in Matt Baum's "gateway" hypothesis.[84] Stemming from his research in the early 2000s on the effects of "soft news" exposure (like talk shows) on attention to foreign affairs, Baum's hypothesis is that because the audiences of these shows are usually less "political" than traditional news audiences, when they encounter political topics through entertainment, the encounter serves as a "gateway" to traditional news exposure. Just as marijuana has been called a "gateway drug," sometimes leading to harder drug use, political entertainment is characterized as a "gateway source," sometimes leading to harder news use. Baum argues that inadvertent exposure—also called "incidental exposure"—to political themes in entertainment programming ignites a motivation in viewers to understand more about these topics, hence triggering information seeking behaviors that increase traditional news consumption. The aforementioned studies of the effects of political humor exposure on subsequent information seeking have shown that Baum's gateway hypothesis holds water.

Satire, Outrage, Political Efficacy, and Trust

In sum, both satire and outrage audiences have high rates of issue-specific political knowledge, interest, and participation. These shows contribute to their audience members' sense of what issues are most important and how they think about them. These audiences also share a unique combination of political traits that have broader democratic implications: these audience members simultaneously have high faith in their own ability to navigate their political worlds (internal political efficacy) and low trust in government and politicians.

In exploring this important combination of political traits among outrage and satire audiences, political communication researchers have rediscovered the work of sociologist William Gamson from the late 1960s.[85] The so-called Gamson hypothesis proposes that "low trust and high efficacy is a 'potent combination' that helps 'stoke the fires of protests.'"[86] Armed with information and the sense that they understand the complexities of the political landscape, these individuals respond to their lack of faith in public officials and governmental institutions with political action: campaigning, petitioning, protesting, and participating. In a study of conservative talk radio audiences,[87] Hollander found high rates of these traits among regular listeners: cynicism,[88] internal efficacy, and political engagement and participation. Hollander concluded: "the results suggest that talk radio may be providing what Gamson described as the optimum condition for political mobilization: higher internal efficacy combined with less trust in government that results in the 'belief that influence is both possible and necessary.'"[89]

In the context of political satire, scholars have disagreed over whether the political distrust that is fueled by viewing shows like *The Daily Show* is good or bad for democracy. Jody Baumgartner and Jonathan S. Morris identified what they called "The *Daily Show* Effect": increased cynicism and more negative ratings of public officials. They described these outcomes as unhealthy for democracy: "although research indicates that soft news contributes to democratic citizenship in America by reaching out to the inattentive public, our findings indicate that *The Daily Show* may have more detrimental effects, driving down support for political institutions and leaders among those already inclined toward nonparticipation."[90] In 2007, Roderick Hart and E. Johanna Hartelius accused Stewart of committing "political heresy" by "making cynicism attractive."[91] They argued that cynics—like Stewart—"place faith in observation, not participation, and see irony as the only stable source of pleasure."[92] Instead of promoting political action or investment in institutions, they wrote, "cynicism . . . promotes only itself, summoning followers to abandon conventional society and its stultifying love of order, predictability, and progress."[93]

While Hart and Hartelius's essay was masterfully written and presented a compelling theoretical proposition, the empirical data painted a very different picture.[94] Stewart's audience did not consist of passive, disengaged observers but active, invested participants in political life.[95] What Hart and Hartelius seemed to ignore was the fact that the combination of low trust in government and high political efficacy found among satire viewers is theoretically and empirically related to more, not less, engagement in politics.[96] So both satire and outrage audiences, for all their ideological and policy differences, have demonstrably little faith in politicians or people in government to do what is right but have high confidence in their own ability to navigate their political world and make things happen. So as a result . . . they *act*.

It is important to note that satire and outrage audiences, in spite of their shared distrust of government institutions and politicians, differ in important ways when it comes to their faith in news media.[97] In a 2011 Pew study, 90 percent of Hannity viewers, 87 percent of Limbaugh listeners, and 81 percent of O'Reilly viewers said that they "saw a lot of bias in news coverage."[98] Spend 10 or so minutes watching or listening to these conservative outrage shows, and you'll understand why. Hannity, Limbaugh, O'Reilly, and Carlson routinely and explicitly characterize mainstream news media as "liberal," "biased," "fake," and—from Hannity—"disgustingly biased, ideological and corrupt."[99] In February 2017, President Trump characterized mainstream news as the "enemy of the American people."[100] Given that citizens take cues from partisan elites on whether to trust news media,[101] it follows that conservative outrage audiences do not trust journalists or journalism as an institution.

Just as audiences of outrage programming have lower faith in news, audiences of satire that overtly criticizes the behavior of the press have lower faith in news as well.[102] Experimental research suggests that viewing satire segments that explicitly criticize press practices reduces viewers' overall trust in news.[103] And, as I showed at the outset of this book, both satire and outrage engage in explicit critiques of the press: conservative outrage hosts rail against liberal media bias, and satire programming mocks the sensationalizing, profit- and ratings-driven practices of the press.

The news media critiques offered by satire and outrage have an important difference, though. Unlike outrage, satire programming often contains another layer of content, a layer that Indiana University's Jason Peifer describes as reinforcing the "epistemic authority" of the press.[104] Peifer concedes that satire sometimes offers "explicit media criticism," in the form of "an overt denouncement of a news media practice or entity in some way."[105] But more common, Peifer argues, is *implicit media criticism*. Satire frequently relies on the products of news (clips and interviews) for its content, in this way "leveraging the credibility of news...in the service of a given parody message's rhetorical strategy."[106] Peifer notes: "through this rhetorical strategy, news parody can implicitly reinforce the legitimacy of news media actors—even if only a temporary characterization—as largely impartial, accurate, and reliable arbiters of truth."[107] The result of this metamessaging across news parody programming, Peifer shows, is an increase in viewers' perceptions of the *importance* of news. By highlighting journalistic practices that are problematic, and articulating the importance of local and investigative journalism, hosts like Bee and Oliver reaffirm the notion that strong journalistic institutions are central to the health of a democracy.

Different Look, Same Great Taste

Rather than conceptualizing satire and outrage as playing entirely different roles in the political environment, this chapter has presented empirical evidence that many of the functions and outcomes of satire and outrage programming—in spite of their distinct look, feel, voice, and content—are quite the same. Regardless of whether you look at the audiences of Oliver or Colbert, Hannity or Limbaugh, you are looking at people who are politically engaged, are knowledgeable about the issues that serve their political side, have confidence in their ability to engage in political life, and lack faith in their leaders and institutions. They come to these programs seeking to satisfy needs for both entertainment and information that are shaped by their underlying psychological traits. They turn to programs that match not only their ideological views but also their aesthetic preferences: for order, structure, and the identification of threats or for ambiguity, play, and rumination. Once they are watching, the shows signal to them what issues and what political events are important for them to think about. The shows frame these issues and events in a way that affects how their audiences interpret them, assign responsibility and blame for them, and look for solutions to them. So satire and outrage, while it may drive audiences of both genres bonkers to hear it, play similar roles in the lives of their viewers and listeners. These genres look different because each is a logical expression of a distinct set of psychological—and epistemological—characteristics. Simply put, these genres look like two different animals because the creators and audiences of outrage and the creators and audiences of satire are—quite literally—*different animals.*

10

Playing against Type

LIBERAL "OUTRAGE" AND CONSERVATIVE "SATIRE"

AT PRECISELY NOON on March 31, 2004, stations across the country were greeted with the voice of Al Franken, former *Saturday Night Live* comedian (and now former Minnesota senator fallen from grace), broadcasting from the newly formed Air America studios in New York City:

> Broadcasting, from an underground bunker 3,500 feet below Dick Cheney's bunker, Air America Radio is on the air. I'm Al Franken and welcome to the O'Franken Factor. Today is both an ending and a beginning. An end to the right wing dominance of talk radio and the beginning of a battle for truth, a battle for justice, a battle indeed for America itself. Folks, you and I know that the radical right wing of the Republican Party has taken over not just the White House, the Congress, and increasingly the courts, but even and perhaps most insidiously, the airwaves. And we know they are lying, lying without shame. Lying with impunity. Safe in the knowledge that there is no watchdog with a platform large enough to call them on their willful untruths. Someday we will find that watchdog. Until then, I will have to do. Now some people have asked me why the name "The O'Franken Factor?" Well, for one reason and one reason only. To annoy and bait Bill O'Reilly.

Air America: Liberal Outrage Can't Escape the Comedy

The corporate story of Air America is a complicated one, featuring a check-bouncing CEO who was eventually arrested on unrelated charges of theft, fraud, and money laundering.[1] And while this financial drama was unfolding backstage, the network was trying to do something without precedent.

Historically, successful political talk radio shows had started small, in one or two markets. Once the shows had a sizable listenership, they were then picked up by other networks across the country. This is how talk radio icon Rush Limbaugh got his start, as did many successful radio hosts after him. But instead of a radio model, Air America seemed to be inspired by a cable news model: the creation—from scratch—of a 24-hour network, including all of the original programming necessary to fill those hours with content. Now there are many factors that contributed to Air America's struggles and ultimate cancellation. But at least part of what limited the network's success as an "outrage machine" can be traced to production and staffing decisions made at the outset. These decisions violated some key features of outrage, and illustrated—yet again—the qualities of a liberal aesthetic.

From its inception, Air America was infused with comedy. From its comedian hosts and comedy writers to its tongue-in-cheek parody and mocking of the right, the left's "outrage" radio network couldn't escape its own penchant for humor. The first talent the station's founders, Sheldon and Anita Drobny, secured was comedian Al Franken. After almost 20 years writing and performing on *Saturday Night Live*, in the late 1990s Franken had become a bestselling author of satirical books, including *Rush Limbaugh Is a Big Fat Idiot* in 1996 and *Lies and the Lying Liars Who Tell Them: A Fair and Balanced Look at the Right* in 2003. He was increasingly recognized as a liberal political activist and a thoughtful and entertaining critic of Republican policies. Once Franken was secured, Air America executives pursued two other well-known comics: stand-up comedian and liberal activist Janeane Garofalo and comedy writer and *Daily Show* cocreator Lizz Winstead. Franken, Garofalo, and Winstead then brought comedy writers and stand-up comics on board, including writers from Winstead's early days at *The Daily Show* and from the San Francisco stand-up comedy scene.[2] At the start, Franken worked with a large team of politically minded college interns, but by 2005 he had hired comedy writer and producer Billy Kimball as executive producer of his radio show.

Not all of Air America's big names or writers came from the comedy world, of course. Some were holdovers from WLIB, the New York station whose studios Air America called home. Others who had been brought in on the "news" side of the operation included reporters like Jo Ann Allen, Bill Crowley, and Wayne Gillman.[3] When these news personalities were reserved for news breaks and straight headlines, the cooperation of the comedy and news staffs was a success. But when news staff were asked to team up with comics and provide shared commentary on the same program, the awkward mixture of journalists and comics revealed the limits of the liberal aesthetic of "hybridity."

At the network's debut, the incendiary comic Marc Maron was partnered with former WLIB radio host Mark Riley and former BBC correspondent Sue Ellicott to cohost a three-hour commentary and call-in morning show, *Morning Sedition*. Just days before the launch of the network on April 1, 2004, Maron, Riley, and producer Jonathan Larsen were reviewing scripts when Maron's frustrations began to mount. In a scene captured in the HBO documentary *Left of the Dial*, Maron said to Larsen: "I don't feel prepared, man...I'm not ready. If it's just him [Riley] and I talking, I think that's great, but these [his hand shaking the papers loaded with news stories] are the kind of things we should be trying *jokes* on...I have expectations of myself."[4] Maron complained that his cohosts "stepped on" his jokes. They sometimes interrupted him, filling in the punchlines he was intending to deliver. Exasperated, Maron once huffed: "I don't know if I can even figure out how to f**king integrate into this thing."[5] Apparently neither could the network. Ellicott was out by June, and by the end of 2005, *Morning Sedition* was canceled and replaced by two solo-hosted shows, one with Mark Riley and another with the young Rachel Maddow.

Recall that according to Berry and Sobieraj, one of the main features of outrage programming is the central role a show's solo host plays.[6] The host drives the show. The host's personality and perspective *are* the show. Yet from the start, Air America execs and programmers seemed to treat the question "Who's hosting?" as an afterthought. When early teams of comedy writers were brought into the studios in the late fall of 2003, former Air America writer Barry Lank recalls, they were writing bits for no one in particular.[7] At that point, it was not even clear who would be hosting the shows, other than Franken and some other heavy hitters. And when the individual programs began taking shape in January and February 2004, they were constructed around teams of hosts—two or three people per program,[8] which often led to tensions like those between Maron and his not-so-comedy-minded cohosts Ellicott and Riley. Given that outrage as a genre is defined by the personality, passions, and perspective of a show's host, it seems that—from the start—Air America had the whole "outrage" thing upside down.

The one exception to the "team-of-hosts" concept in the early days at Air America was Randi Rhodes. Rhodes was best known for her 12 years at WIOD in Miami as a brazen talk radio show host who reached millions of listeners each week.[9] Her tone was unapologetic, in-your-face, and often uncivil. She was angry more than she was playful or funny. She used her show to highlight perceived injustices and enrage the audience. As writer Barry Lank recalls, "Randi was the person at the network who was really doing outrage. The thing she is good at is being angry for people and she did outrage better than anyone else at the network."[10] *Time*'s Barry Corliss writes: "the one solo flyer, Randi Rhodes, in the afternoon drive-time slot, showed the network how it's done. Braying and abrasive, funny and whip-smart, Rhodes had what Limbaugh had: a distinctive voice that made people tune in for her next insight or outrage. She built a large, loyal audience—Air America's only show with more than 1.5 million listeners."[11] Rhodes's success in the solo format might explain why Air America's programming lineup soon integrated other solo hosts, including Maddow, Thom Hartmann, Jerry Springer, and Ron Reagan (son of the former president). Rhodes's show remained one of the network's most successful programs until her termination in 2008 for "inappropriate statements."[12] At an event in San Francisco, Rhodes had called Hillary Clinton and former congresswoman and Democratic vice-presidential candidate Geraldine Ferraro "big f**king whores."

Well, at least *somebody* at Air America knew how to do outrage right.

The ½ Hour News Hour: Conservative Comedy Can't Escape the Outrage

On February 18, 2007, Fox News introduced its viewers to a new show—a new genre of programming for a network dedicated to conservative news and analysis. *The ½ Hour News Hour* was styled as a news parody show in the spirit of *The Daily Show* and was designed to offer humorous conservative takes on political issues. The show was created by Joel Surnow, creator of the popular Fox thriller *24*.[13] In the mid-2000s, *24* was the television show to watch and the television show to beat. It was an action-packed thriller that followed counterterrorist agent Jack Bauer (played by Kiefer Sutherland) in real time. Each episode gave you one hour of Jack Bauer frantically racing against the clock to diffuse bombs, foil terrorist plots, and rescue innocent people and loved ones. It was hailed by critics;[14] it was also a ratings bonanza, regularly attracting between 10 and 15 million viewers per episode.[15]

Given *24*'s tough-on-terror plot lines and unapologetic depictions of violent (and always successful) interrogation techniques,[16] it is not surprising that Surnow leaned more to the right than the left. It is also understandable that someone with such a successful track record in television programming would want to "try to stake out some new territory" and "do something that's not out there," as Surnow described his news parody project to conservative radio host Hugh Hewitt in 2007.[17]

In his talk with Hewitt, Surnow called the project a "conservative comedy show, something like *The Daily Show*." Hewitt gently suggested that writing for a comedy show might be more difficult than writing drama, telling Surnow, "a drama that remains interesting for six years is hard, but funny is really hard. I mean, Colbert is really funny, Stewart is really funny."

"They're great," Surnow agreed. "They're really brilliant...and the reason they're successful is not because they have a liberal bias, or that they tilt one way or another, but because they're funny."[18]

Unfortunately for Surnow, it seems Hewitt was right about the fact that "funny is really hard." *The ½ Hour News Hour* was canceled after just 13 episodes and, as the *Atlantic*'s Oliver Morrison delicately noted, "has remained the worst-rated show of all time on Metacritic."[19] *Vulture*'s Matt Schimkowitz wrote: "looking at The 1/2 Hour News Hour objectively, one would be hard pressed to give up a snort to what constitutes as [*sic*] a joke on this show."[20] The *Philadelphia Inquirer*'s Jonathan Storm wrote: "*The ½ Hour News Hour* is slow torture all by itself."[21] Meanwhile, Barry Garron at the *Hollywood Reporter* was apparently writing my book for me back in 2007 when he assessed the show this way: "a look at the first episode suggests that, just as A.M. radio is the unassailable province of the right, TV might better be left to the left."[22]

Alluding to the fact that Fox's viewers are typically far older than a typical late-night audience (68 years old compared to Stewart's 36-year-old median viewer), Jeremy Griffin of *Pop Matters* surmised that the show's failure wasn't just due to the fact that it wasn't that funny. Instead, "*The ½ Hour News Hour* was a comedy program chasing an audience that wasn't interested in comedy."[23] I imagine that Griffin is partly right. But it's not because Fox viewers are old. It's because Fox viewers are conservative and thus are endowed with all the psychological traits that make people less comfortable with and less appreciative of political satire as a mode of political expression and argumentation.

The other reason for the show's failure, though, was not about the audience at all but about the writers—and the way those writers approached the formulation of the show's jokes. Just as liberals at Air America fundamentally misunderstood the central role of the solo host in the articulation of outrage, the conservatives at *The ½ Hour News Hour* in their articulation of satire fundamentally misunderstood humorous incongruities in their articulation of satire.

Remember how the magic of satire is that the judgment—the critique that is advanced through satire—is not explicitly made in the text itself? Instead, humorous juxtapositions invite the audience to draw conclusions so as to be able to "see the joke." In drawing these conclusions, *we the audience* issue the judgment. *We* advance the critique. *The ½ Hour News Hour*'s sketches routinely abandoned the concept of incongruity altogether, instead featuring, for example, a joke about Nancy Pelosi's bad facelift or a parody prescription drug ad for liberal voters suffering from "Hillary Ambivalence Syndrome." Other times, the bits would start with a decent joke "setup," only to fail in their execution.[24] Host Kurt Long (in character as coanchor Kurt McNally), for instance, aimed this joke at then Democratic candidate for president Hillary Clinton: "dispelling reports that she would staff her White House with longtime cronies and political appointees, presidential candidate Hillary Clinton vowed that if she becomes president, she will surround herself with a diverse, multi-ethnic, multi-generational group...of angry lesbians." The setup here is perfect. But there is no logical incongruity juxtaposed with the concept of cronyism. It's missing the logical gap that could be woven together by the audience. For instance, the text could have said: "dispelling reports that she would staff her White House with longtime cronies and political appointees, presidential candidate Hillary Clinton vowed that if she becomes president, she will...hire people she doesn't even really know or like. To which Bill replied: 'Sorry, honey, I'm too busy.'" This version of the joke would have posed a question the audience would have had to answer. It would also have encouraged the audience to issue a judgment: "Hillary doesn't really know or like her own husband," or "Even when she vows to not engage in nepotism, she does it anyway." Here is another example of a *½ Hour News Hour* joke that fails the humorous incongruity test: "according to the latest polls, only 8 percent of Americans are bothered by the fact that Barack Obama's middle name is Hussein. However almost two-thirds of voters were disappointed to learn that his nickname in college was 'gassy.'" Gassy has nothing to do with Hussein. There is no logical overlap between these concepts, hence no reconciliation of incongruity for the audience to discover. And the joke doesn't issue a substantive judgment and so isn't even technically "satire." Imagine if instead the joke had read: "according to the latest polls, only 8 percent of Americans are bothered by the fact that Barack Obama's middle name is Hussein...and in unrelated news, 92 percent of Americans want the U.S. to convert to sharia law." What could be more incongruous or require more of a cognitive contribution than an actual *math* problem that invited listeners to equate support for Obama with support for Islamic religious law?

Not all the show's jokes fell flat, of course. Some were well-crafted in terms of incongruity. But those jokes often punched down (at marginalized groups) instead of up (at people in positions of power). And when comedy punches down, it runs the risk of activating empathy or even a threat response, which prohibits some audience members from entertaining an idea while remaining in the state of play. Coanchor Jennifer Robertson told one such joke: "During this week's Miss Universe Pageant in Mexico City, Miss USA Rachel Smith was booed by a mostly Mexican audience. Probably because, for the pageant's talent competition, she built a 700-mile fence." McNally then chimed in: "three more of those and we're good."

Life under Trump: Is Comedy Getting Outrageous?

Over the last two decades, Americans have become accustomed to their late-night comedians temporarily abandoning humor in the face of tragedy. In September 2001, a week after the 9/11 terror attacks, late-night hosts returned with emotional opening monologues that sought to acknowledge the tragedy and bring the country together in grief and resilience. On *The Daily Show*, Stewart engaged in a tearful monologue about the resilience of New York City and its residents. "To see these guys, these firefighters, these policemen and people from all over the country, literally, with buckets rebuilding. That's extraordinary. That's why we've already won. It's light. It's democracy. We've already won."[25] Stewart's monologue that day set the tone for how late-night comedy hosts would respond to tragedy—with increasing frequency—for years to come. Following terror attacks, mass shootings, and hate crimes, late-night hosts use their monologues to mourn and to remind Americans "who we are." "We need to get back to being brave enough to accept that we have different opinions and that's OK because that's what America is built on," said Jimmy Fallon after the June 2016 nightclub shooting in Orlando, Florida.[26] After the 2017 white supremacist rally in Charlottesville, Virginia, when a white supremacist drove his car into a peaceful protest, killing 22-year-old Heather Heyer,[27] Fallon implored his audience: "we cannot do this. We can't go backward. We can't go backward."[28]

In the aftermath of tragedy, dropping the mask and acknowledging our collective pain seems necessary. It helps to establish the comedy as a respite from events that make the world seem cruel and chaotic, without pretending that everything is normal and fine. But in the years following President Trump's election, for many progressive comics, it seems that nothing is perceived as normal or fine.

At first, when Trump announced his bid for the Republican presidential nomination in June 2015, comedians were giddy. Stewart opened his show: "like many of you, I heard some interesting, let's call it 'news,' about a certain, let's say, 'gift from heaven' entering the presidential race." As Stewart showed footage of Trump descending the escalator of the Trump Tower to announce his candidacy, Stewart feigned tears of joy, gesturing up toward the heavens and squeaking out an emotional "I'm just really happy right now!" But comedians' reactions to the Trump presidency have contrasted markedly with their initial reactions to his candidacy. While most liberals assumed that Hillary Clinton would win the 2016 presidential race, on the evening of November 8, 2016, half of the country quickly had to come to terms with a very different political, social, and cultural reality.

Trump's victory signaled a seismic shift for many liberals. In the post–November 8 world, progressive ideals that were assumed (by many on the left) to be shared societal goals—like social and cultural diversity, feminism, and environmentalism—all suddenly seemed under threat. Instead of conservatives feeling muzzled by "political correctness" or criticized by "social justice warriors," suddenly it was liberals, with their values of tolerance, equality, and social justice, who perceived themselves to be under attack. In chapter 5, I mentioned that humor appreciation requires a willingness to enter a "playful mode." If you feel threatened or aggrieved, if your ego is involved, if your empathy is activated, you will be less willing—and able—to operate in a playful mode. My own sense is that when an event or issue activates a comic's own threat response, coupled with empathy, that comic will likely avoid that topic completely, or treat it without any humor at all.

Take Jimmy Kimmel, for example. In May and September 2017, in response to Republicans' efforts in Congress to repeal the Affordable Care Act, Kimmel opened his show with emotional stories of his infant son Billy's battles with a congenital heart defect. Kimmel discussed how, without the Affordable Care Act, thousands of children like Billy would be uninsured due to their "preexisting condition" and so might not survive. He did so without any humor at all: "let's stop with the nonsense. This isn't football. There are no teams. We are the team. It's the United States. Don't let their partisan squabbles divide us on something every decent person wants. No parent should ever have to decide if they can afford to save their child's life. It just shouldn't happen. Not here."[29] Following the February 2018 shooting at Marjory Stoneman Douglas High School in Parkland, Florida, that killed 17, Colbert did not employ humor in his assessment of solutions and blame. Referring to the students at the school who had launched a gun reform movement called #NeverAgain in the wake of the shooting, Colbert suggested that these young people would be the ones to act on the issue of gun control because "the adults aren't cutting it anymore." And he said: "I hope these kids don't give up, because this is their lives and their future. Someone else may be in power, but this country belongs to them. . . . This is an election year. So if you want to see change, you have to go to the polls and tell the people who will not protect you that their time is up."[30]

While feeling threatened may make it difficult for comics to operate in a "playful mode," threat is exceptionally compatible with the anger and moral seriousness of outrage programming. When Berry and Sobieraj first wrote about the characteristics of outrage, they argued that the genre is fueled by a palpable sense of threat.[31] And for conservative outrage hosts, these perceived threats have loomed large for many years: they feel that traditional social values are under threat from policies like gay marriage, cultural values are under threat from immigration, and fairness is under threat from government entitlement programs.[32] For conservative audiences, these perceived threats have been coupled with fears of being labeled as bigoted or racist. In Berry and Sobieraj's study, when they talked with respondents about their experiences discussing politics, all of the nine viewers of conservative outrage whom they interviewed mentioned their fear of being called a racist—without even being asked.[33]

Thus far, I have argued that liberals' and conservatives' distinct preferences for engaging in political expression through humor versus outrage stem from underlying psychological—even physiological—characteristics. However, political psychologists have been careful to acknowledge that these underlying psychological predispositions interact with your social and cultural context to affect your ultimate attitudes and behaviors.[34] For example, even though it is known that conservatives are more physiologically reactive to perceptions of threat,[35] the extent to which they feel threatened is certainly shaped in part by the political climate of the moment. Similarly, whether or not liberals' high tolerance for ambiguity and uncertainty can itself be maxed out is also contingent on context (a Trump presidency, for example). As a scholar of political psychology, my inclination is to explain this in terms of psychological causes. But in my discussions of these issues with my friend the sociologist Sarah Sobieraj, she has challenged the notion that these are exclusively psychological phenomena. She wrote to me: "perhaps the left is not altogether immune to the impact of threat. Maybe they become less comfortable with ambiguity if they perceive their values and way of life to be under siege."[36] And maybe this is why, just as Fox's ratings increased in the early years of Obama's presidency, so did Maddow's in the early years of Trump. Threat might make play more difficult, but it does wonders for outrage.

In the era of Trump, progressives have found their core beliefs, value systems, and social identities challenged—by executive orders and legislative outcomes and even by the nature of political discourse itself. In such a climate, it shouldn't be surprising the country's left-leaning comics, in a state of existential threat and armed with political beliefs and a microphone, occasionally exited the state of play and began adopting some of the tropes of outrage. No, not all comics. No, not all the time. But frequently enough that political and cultural commentators—and comics—have started to take note.

Vulture's Jesse David Fox has described Trump's impact as "one of the worst things ever to happen to comedy."[37] Alluding to the negative interaction between threat and play, Fox writes: "Trump, because of the feeling of constant danger he projects, makes us more vigilant. But comedy needs room to fail, and these days, we're less likely to afford it the time to be ambiguous or complicated." Writing in the *Scotland Herald*, stand-up comedian Sara Schaefer has described the trouble this way: "comedians are now struggling to get the distance needed to make something awful hilarious."[38] Describing how she and her fellow comics are struggling to deal with Trump in their work, she explains: "we're too angry and scared to find the funny in Donald Trump's rule. For me, dark material has to incubate for a really long time before it can make its way to the stage."[39] Referring to the role of the comedian during times of tragedy or injustice, comedian Mindy Kaling tweeted after the Las Vegas massacre: "our late talk show hosts are now de facto activists, not because they want to, but because it would be incomprehensible to not be."[40]

And some satire hosts in the age of Trump are getting angry and becoming more like the outrage hosts they often mock. On the May 30, 2018, episode of *Full Frontal* on TBS, Bee made headlines with her criticism of the Trump administration's "zero-tolerance" immigration policy and the resulting forced separation of immigrant children from their parents at the US-Mexico border. In reference to a tweet from Trump's daughter, Ivanka, which featured a picture of Ivanka and her young son, Bee exclaimed: "You know that's a beautiful picture of you and your child, but let me say, one mother to another.... *Do something* about your dad's immigration policies, you *feckless cunt*! He listens to you. Put on something tight and low cut and tell your father to fucking stop it. Tell him it was an Obama thing and see how it goes."[41] The live studio audience responded with a combination of shrieks and applause. But outside the studio, the blowback against Bee was immediate. Media personalities from the left and the right criticized her use of such a "gross" and "distasteful" insult against the president's daughter. The president responded to Bee's vitriol, tweeting: "why aren't they firing no talent Samantha Bee for the horrible language used on her low ratings show?" (photo 10.1).

Bee spent the better part of the following week apologizing for using the C-word. In one of her many apologies, she lamented that her statement had taken attention away from the focus of the segment, the separation of immigrant

PHOTO 10.1 The set of *Full Frontal with Samantha Bee*, 2018. Courtesy of Olivia Nyce Roth.

children from their parents: "we spent the day wrestling with the repercussions of one bad word, when we all should have spent the day incensed that as a nation we are wrenching children from their parents and treating people legally seeking asylum as criminals."[42]

When colleagues and journalists asked me for my thoughts about this incident, I was less interested in Bee's use of the C-word than in the fact that Bee appeared to abandon humorous incongruities altogether. It seemed that her use of the term "feckless" may have been an attempt at play, but the structure of the statement that brought her to that insult wasn't formulated as a joke at all. There was no incongruity. No punchline. It wasn't humor.

In fact, it looked an awful lot like outrage.

In June 2018, *Daily Show* host Trevor Noah publicly discussed the advice he had received from his mentor, Jon Stewart, before taking over as host of the show. According to Noah, Stewart told him: "I'm leaving because I'm tired. I'm tired of being angry. I'm angry all the time. I don't find any of this funny. I do not know how to make it funny right now, and I don't think the show deserves a host who does not feel that it is funny." Noah said Stewart urged him to "relish the fact that you can make jokes about these things, because there will come a day when you are too angry to laugh. But don't rush to get there."[43]

I am reminded of the political awakening of Tommy and Dick Smothers, when their comic sensibility ran head first into the Vietnam War and the CBS network censors. The tone of their show changed rapidly between 1967 and 1969, in response partly to heavy-handed censors and partly to what they perceived as a threatening and unjust political world. The two lighthearted hosts became increasingly serious and strident as the weeks went on. As Tommy conceded, looking back, "I was young, and I was angry. I was trying to make my voice heard from this particular viewpoint." The result was an ongoing battle between Tommy and the network censors that left little room for play. "Looking back, Tommy cringes at how serious he became in the last year [of the show]," Lyndon Stambler writes. "I was too involved with fighting with the censors," Tommy told Stambler. "I sacrificed our comedy team in the name of the show."[44]

After spending several years looking at the research on the psychology of the left and the right, I can't escape the feeling that when comics abandon humor in favor of an approach more characteristic of outrage, it may work against them. Threat-oriented, explicitly angry political speech does not take advantage of the unique profile of (many on) the left—high in tolerance for ambiguity and high in need for cognition. Sure, liberals cheered when MSNBC's ratings increased under Trump, but is didactic outrage programming really compatible with the psychology and physiology underlying liberalism? When MSNBC hosts issue increasingly dire warnings about the danger Trump poses to democracy and spend hours railing against the administration and its supporters as threats to progressive values, aren't these tactics themselves appealing to a more conservative than liberal orientation to the world? One telling observation is that some of the most ominous warnings about the threat posed by President Trump actually come from political *conservatives*. Conservative opinion writer Jennifer Rubin at the *Washington Post* has warned that "journalists are at risk around the globe and Trump keeps adding fuel to the fire."[45] Former GOP strategist Steve Schmidt called President Trump "an agent de facto of Russia." Republican strategist Rick Wilson published a book titled *Everything Trump Touches Dies*. And conservative radio host Charlie Sykes wrote: "Trumpism poses an existential threat to the conservative vision of ordered liberty."[46]

Tapping into negative, threat-based emotions might motivate and mobilize liberals in the short term, but the physiological and psychological systems that such appeals tap into are fundamentally at odds with a liberal orientation to the world. To articulate threats through emotion-based appeals that leave no room for play or uncertainty is to operate according to the logic and epistemology of conservatism. Perhaps this is why it struck me as so odd when Bee called Ivanka Trump a "cunt." It was explicit. It was emotion-fueled. There was no irony. There was very little humor. In fact, this was the very thing that Glenn Beck had warned Bee about back when they chatted in December 2016.[47]

Comics Try to Strike a Balance

In spite of the fact that some late-night comics under Trump have occasionally invoked gravity, sincerity, and even anger, most of them are staying true to the underlying logic and structure of humor. *Late Show* host Colbert has been a consistent critic of the Trump presidency and of the man himself, often delivering scathing critiques with riddles, puns, and punchlines. ("Sir, you attract more skinheads than free Rogaine"; "You have more people marching against you than cancer"; "You talk like a sign language gorilla that got hit in the head.")[48] Colbert drew a backlash in May 2017 when he said of Trump: "the only thing your mouth is good for is being Vladimir Putin's c*ck holster." And while that joke was offensive to some audience members, it is still technically "humor," as it offers an incongruity that the listener has to complete to understand the argument (that President Trump's only job is to please Russia's President Vladimir Putin).

On August 2017, after anti-Nazi protester Heather Heyer was killed by a white supremacist in Charlottesville, Trump addressed the public, stating: "we condemn in the strongest possible terms this egregious display of hatred, bigotry and violence on many sides," and he repeated, "on many sides." Colbert responded to Trump's statement in his *Late Show* monologue, finding ways to be earnest while still capitalizing on comic juxtaposition. He explained that what was most disturbing about Trump's response was that "after [Trump] made his statement, reasonable people *could not tell* if he was condemning Nazis." Colbert went on to contrast Trump's silence about Nazis to his unchecked anger at just about everything else. The result was a naturally comedic juxtaposition: "if only the president was as mad about neo-Nazis murdering people in the streets as he's been about... Hillary Clinton, the New York Times, CNN, Joe Scarborough, Kristen Stewart, the cast of 'Hamilton,' Diet Coke, Nordstrom not selling his daughter's clothes, Arnold Schwarzenegger, the mayor of London Sadiq Khan, me, the state of New Hampshire, Gold Star families, Penn Jillette's Las Vegas show, the movie 'Django Unchained,' Meryl Streep and lady 'Ghostbusters.'"

Following the public outcry in response to the Trump administration's zero-tolerance immigration policy in the summer of 2018, Colbert walked a similar line between sincerity and humor. Attorney General Jeff Sessions had cited a biblical verse (Romans 13) in his justification of the child-separation policy: "obey the laws of the government because God has ordained the government for his purposes." Colbert pointed out that later in that same passage the verse states: "love your neighbor as yourself. Love does no harm to a neighbor. Therefore, love is the fulfillment of the law."[49] Then, returning to the state of play, Colbert joked: "I'm not surprised Sessions didn't read the whole thing. After all, Jesus said, 'Suffer the children to come unto me.' But I'm pretty sure all Sessions saw were the words 'children' and 'suffer' and said, 'I'm on it!'"

That same week, *Last Week Tonight* host John Oliver challenged the administration's claim that the zero-tolerance immigration policy was merely enforcing existing law. Even in his scathing takedown of the policy and of the administration's doublespeak, Oliver kept one foot firmly planted in the state of play: "I cannot stress this enough. There is no law that suddenly required separating parents from their children. This was the result of a deliberate policy choice by *Jeff Sessions*—a man so small that he can wear... *and this is true...* a *raspberry* as a hat." Oliver, also critical of Sessions's invocation of Romans 13, continued: "lots of things are said in the Bible, but that doesn't mean you should do them. At one point the Bible demands that the head of government get 100 foreskins, but I don't think that [press secretary Sarah Huckabee] Sanders is looking for Congress to gather together and start *slicing dicks.*"[50]

Even in their passionate critiques of the White House's policy to separate children from their parents, these comedians were capitalizing on the unique elements that make humor subtle, effective, and distinct from outrage: playful incongruities and comic juxtapositions.

In what may be the surest sign that satire would endure a Trump presidency, if only satirists could get enough distance, comic Michelle Wolf used a segment on her Netflix series *The Break* to parody political satirists' use of their platforms to angrily criticize politics and media. Yes, you read that right. This is awfully meta, so buckle your seat belts. Sitting behind a desk in a segment aptly titled "Segment Time," Wolf began by describing the nature, positioning, and tone of what she was about to do: "I just finished the monologue. I addressed all the news this week, and now I'm at a desk. So you know what that means... It's segment time!" Then, explicitly capturing the increased anger and outrage among practitioners of the satire genre under Trump, Wolf continued: "and since this is a comedy show in 2018, you know one thing for sure: This comedy segment is going to be sincere and angry."[51] Wolf described the template that has come to dominate the televised political satire genre—from *The Daily Show* with Trevor Noah to the *Late-Show* with Colbert and to *Late-night* with Seth Meyers and *Last Week Tonight* with John Oliver: "and you can also tell that it will be funny because I'm sitting down, there will be graphics and facts, and it will feel a little bit like school." Wolf showed clips to illustrate how cable and network news outlets covered Trump's Supreme Court selection in the same way media might report on the winner of a beauty pageant. She even equated media outlets to both puppets and tampons—neither of which are troubled by their strings being pulled. She then called attention to this classic shift away from straight political satire to media satire: "that's right! You probably thought I was only going to go after the orange clown, Trump. But I'm *also* calling out the *liberal media*! Whah-*bam*! Unexpected pivot!" (on-screen graphic reads: UNEXPECTED PIVOT). When the segment ends, you're not totally sure who she's criticizing... or for what. You're thinking: "wait. Is she criticizing comedians for mocking politicians and the press? Is she criticizing the press for abdicating responsibility to such an extent that we are all now familiar with late-night comics playing this role? Is she criticizing the Trump administration for manipulating the media in this way in the first place? Is she criticizing *us* for being willing to serve as the spectators for *all of this*?"

Maybe she is saying all of these things.

We. Just. Don't. Know. But as listeners, we entertain all of these possibilities and, in so doing, issue each of these judgments—at least for a moment.

In sum, when they have tried to dabble in the preferred genre of the "other side," liberals and conservatives have often struggled. Liberals brought play, experimentation and collaboration to their attempt at outrage at Air America. Conservatives brought straightforward insult, directness, and very little humor to their attempt at satire at the *½ Hour News Hour.* Under the Trump administration, though, as liberals' high tolerance for ambiguity has most certainly been tested by conservative social and cultural policy and rhetoric, some liberal comics have eschewed humor, at times invoking the tropes of outrage. But if the characteristics of the outrage genre are indeed better suited to a conservative orientation to the world, perhaps liberals should proceed with caution before substituting funny with angry.

11

Irony and Outrage

A WILD RACCOON VERSUS A WELL-TRAINED ATTACK DOG

"Why is there no satire on the right?"
"Why do liberals fail at talk radio?"

IN WRITING THIS book, I have highlighted the ways irony and outrage are the logical extensions of the psychology of liberalism and conservatism. I have proposed that the two genres have parallel histories, encouraged by the same technological and political transformations, and serve similar political functions for their audiences. But make no mistake: satire and outrage are *not* the same. They look, feel, and sound different because—in keeping with the distinct values and psychological profiles of their audiences—they serve different needs and gratifications. However, rather than thinking about satire and outrage as occupying two divergent spaces in the media landscape, this book argues that these two genres should be thought of as natural expressions of the psychologies and personalities of the left and right.

There is no conspiracy to keep conservatives out of the world of satire, just as there is no conspiracy to keep liberals out of the outrage business. Instead, liberals, comfortable with ambiguity, rumination, experimentation, and hybridity, gravitate toward and appreciate aesthetic forms that are themselves incomplete or messy. Abstract art. Stories without a clear ending. Improvisation. Irony. Combinations of the serious and the playful, the informative and the entertaining. The Committee. Lenny Bruce. John Oliver. Liberals see these forms as invitations to participate, to think, and to play. And conservatives (most notably social and cultural conservatives), with a strong desire for certainty and order, are drawn to aesthetic forms that follow the rules and emerge "fully cooked." Realistic art. Stories with a clear ending. Texts that are literal and didactic. Conservatives make efficient use of heuristics and are acutely affected by negative and threatening stimuli. They appreciate and gravitate toward aesthetic forms that are themselves unambiguous, didactic, firm, and clear. They also prefer political sources that "stay in their lane," abiding by the boundaries that "ought to exist" between politics and play. Dan Smoot. Rush Limbaugh. Sean Hannity.

To Hell with the Other Side? Not So Fast.

After several years studying the psychology, physiology, and aesthetic preferences of the left and the right, I am not convinced that a liberal aesthetic preference is objectively "better than" a conservative one. Liberals' rejection of categories and boundaries—their penchant for hybridity and experimentation—can be chaotic, messy, and unfinished. And as conservatives, with their high need for closure, have always known, watching a painter capture—with photographic realism—the contours of a landscape with only a paintbrush is truly awe-inspiring. Who hasn't seen an abstract "masterpiece" on exhibit in a modern art museum and thought: "this looks like something my two-year-old could do?" Indeed, as the *National Review*'s film critic Kyle Smith might argue, liberals can't even seem to provide a satisfying ending to a story, instead opting for ambiguity and untied ends.

The United States' political climate is so toxic that liberal and conservative opinion leaders would have each side believe that if the other side just disappeared, things would be fine. But unpacking these differences between the left and the right reveals how these ideologies might reflect distinct and necessary psychological and physiological systems that contribute to the healthy functioning of the larger organism: democratic society. In fact, reflecting on the very different psychologies, lifestyles, and values of the left and the right invites a thought experiment: is it possible that conservatives manage those aspects of society that make it possible for artists, musicians, and comics to enter the state of play and experiment with hybrid aesthetic forms in the first place? Perhaps liberals' comfort with uncertainty and ambiguity is a luxury made possible—in part—by the fact that those higher in "need for closure and order" are minding the store. And maybe regular artistic expression is facilitated by a society that has some semblance of stability—maintained by vigilant individuals whose need for order and certainty helps make it so. On the other hand, perhaps a world without liberals would be so driven by vigilance and threat-monitoring that it would leave less room for music, art, or comedy. Taken to their extreme, societies that are focused exclusively on law and order would certainly lack play and experimentation—ultimately slowing the kinds of innovations that contribute to cultural enrichment and economic growth.

The Limits of Satire and the Dangers of Outrage

The proposition that the aesthetics of the left and the right stem from psychological predispositions is an argument about people's natural tendencies— their innate inclinations. However, the increased popularity of the genres of satire and outrage—the fact that they are no longer relegated to dark smoky comedy clubs or the far end of a radio dial—is what happens when media executives capitalize on these psychological predispositions in a splintered media environment. With journalism decimated by profit motives, trust in institutions at historic lows, and political polarization at its peak, satire and outrage have become viable vehicles for political information. Media executives and political strategists, having come to understand the unique ways the left and the right orient to the world, have made it their goal to use this knowledge to create messages and content that serve their political and financial interests. In the process, they push the nation's citizens farther apart. This is the heart of the business model that creates enormous profit for 21st Century Fox through programming at Fox News (and to a lesser extent for Comcast through its programming at MSNBC). It is also how Russian intelligence tried to exploit Americans' ideological divisions in their effort to undermine America's democracy in the 2016 election.[1] By persuading Americans on both the left and the right to frame their differences as fatal flaws of the opposing side rather than necessary features of a cohesive system, these entities and others seek to destabilize American society in an effort to obtain power and financial reward.

Yet the potential for outrage and satire to be strategically employed for such political and financial gains is not symmetrical. Politicians, political parties, and political strategists might want to use both of these genres as attack dogs that they can sic on enemies or trespassers. But because satire requires staying in the state of play, downplaying its own moral certainty and issuing judgments through implication rather than proclamation, political elites' ability to harness satire and use it to their own ends is by definition compromised. I would contend that satire is far more difficult than outrage to exploit for attaining large-scale political influence. Argumentation through play and insinuation through irony are hard to use for political gain. Any form of organic, hybrid artistic expression with radical or political themes is intrinsically difficult to employ purposefully. It's experimental. It's messy. And it's not conducive to goal-driven propaganda.

When Ellul wrote about hate as the most profitable resource of agitation propaganda,[2] he certainly was not talking about ironic segments praising the humanity of the death penalty or radical performance art with antiwar themes. Ellul was talking about didactic, emotion-filled (typically hate- and anger-filled) speech. Speech that explicitly identifies out-groups and threats and that proposes specific courses of action. Speech that is cloaked in moral certainty and purports to present an unequivocal truth. Ellul described such propaganda as producing "rapid and spectacular effects" and as the preferred propaganda of elites seeking war or social upheaval. "Propaganda of agitation unleashes an explosive movement; it operates inside a crisis or actually provokes the crisis itself."[3] Satire and irony on the other hand are more akin to Ellul's concept of "sociological propaganda," a form of diffuse, spontaneous messaging that is not created by elites seeking to mobilize the public toward a political goal but originates organically from the culture and people themselves. Sociological propaganda operates "in reverse," such that "existing economic, political and sociological factors progressively allow an ideology to penetrate individuals."[4] It is aimed at an entire "style of life" rather than at "opinions or one particular course of behavior."

The underlying logic and aesthetic of outrage make it an ideal mechanism for tactical, goal-driven political mobilization. Importantly, though, it is the symbiosis between outrage and the underlying psychology of social and cultural conservatism that renders conservative outrage especially fruitful as an avenue for strategic political persuasion. It's why it worked well for Dan Smoot and Clarence Manion with their (admittedly small) audiences in the early 1960s and why it's working well for Limbaugh and Hannity today.

But just as it is the symbiosis between outrage and conservatism that lends itself to strategic persuasion and mobilization, the symbiosis between the aesthetic of irony and the underlying psychology of liberalism render liberal satire especially fruitful as a forum *not* for mobilization but for exploration and rumination. Consider one of the most critically acclaimed and influential pieces of satire of the past decade: Colbert's 2011 creation of an actual super PAC, Americans for a Better Tomorrow, Tomorrow. As discussed in chapter 9, Colbert's coverage of super PACs and *Citizens United* influenced public opinion and knowledge of the topic. But, according to Colbert, he didn't create his super PAC with political or persuasive intentions at all. He didn't push the limits of campaign finance in an effort to fuel activism on the issue of campaign finance reform. Rather, the whole thing came about by accident. After having mentioned a fictional super PAC at the end of a political parody on *The Colbert Report*, Comedy Central expressed resistance to the idea of an actual Colbert super PAC. "Are you really going to get a PAC?" a network representative asked Colbert. "Because if you actually get a PAC, that could be trouble." To which Colbert replied: "well then, I'm definitely doing to do it."[5] And so began the largely organic and experimental process of launching and raising funds for an actual super PAC and learning about the (nearly nonexistent) limits of campaign financing. As Colbert explained, "at every stage of [the super PAC], I didn't know what was going to happen next. It was just an act of discovery. It was purely improvisational. People would say 'what is your plan?' My plan is to see what I can and cannot do with it."[6]

This is the essence of the liberal aesthetic: experimentation. An act of discovery. Not knowing what is going to happen next. I can see how this would be extremely frustrating to liberal political strategists. Whereas the preferred aesthetic form among conservatives is perfectly suited to elite strategic persuasion, the preferred aesthetic form among liberals is absolutely *not*. Satire especially, when functioning at its best, is not explicitly goal-driven but is exploratory. And it remains outside the system, not beholden to political interests or parties. *Last Week Tonight*'s John Oliver has even argued: "a comedian is supposed to be an outsider. He's supposed to be outside looking in. I don't want to be at parties in D.C. with politicians. Comedians shouldn't be there. If you feel comfortable being in a room like that, there's a big problem."[7]

When satirists *do* step into the realm of organized politics or political activism, it doesn't seem to go particularly well. In October 2010, after Stewart and Colbert hosted the Rally to Restore Sanity and/or Fear on the National Mall in Washington, DC, journalists asked them how successful they thought the rally had been. They laughed at the frame surrounding such questions. "Our currency is not this town's [Washington, DC's] currency," Stewart replied. "We aren't running for anything. We don't have a constituency. We do television shows for people who like them."[8]

Some of the most uncomfortable interactions among satirists, politicians, and the press in American politics have come at the annual White House Correspondents' Association Dinner. When the Association invited Colbert to serve as the featured speaker in 2006, he performed in his ironic persona, "praising" then-president George W. Bush: "most of all, I believe in this president. Now, I know there are some polls out there saying that this man has a 32 percent approval rating. But guys like us, we don't pay attention to the polls. We know that polls are just a collection of statistics that reflect what people are thinking in 'reality.' And reality has a well-known liberal bias." In 2018, comedian Michelle Wolf used her speech at the dinner to invite the audience to question the integrity of White House press secretary Sarah Huckabee Sanders, saying: "I actually really like Sarah. I think she's very resourceful. Like she burns facts, and then she uses that ash to create a perfect smoky eye. Like 'maybe she's born with it, maybe it's lies.' It's probably lies." In response to the backlash against Wolf's comments, the Association's president, Margaret Talev, issued a statement in which she said: "last night's program was meant to offer a unifying message about our common commitment to a vigorous and free press while honoring civility, great reporting and scholarship winners, not to divide people. Unfortunately, the entertainer's monologue was not in the spirit of the mission."[9] In an interview, the comedian, author, and former *Colbert Report* writer Frank Lesser described getting roped into the world of political activism in 2017. In response to White House spokesperson Kellyanne Conway suggesting that "people don't care" about President Trump's tax returns, Lesser tweeted: "Trump claims no one cares about his taxes. The next mass protest should be on Tax Day to prove him wrong."[10] The tweet went viral, and suddenly the Tax March was an actual event. As the author of the tweet, Lesser found himself at the center of the organizing. "This was the only time I actually got sort of involved in actual politics," he admitted, "and I was frustrated by the experience and met some very unpleasant people."[11] "I'm thinking of making a mockumentary about the whole thing, inspired by the protest chant, called *This Is What Democracy Looks Like?* with a *question mark* at the end. It was all so very frustrating."[12]

Compare these uncomfortable partnerships between satirists and the political establishment to the exceedingly comfortable partnership between conservative outrage hosts and the Trump administration. At a rally in Cape Girardeau, Missouri, on the night before the 2018 midterm elections, the conservative crowd was greeted by the familiar voice of Limbaugh. He quickly hit all the classic markers of outrage, warming up the crowd with dire talk of "risk," "danger," and "hanging on by a thread": "We are a great nation at risk in a dangerous world. We are hanging by a thread. Do you realize, folks, there is nobody...who would do what Donald Trump has done—nobody who would buck the system? Who among anybody in politics, who could you have glommed onto that would have this kind of chance to make America great again?"[13] Once on stage, President Trump acknowledged the support of "a few people" he described as "very special"; people who "have done an incredible job for us. They've been with us from the beginning....Come on up, Sean Hannity" (photo 11.1). At the microphone before the raucous crowd, Hannity

PHOTO 11.1 Presidential candidate Donald Trump and Sean Hannity at the Conservative Political Action Conference, National Harbor, Maryland, February 27, 2015. Photo courtesy of Gage Skidmore via Wikimedia Commons.

campaigned for the president's agenda: "the one thing that has made and defined your Presidency more than anything else: Promises made. Promises kept. 4 and a half million new American jobs. 4.3 million Americans off of food stamps. 4 million Americans out of poverty. And we're not dropping cash loads, cargo planes of cash to Iranian mullahs who chant 'death to America.' Mr. President, thank you."[14]

Hannity was followed onstage by yet another outrage host, Jeanine Pirro, host of Fox News's *Justice with Judge Jeanine*. On her show, Pirro warns of the threat of migrant caravans crossing the southern border and refers to the Mueller investigation as the "Russian collusion delusion."[15] On the stage at the rally, she engaged in straight electioneering rhetoric—or, to quote myself from a couple of pages ago, "tactical, goal-driven political mobilization": "if you like the America that he is making now, you've got to make sure you get out there tomorrow, if you haven't voted yet. Everyone you know: your grandmother, your cousin, your kids, even your next door neighbor if you don't like 'em—get them out to vote for Donald Trump and all the people who are running for the Republican Party."[16]

In Sum: A Wild Raccoon versus a Well-Trained Attack Dog

It is time to recognize these ideologies as overlapping and necessary systems that both contribute to everyone's cultural and societal well-being. The fact that one of these ideologies cultivates particularly fertile ground in which political operatives can more readily sow the seeds of hate and division—*this* is where things go off the rails. But instead of seeing conservatism as problematic for societal health—which it most certainly is not—I would argue that people should consider how, through the genre of outrage, the psychology of conservatism is more readily exploited by those seeking political power, financial reward, and cultural dominance. Conversely, satire thrives outside the system and emerges from the bottom up largely through experimentation and improvisation.

If outrage is a well-trained attack dog that operates on command, satire is a raccoon—hard to domesticate and capable of turning on anyone at any time.

Does satire have a liberal bias? Sure. Satire has a liberal psychological bias. But the only person who can successfully harness the power of satire is the satirist. Not political strategists. Not a political party. Not a presidential candidate.

Outrage is the tool of conservative elites.

But ironic satire is the tool of the liberal satirist alone.

Notes

PROLOGUE

1. Shane, S. (2009). Conservatives draw blood from Acorn. *New York Times.* September 15.
2. Glenn Beck: Obama is a racist. (2009). Associated Press. July 29. https://www .cbsnews.com/news/glenn-beck-obama-is-a-racist/.
3. Weinstein, J. (2014). Glenn Beck: "I think I played a role, unfortunately, in helping tear the country apart." *Daily Caller.* January 21.
4. Schmidle, N. (2016). Glenn Beck tried out decency. *New Yorker.* November 14.
5. Berry, J. M., & Sobieraj, S. (2014). *The outrage industry: Political opinion media and the new incivility.* New York: Oxford University Press.
6. Hesse, J. (2013). Why does every "conservative *Daily Show*" fail? Vulture. December 2. http://www.vulture.com/2013/12/why-does-every-conservative-daily -show-fail.html.
7. Nevins, J. (2017). Why can't rightwing comics break into US late-night TV? *Guardian.* September 27. https://www.theguardian.com/global/2017/sep/27/why -cant-rightwing-comics-break-into-us-late-night-tv.
8. Green, J. (2012). Why aren't conservatives funny? *Washington Monthly.* September/October 2012. https://washingtonmonthly.com/magazine/septoct -2012/why-arent-conservatives-funny/.
9. Bershad, J. (2011). Why conservative comedy doesn't work and likely never will. *Mediaite.* December 21. https://www.mediaite.com/online/why-conservative -comedy-doesnt-work-and-likely-never-will/.
10. Morrison, O. (2015). Waiting for the conservative Jon Stewart. *Atlantic.* February 14. https://www.theatlantic.com/entertainment/archive/2015/02/why-theres-no -conservative-jon-stewart/385480/.
11. Brown, A. (2015). Why all the talk-radio stars are conservative. *Forbes.* July 13. https:// www.forbes.com/sites/abrambrown/2015/07/13/why-all-the-talk-radio-stars -are-conservative/#7a076ee52788.

12. Lowry, B. (2014). How conservatives dominate the TV/radio talk game. *Variety*. January 3. https://variety.com/2014/voices/columns/how-conservatives-dominate-tvradio-talk-game-1201022387/.

13. Romero, D. (2010). Air America goes down; Liberal talk radio a fail. *LA Weekly*. January 21. http://www.laweekly.com/news/air-america-goes-down-liberal-talk-radio-a-fail-2398422.

14. Mordock, J. (2017). Conservatives get canceled, liberals quit laughing: How Trump's election killed comedy. *Washington Times*. December 24. https://www.washingtontimes.com/news/2017/dec/24/conservatives-banished-comedy-industry/. Nevins, Why can't rightwing comics break into US late-night TV?

15. Hesse, Why does every "conservative *Daily Show*" fail?

16. Colbert, S. (2006). Lecture at Institute of Politics, Kennedy School, Harvard University. December 1. http://iop.harvard.edu/forum/conversation-stephen-colbert.

CHAPTER 1

1. Kreps, D. (2018). Samantha Bee addresses Ivanka controversy, regrets "one bad word." *Rolling Stone*. June 1. https://www.rollingstone.com/tv/news/samantha-bee-addresses-ivanka-controversy-regrets-one-bad-word-w520972 Glenn Beck: Obama is a racist. (2009). Associated Press. July 29. https://www.cbsnews.com/news/glenn-beck-obama-is-a-racist/.

3. Nelson, L. (2016). Glenn Beck regrets "freaking out about Barack Obama." Vox.com. November 7. https://www.vox.com/policy-and-politics/2016/11/7/13556876/glenn-beck-obama-trump.

4. Hemmer, N. (2016). *Messengers of the right: Conservative media and the transformation of American politics*. Philadelphia: University of Pennsylvania Press, 221.

5. Hemmer, *Messengers of the right*, 111.

6. Brock, D. (2005). *The Republican noise machine: Right-wing media and how it corrupts democracy*. New York: Three Rivers Press.

7. Minutaglio, B., & Davis, S. L. (2013). *Dallas 1963*. London: Hachette UK, 231.

8. Minutaglio & Davis, *Dallas 1963*, 74.

9. Cray, E. (1997). *Chief justice: A biography of Earl Warren*. New York: Simon and Schuster, 390.

10. Cray, *Chief justice*.

11. Hemmer, *Messengers of the right*, 22.

12. Hemmer, *Messengers of the right*, 22.

13. Hemmer, *Messengers of the right*, 111.

14. Hemmer, *Messengers of the right*, 29.

15. Hemmer, N. (2016). The birth of conservative media as we know it. *New Republic*. September 2. https://newrepublic.com/article/136390/birth-conservative-media-know.

16. Hemmer, *Messengers of the right*, 110–111.

17. Minutaglio & Davis, *Dallas 1963*, 251.

19. Minutaglio & Davis, *Dallas 1963*, 303.

20. Stahl, J. (2016). *Right moves: The conservative think tank in American political culture since* 1945. Chapel Hill: University of North Carolina Press .

21. Sykes, C. J. (2017). *How the right lost its mind.* New York: St. Martin's Press, 49.

22. Felzenberg, A. S. (2017). *A man and his presidents: The political odyssey of William F. Buckley Jr.* New Haven: Yale University Press.

23. Felzenberg, *A man and his presidents*, 137.

24. Felzenberg, *A man and his presidents*, 137.

25. Sykes, *How the right lost its mind*, 41.

26. Jurem, L. R. (2015). Reagan and his favorite magazine. *National Review.* December 5. https://www.nationalreview.com/2015/12/paving-way-reagan/.

27. Continetti, Matthew (2016). The coming conservative dark age. *Commentary.* April 12. https://www.commentarymagazine.com/articles/coming-conservative -dark-age/.

28. Test, G. A. (1991). *Satire: Spirit and art.* Gainesville: University Press of Florida.

29. Nesteroff, K. (2015). *The comedians: Drunks, thieves, scoundrels, and the history of American Comedy.* Grove/Atlantic.

30. Sweet, J. (1978). Editor's introduction to *Something wonderful right away.* New York: Avon Books, xvii.

31. Taormina, L. (2017). Personal communication. July 27.

32. Interview with Carl Gottlieb, excerpted in documentary *The Committee: A Secret History of American Comedy* (in production). Dir. Sam Shaw and Jamie Wright.

33. Excerpt from The Committee's *Wide World of War* (LP, 1973), in documentary *The Committee.*

34. Excerpt from The Committee's *Wide World of War*, in documentary *The Committee.*

35. Nesteroff, *The comedians*, 160.

36. Nesteroff, *The comedians*, 160.

37. Robinson, P. M. (2010). *The dance of the comedians: The people, the president, and the performance of political standup comedy in America.* Amherst: University of Massachusetts Press, 150.

38. Robinson, *The dance of the comedians*, 150.

39. Cited in Krassner, P. (2011). *One hand jerking: Reports from an investigative journalist.* New York: Seven Stories Press, 123.

40. Johnson, K. H. (2008). *The funniest one in the room: The lives and legends of Del Close.* Chicago: Chicago Review Press, 133.

41. Myerson, A. (2018). Interview with author. February 2.

42. Quoted in Nesteroff, *The comedians*, 243.

43. Sweet, editor's introduction to *Something wonderful right away*, xlii.

44. Personal correspondence with author, January 31, 2018.

45. Excerpted in documentary *The Committee.*
46. Greenberg, E. (2017). Interview with author. September 8.
47. Greenberg, E. (2017). Interview with author. September 8.
48. Kercher, S. E. (2010). *Revel with a cause: Liberal satire in postwar America.* Chicago: University of Chicago Press, 253.
49. Sweet, J. (ed.) (1978). *Something wonderful right away.* New York: Avon Books, 284–285.
50. Von Hoffman, N. (1988). *We are the people our parents warned us against.* New York: Ivan R. Dee, 133.
51. Nesteroff, *The comedians*, 160, 217.
52. Nesteroff, *The comedians*, 160, 219.
53. Personal correspondence with author, February 2, 2018.
54. Thomas, M. (2012). *The Second City unscripted: Revolution and revelation at the world-famous comedy theater.* Evanston, IL: Northwestern University Press, 140.
55. Nesteroff, *The comedians*, 160, 243.
56. Robinson, *The dance of the comedians*, 172.
57. Robinson, *The dance of the comedians*, 172.
58. Bianculli, D. (2009). *Dangerously funny: The uncensored story of "The Smothers Brothers Comedy Hour."* New York: Simon and Schuster, xi.
59. Robinson, *The dance of the comedians*, 173.

CHAPTER 2

1. Colbert, Stephen (2006). Interview with N. Rabin. *A.V. Club.* January 25. https://tv.avclub.com/stephen-colbert-1798208958.
2. Guthrie, M. (2015). TV ratings: Bill O'Reilly to finish year with top-rated cable news show. *Hollywood Reporter.* December 21. https://www.hollywoodreporter.com/news/tv-ratings-bill-oreilly-finish-850467.
3. Today the FCC's rules place no limit on the number of television stations that can be owned by a single entity, as long as "the station group collectively reaches no more than 39 percent of all U.S. TV households." FCC Broadcast Ownership Rules. Federal Communications Commission, www.fcc.gov. Updated December 27, 2017. https://www.fcc.gov/consumers/guides/fccs-review-broadcast-ownership-rules. Accessed March 28, 2019.
4. McChesney, R. (1999). *Rich media, poor democracy: Communication politics in dubious times.* Urbana: University of Illinois Press, 17.
5. Bagdikian, B. (2000). *The media monopoly.* 6th ed. Boston: Beacon Press.
6. Bagdikian, *The media monopoly*, 4.
7. McChesney, *Rich media, poor democracy*, 48.
8. Bagdikian, *The media monopoly*, xii.
9. Kovach, B., & Rosenstiel, T. (2014). *The elements of journalism: What newspeople should know and the public should expect.* New York: Three Rivers Press, 50.

10. McChesney, *Rich media, poor democracy*, 49.

11. ASNE Statement of Principles (1975) (2011). October 24. Website of Center for the Study of Ethics in the Professions, Illinois Institute of Technology. http://ethics.iit.edu/ecodes/node/3588.

12. Press widely criticized, but trusted more than other information sources: Views of the news media: 1985–2011 (2011). Pew Research Center. September 22. http://www.people-press.org/2011/09/22/press-widely-criticized-but-trusted-more-than-other-institutions/#long-term-views-of-the-press.

13. Kovach, *The elements of journalism*, 59.

14. McChesney, *Rich media, poor democracy*, 51.

15. Gans, H. J. (2004). *Deciding what's news: A study of CBS Evening News, NBC Nightly News, Newsweek, and Time.* Evanston, IL: Northwestern University Press, 51.

16. Gans, *Deciding what's news*, 27.

17. Downie, L., Jr., & Kaiser, R. G. (2002). *The news about the news: American journalism in peril.* New York: Knopf.

18. Downie & Kaiser, *The news about the news*, 10.

19. Downie & Kaiser, *The news about the news*, 11.

20. Kovach & Rosenstiel, *The elements of journalism*, 61.

21. McChesney, *Rich media, poor democracy*, 54.

22. Downie & Kaiser, *The news about the news*, 231.

23. Downie & Kaiser, *The news about the news*, 10.

24. Bennett, W. L. (2016). *News: The politics of illusion.* Chicago: University of Chicago Press.

25. Bennett, *News*, 46.

26. Bennett, *News*, 47.

27. Edelman, M. (1988). *Constructing the political spectacle.* Chicago: University of Chicago Press.

28. Edelman, *Constructing the political spectacle*, 63.

29. Bennett, *News*, 23.

30. Bennett, *News*, 24.

31. Arceneaux, K., Johnson, M., & Murphy, C. (2012). Polarized political communication, oppositional media hostility, and selective exposure. *Journal of Politics*, 74(1), 174–186. Vallone, R. P., Ross, L., & Lepper, M. R. (1985). The hostile media phenomenon: Biased perception and perceptions of media bias in coverage of the Beirut massacre. *Journal of Personality and Social Psychology*, 49(3), 577–585. Tsfati, Y., & Cohen, J. (2005). Democratic consequences of hostile media perceptions. *Harvard International Journal of Press/Politics*, 10(4), 28–51.

32. Political polarization, 1994–2017 (2017). Pew Research Center. October 20. http://www.people-press.org/interactives/political-polarization-1994–2017/.

33. Carmines, E. G., & Stimson, J. A. (1989). *Issue evolution: Race and the transformation of American politics.* Princeton: Princeton University Press.

34. Layman, G. C., Carsey, T. M., & Horowitz, J. M. (2006). Party polarization in American politics: Characteristics, causes, and consequences. *Annual Review of Political Science, 9*, 86.

35. Desilver, D. (2016). *Turnout was high in the 2016 primary season, but just short of 2008 record.* Pew Research Center. http://www.pewresearch.org/fact-tank/2016/06/10/turnout-was-high-in-the-2016-primary-season-but-just-short-of-2008-record/.

36. Sides, J., Tausanovitch, C., Vavreck, L., & Warshaw, C. (2018). On the representativeness of primary electorates. *British Journal of Political Science*, 1–9.

37. Outside spending (n.d.). Open Secrets.org. Center for Responsive Politics. https://www.opensecrets.org/outsidespending/.

38. Fiorina, M. (2017). *Unstable majorities: Polarization, party sorting, and political stalemate.* Stanford, CA: Hoover Press.

39. Converse, P. E. (2006). The nature of belief systems in mass publics (1964). *Critical Review, 18*(1–3), 1–74.

40. Iyengar, S., Sood, G., & Lelkes, Y. (2012). Affect, not ideology: A social identity perspective on polarization. *Public Opinion Quarterly, 76*(3), 405–431.

41. History of cable (2018). California Cable and Telecommunications Association. https://www.calcable.org/learn/history-of-cable/.

42. Ismail, S. (2010). Transformative choices: A review of 70 years of FCC decisions. Federal Communication Commission. October. https://apps.fcc.gov/edocs_public/attachmatch/DOC-302496A1.pdf.

43. Ismail, Transformative choices, 12.

44. The Cable Center (2014). The cable history timeline. http://www.cablecenter.org/images/files/pdf/CableHistory/CableTimelineFall2015.pdf.

45. The Hollywood Reporter Staff (2011). How *I Love Lucy* dominated ratings from its start. *Hollywood Reporter.* August 15. https://www.hollywoodreporter.com/news/how-i-love-lucy-dominated-222960.

46. Nielsen (2017). Tops of 2017: Television and social media. December 18. http://www.nielsen.com/us/en/insights/news/2017/tops-of-2017-television-and-social-media.html?afflt=ntrt15340001&afflt_uid=rMOU3B5yhVA.rF_yoLAKyVVbVxK4bGZ9aF7YyLCTSblb&afflt_uid_2=AFFLT_ID_2.

47. Nielsen (2016). Nielsen estimates 118.4 million TV homes in the U.S. for the 2016–17 TV season. August 26. http://www.nielsen.com/us/en/insights/news/2016/nielsen-estimates-118-4-million-tv-homes-in-the-us—for-the-2016-17-season.html.

48. Bolin, G. (2014). The death of the mass audience reconsidered: From mass communication to mass personalisation. In S. Eichner & E. Prommer (eds.), *Fernsehen: Europäische Perspectiven*, 159–172. Munich: UVK.

49. Turow, J. (2007). *Breaking up America: Advertisers and the new media world.* Chicago: University of Chicago Press.

50. Turow, *Breaking up America.*

51. Turow, *Breaking up America.*

52. Crank Yankers was on the air as the lead-in program, airing in the slot before *The Daily Show* with Jon Stewart from 2002 to 2007.

CHAPTER 3

1. Edelman, M. (1988). *Constructing the political spectacle.* Chicago: University of Chicago Press.

2. Berry, J. M., & Sobieraj, S. (2013). *The outrage industry: Political opinion media and the new incivility.* New York: Oxford University Press.

3. Berry & Sobieraj, *The outrage industry,* 67.

4. Jamieson, K. H., & Cappella, J. N. (2008). *Echo chamber: Rush Limbaugh and the conservative media establishment.* New York: Oxford University Press, 46.

5. Talkers Estimetrix: Most-listened-to radio talk show hosts in America (2019). Talkers. http://www.talkers.com/top-talk-audiences/.

6. Hemmer, N. (2016). *Messengers of the right: Conservative media and the transformation of American politics.* Philadelphia: University of Pennsylvania Press, 265.

7. Jamieson & Cappella, *Echo chamber.*

8. Jamieson & Cappella, *Echo chamber.*

9. Jamieson & Cappella, *Echo chamber.*

10. Sherman, G. (2014). *The loudest voice in the room: How the brilliant, bombastic Roger Ailes built Fox News—and divided a country.* New York: Random House.

11. Sherman, *The loudest voice in the room,* 136.

12. Sherman, *The loudest voice in the room.*

13. Jones, J. (2005). *Entertaining politics: New political television and civic culture.* Lanham, MD: Rowman & Littlefield.

14. Hall, J. (1993). CNBC chief and former GOP media strategist Roger Ailes is executive producer for Rush Limbaugh's show. *Los Angeles Times.* October 18. http://www.latimes.com/business/hollywood/la-fi-ct-roger-ailes-rush-limbaugh-19931018-story.html.

15. Sherman, *The loudest voice in the room,* 151.

16. Hemmer, *Messengers of the right,* 265.

17. Hemmer, *Messengers of the right.*

18. Sherman, *The loudest voice in the room,* 176.

19. Moore, F. (1995). Trying to cure what Ailes you. Associated Press. August 6.

20. Sherman, *The loudest voice in the room,* 178.

21. Sella, M. (2001). The red-state network. *New York Times Magazine.* June 24. https://www.nytimes.com/2001/06/24/magazine/the-red-state-network.html.

22. Sherman, *The loudest voice in the room,* 178.

23. Sella, The red-state network.

24. Sella, The red-state network.

25. Sella, The red-state network.

26. Jamieson & Cappella, *Echo chamber*, 49.

27. Sherman, *The loudest voice in the room*, 194.

28. Sherman, *The loudest voice in the room*, 194.

29. O'Reilly Talking Points: White privilege. (2014). *The O'Reilly Factor*, Fox News. September 13.

30. O'Reilly Talking Points: How to oppose the totalitarian left on college campuses. (2016). *The O'Reilly Factor*, Fox News. December 4.

31. O'Reilly Talking Points: The pro–illegal immigration movement. (2017). *The O'Reilly Factor*, Fox News. January 26.

32. Steel, E., & Schmidt, M. (2017). Bill O'Reilly is forced out at Fox News. *New York Times*. April 19. https://www.nytimes.com/2017/04/19/business/media/bill-oreilly-fox-news-allegations.html.

33. Fisher, M. (2017). The making of Sean Hannity: How a Long Island kid learned to channel red-state rage. *Washington Post*. October 10. https://www.washingtonpost.com/lifestyle/style/the-making-of-sean-hannity-how-a-long-island-kid-learned-to-channel-red-state-rage/2017/10/09/540cfc38-8821-11e7-961d-2f373b3977ee_story.html?noredirect=on&utm_term=.8b1572586f3.

34. Fisher, The making of Sean Hannity.

35. Fisher, The making of Sean Hannity.

36. Schmidt, S. (2018). Trump touts Hannity's show on "Deep State crime families" led by Mueller, Comey and Clintons. *Washington Post*. April 12. https://www.washingtonpost.com/news/morning-mix/wp/2018/04/12/trump-touts-hannitys-show-on-deep-state-crime-families-led-by-mueller-comey-and-clintons/?utm_term=.f98463910014.

37. Stelter, B. Beck leaving CNN for Fox News. *New York Times*. October 16. https://mediadecoder.blogs.nytimes.com//2008/10/16/beck-leaving-cnn-for-fox-news.

38. Gold, M. (2009). Fox News' Glenn Beck strikes ratings gold by challenging Barack Obama. *Los Angeles Times*. March 6. http://articles.latimes.com/2009/mar/06/entertainment/et-foxnews6.

39. Farley, R. (2011). Glenn Beck's greatest hits (and misses). *Politifact*. June 30. http://www.politifact.com/truth-o-meter/article/2011/jun/30/glenn-becks-greatest-hits-and-misses/.

41. Gold, Fox News' Glenn Beck strikes ratings gold by challenging Barack Obama.

42. Chasmar, J. (2016). Glenn Beck on leaving Fox News: I was told to stop talking about God. *Washington Times*. February 15. https://www.washingtontimes.com/news/2016/feb/15/glenn-beck-on-leaving-fox-news-i-was-told-to-stop-/.

43. Beinart, P. (2017). Glenn Beck's regrets. *Atlantic*. January/February. https://www.theatlantic.com/magazine/archive/2017/01/glenn-becks-regrets/508763/?utm_source=nl-atlantic-daily-120816.

44. Beinart, Glenn Beck's regrets.

45. *Tucker Carlson Tonight* (2018). February 22.

46. *Tucker Carlson Tonight* (2018). January 3.

47. Ahmed, T. (2017). Fox News' Tucker Carlson strikes again: "Feminism is insincere." *Newsweek*. October 12. http://www.newsweek.com/fox-news-tucker-carlson-strikes-again-feminism-insincere-683017.

48. Coaston, J. (2018). Watch: Tucker Carlson rails against America's demographic changes. Vox.com. March 21. https://www.vox.com/2018/3/21/17146866/tucker-carlson-demographics-immigration-fox-news.

49. *Tucker Carlson Tonight*. (2018). June 14.

50. Wang, A., Chiu, A., & Jan, T. (2018). Facing boycott, Laura Ingraham apologizes for taunting Parkland teen over college rejections. March 29. https://www.washingtonpost.com/news/morning-mix/wp/2018/03/29/laura-ingraham-savaged-for-taunting-parkland-activist-over-college-rejections/?utm_term=.217a78e1c632.

51. *Ingraham Angle* (2018). March 28.

52. Sullivan, E. (2018). Laura Ingraham told LeBron James to shut up and dribble; He went to the hoop. NPR. February 19. https://www.npr.org/sections/thetwo-way/2018/02/19/587097707/laura-ingraham-told-lebron-james-to-shutup-and-dribble-he-went-to-the-hoop.

53. Wang, Chiu, & Jan, Facing boycott, Laura Ingraham apologizes for taunting Parkland teen over college rejections.

54. PunditFact checks in on the cable news channels. (2015). Politifact.com. https://www.politifact.com/truth-o-meter/article/2015/jan/29/punditfact-checks-cable-news-channels/.

55. Berry & Sobieraj, *The outrage industry*, 8.

56. Marans, D. (2016). Sean Hannity: "I'm not a journalist. I'm a talk show host." *Huffington Post*. April 14. https://www.huffingtonpost.com/entry/sean-hannity-not-a-journalist_us_570fc4f3e4b0ffa5937e6cd2.

57. Farhi, P. (2017). Sean Hannity thinks viewers can tell the difference between news and opinion. Hold on a second. *Washington Post*. March 28. https://www.washingtonpost.com/lifestyle/style/sean-hannity-thinks-viewers-can-tell-the-difference-between-news-and-opinion-hold-on-a-moment/2017/03/27/eb0c5870-1307-11e7-9e4f-09aa75d3ec57_story.html?utm_term=.9739b066fda9.

58. Mitchell, A., Gottfried, J., Barthel, M., & Sumida, N. (2018). Distinguishing between factual and opinion statements in the news. Pew Research Center. June 18. http://www.journalism.org/2018/06/18/distinguishing-between-factual-and-opinion-statements-in-the-news/.

59. Mitchell et al., Distinguishing between factual and opinion statements in the news. Pew Research Center. June 18. http://www.journalism.org/2018/06/18/distinguishing-between-factual-and-opinion-statements-in-the-news/.

60. Key indicators in media and news. (2014). Pew Research Center. March 26. http://www.journalism.org/2014/03/26/state-of-the-news-media-2014-key-indicators-in-media-and-news/.

61. Berry & Sobieraj, *The outrage industry*, 8.

62. The show moved to advertiser-free HBO under the moniker *Real Time* in 2002, after ABC canceled the show in response to pressures from audiences' boycotts of sponsors. On the September 17, 2001, episode of *Politically Incorrect* on ABC, Maher had made controversial comments following the 9/11 attacks that angered audiences. "We have been the cowards, lobbing cruise missiles from 2,000 miles away. That's cowardly," Maher said. "Staying in the airplane when it hits the building, say what you want about it, it's not cowardly."

63. Roy, J. (2015). Lizz Winstead, *Daily Show* creator, on women in comedy and the end of the Jon Stewart era. *The Cut*. August 6. https://www.thecut.com/2015/08/daily-show-creator-on-the-end-of-the-stewart-era.html.

64. Roy, Lizz Winstead, *Daily Show* creator, on women in comedy and the end of the Jon Stewart era.

65. Jones, *Entertaining politics*, 48.

66. Baym, G. (2010). *From Cronkite to Colbert: The evolution of broadcast news.* Boulder, CO: Paradigm.

67. Baym, *From Cronkite to Colbert*, 121.

68. Hagan, J. (2012). "It Won't Hurt You. It's Vapor." *New York Magazine*, April 6. http://nymag.com/news/features/bill-maher-2012-4/.

69. Jones, *Entertaining politics*.

70. Young, D. G. (2008). *The Daily Show* as the new journalism: In their own words. In J. Baumgartner & J. Morris (eds.), *Laughing matters: Humor and American politics in the Media Age*, 241–259. New York: Routledge, 252.

71. Young, D. G. (2008). *The Daily Show* as the new journalism, 253.

72. *Nightline* (2004). July 28.

73. *Nightline* (2004). July 28.

74. *Newhouse School Forum with Jon Stewart* (2004). C-Span. October 14.

75. *The Daily Show with Jon Stewart* (2004). August 23. http://www.cc.com/video-clips/qsowxe/the-daily-show-with-jon-stewart-kerry-controversy. See Young, D. G. (2008). The *Daily Show* as the new journalism, 247–248.

76. Jones, *Entertaining politics*, 75.

77. "The Colbert Report" wins Emmy for Outstanding Variety Series (2013). *Huffington Post*. September 22. https://www.huffingtonpost.com/2013/09/22/colbert-report-emmy-win-2013_n_3966008.html?ir=Entertainment.

78. Gross, T. (2012). Colbert: "Re-becoming" the nation we always were. *Fresh Air*. NPR. October 4. https://www.npr.org/2012/10/04/162304439/colbert-re-becoming-the-nation-we-always-were.

79. "The Colbert Report" wins Emmy for Outstanding Variety Series.

80. Weprin, A. (2015). Jon Stewart to serve as executive producer of Colbert's *Late Show*. Politico. September 9. https://www.politico.com/media/story/2015/09/jon-stewart-to-serve-as-executive-producer-of-colberts-late-show-004106.

81. Stewart, Jon (2002). Interview. *Larry King Live*. March 22. http://transcripts.cnn.com/TRANSCRIPTS/0203/22/lkl.00.html.

CHAPTER 4

1. Test, G. A. (1991). *Satire: Spirit and art*. Gainesville: University Press of Florida.
2. Test, *Satire*, 5.
3. Caufield, R. (2008). The influence of "infoenterpropagainment": Exploring the power of political satire as a distinct form of political humor. In J. C. Baumgartner & J. S. Morris (eds.), *Laughing matters: Humor and American politics in the Media Age*, 3–20. New York: Routledge, 10.
4. Bergson, H. (1911). *Laughter: An essay on the meaning of the comic*. London: Macmillan, 96.
5. Koestler, A. (1964). *The act of creation*. London: Hutchinson.
6. Koestler, *The act of creation*, 35.
7. Martin, R. A. (2007). *Psychology of humor: An integrative approach*. Burlington, MA: Elsevier Academic Press.
8. Schmidt, S. R. (2002). The humour effect: Differential processing and privileged retrieval. *Memory*, 10(2), 127–138.
   Eisend, M. (2009). A meta-analysis of humor in advertising. *Journal of the Academy of Marketing Science*, 37(2), 191–203.
   Blanc, N., & Brigaud, E. (2014). Humor in print health advertisements: Enhanced attention, privileged recognition, and persuasiveness of preventive messages. *Health Communication*, 29(7), 669–677. Strick, M., Holland, R. W., Van Baaren, R., & Van Knippenberg, A. (2009). Humor in the eye tracker: Attention capture and distraction from context cues. *Journal of General Psychology: Experimental, Psychological, and Comparative Psychology*, 137(1), 37–48.
9. Kant, E. (1951). *Critique of judgement* (1790). Trans. J. H. Bernard. New York: Hafner.
10. Sweet, J. (ed.) (1978). *Something wonderful right away*. New York: Avon Books, xxxix.
11. Bergson, *Laughter*, 127.
12. Griffin, D. H. (1994). *Satire: A critical reintroduction*. Lexington: University Press of Kentucky, 36.
13. Simpson, P. (2003). *On the discourse of satire: Towards a stylistic model of satirical humour*. Vol. 2. Amsterdam: John Benjamins, 52.
14. Colbert, Stephen (2005). Interview. *Fresh Air*. NPR. December 5.
15. Burgers, C., van Mulken, M., & Schellens, P. J. (2012). Type of evaluation and marking of irony: The role of perceived complexity and comprehension. *Journal of Pragmatics*, 44(3), 231–242.
16. Burgers, van Mulken, & Schellens, Type of evaluation and marking of irony.
17. Children do not comprehend irony. At least not until they are about ten years old (it's a rather sophisticated form of communication, which I will discuss in the coming pages). Prior to your child's tenth birthday, you'll only find yourself frustrated, as I did when used the "Go ahead! Leave your dirty plates on the table for me to clear! I'm only here to do your bidding, after all" approach with my

then five-year-old son. He looked at me for a second, paused, and said, "Thanks Mom," before retreating to his toys again.

18. Meyer, J. C. (2000). Humor as a double-edged sword: Four functions of humor in communication. *Communication Theory*, 10(3), 310–331.

19. Howrigan, D. P., & MacDonald, K. B. (2008). Humor as a mental fitness indicator. *Evolutionary Psychology*, 6(4), doi: 147470490800600411.

20. Greenwald, A. G. (1990). What cognitive representations underlie social attitudes? *Bulletin of the Psychonomic Society*, 28(3), 254–260.

21. Schmidt, S. R. (2002). The humour effect: Differential processing and privileged retrieval. *Memory*, 10(2), 127–138. Eisend, A meta-analysis of humor in advertising. Blanc, N., & Brigaud, E. (2014). Humor in print health advertisements: Enhanced attention, privileged recognition, and persuasiveness of preventive messages. *Health Communication*, 29(7), 669–677.

22. Nabi, R. L., Moyer-Gusé, E., & Byrne, S. (2007). All joking aside: A serious investigation into the persuasive effect of funny social issue messages. *Communication Monographs*, 74(1), 29–54. doi: 10.1080/03637750701196896.

23. Young, D. G. (2008). The privileged role of the late-night joke: Exploring humor's role in disrupting argument scrutiny. *Media Psychology*, 11(1), 119–142. doi: 10.1080/15213260701837073.

24. Coulson, S., & Kutas, M. (2001). Getting it: Human event-related brain response to jokes in good and poor comprehenders. *Neuroscience Letters*, 316, 71.

25. Coulson & Kutas, Getting it, 74.

26. Coulson, S., & Lovett, C. (2004). Handedness, hemispheric asymmetry, and joke comprehension. *Cognitive Brain Research*, 19, 277.

27. Chan, Y. C., Chou, T. L., Chen, H. C., & Liang, K. C. (2012). Segregating the comprehension and elaboration processing of verbal jokes: An fMRI study. *NeuroImage*, 61(4), 899–906, 904. doi: 2012.03.052.

28. Coulson, S., & Williams, R. F. (2005). Hemispheric asymmetries and joke comprehension. *Neuropsychologia*, 43, 128.

29. Fiske, S. T., & Taylor, S. E. (2013). *Social cognition: From brains to culture.* Los Angeles: Sage.

30. Graesser, A., & Mandler, G. (1978). Limited processing capacity constrains the storage of unrelated sets of words and retrieval from natural categories. *Journal of Experimental Psychology: Human Learning & Memory*, 4, 86–100.

31. Or just try to have a coherent phone conversation while your kid is in the room with you.

32. Polk, J., Young, D. G., & Holbert, R. L. (2009). Humor complexity and political influence: An elaboration likelihood approach to the effects of humor type in the *Daily Show* with Jon Stewart. *Atlantic Journal of Communication*, 17(4), 202–219. doi: 10.1080/15456870903210055.

33. LaMarre, H. L., & Walther, W. (2013). Ability matters: Testing the differential effects of political news and late-night political comedy on cognitive responses

and the role of ability in micro-level opinion formation. *International Journal of Public Opinion Research*, 25(3), 303–322.

34. Boukes, M., Boomgaarden, H. G., Moorman, M., & de Vreese, C. H. (2015). At odds: Laughing and thinking? The appreciation, processing, and persuasiveness of political satire. *Journal of Communication*, 65(5), 721–744.

35. Bergen, B., & Binsted, K. (2003). The cognitive linguistics of scalar humor. *Language, Culture, and Mind*, 79–92.

CHAPTER 5

1. Comprehending the joke does *not* require that you comprehend it in the way the speaker intended you to. It's possible to "make sense of a joke" on your own in a way that is inconsistent with the speaker's intended meaning. More on this later.

2. Wu, Z. (2013). The laughter-eliciting mechanism of humor. *English Linguistics Research*, 2(1), 52–63.

3. Wu, The laughter-eliciting mechanism of humor, 57.

4. Berlyne, D. E. (1960). Conflict, arousal, and curiosity. New York: McGraw Hill. doi: 10.1037/11164–000. McGhee, P. E. (1976). Sex differences in children's humor. *Journal of Communication*, 26(3), 176–189.

5. Dunbar, R. I. M., Launay, J., & Curry, O. (2016). The complexity of jokes is limited by cognitive constraints on mentalizing. *Human Nature*, 27(2), 130–140.

6. Dunbar, Launay, & Curry, The complexity of jokes is limited by cognitive constraints on mentalizing, 136.

7. Attardo, S. (2009). Salience of incongruities in humorous texts and their resolution. In E. Chrzanowska-Kluezewska & G. Szpila (eds.), *In search of (non) sense*. Cambridge: Cambridge Scholoars Publishing.

8. Attardo, Salience of incongruities in humorous texts and their resolution, 165–166.

9. Brownell, H. H., Potter, H. H., Bihrle, A. M., & Gardner, H. (1986). Inference deficits in right brain-damaged patients. *Brain and Language*, 27(2), 310–321. Dagge, M., & Hartje, W. (1985). Influence of contextual complexity on the processing of cartoons by patients with unilateral lesions. *Cortex*, 21(4), 607–616. Shammi, P., & Stuss, D. T. (1999). Humour appreciation: A role of the right frontal lobe. *Brain*, 122(4), 657–666.

10. Brownell et al., Inference deficits in right brain-damaged patients.

11. Giora, R., & Fein, O. (1999). Irony: Context and salience. *Metaphor and Symbol*, 14(4), 241–257.Giora, R., Fein, O., & Schwartz, T. (1998). Irony: Grade salience and indirect negation. *Metaphor and Symbol*, 13(2), 83–101.

12. Wang, A. T., Lee, S. S., Sigman, M., & Dapretto, M. (2006). Neural basis of irony comprehension in children with autism: The role of prosody and context. *Brain*, 129(4), 932–943. Wang, A. T., Lee, S. S., Sigman, M., & Dapretto, M. (2007).

Reading affect in the face and voice: Neural correlates of interpreting communicative intent in children and adolescents with autism spectrum disorders. *Archives of General Psychiatry, 64*(6), 698–708.

13. Wang et al., Reading affect in the face and voice, 698.

14. Cacioppo, J. T., & Petty, R. E. (1982). The need for cognition. *Journal of Personality and Social Psychology, 42*(1), 116.

15. The following is a sample of the items typically used to create the need for cognition measure, taken from Cacioppo and Petty's original scale: *I would prefer complex to simple problems. I like to have the responsibility of handling a situation that requires a lot of thinking. I really enjoy a task that involves coming up with new solutions to problems. I would prefer a task that is intellectual, difficult, and important to one that is somewhat important but does not require much thought.* The scale also includes items that are measured in reverse. If an individual strongly agreed with these items, it indicates a *lower* need for cognition: *I would rather do something that requires little thought than something that is sure to challenge my thinking abilities. I try to anticipate and avoid situations where there is a likely chance I will have to think in depth about something. I prefer to think about small, daily projects to long-term ones. I like tasks that require little thought once I've learned them. I feel relief rather than satisfaction after completing a task that required a lot of mental effort. It's enough for me that something gets the job done; I don't care how or why it works. Thinking is not my idea of fun.*

16. Cacioppo, J. T., Petty, R. E., Feinstein, J. A., & Jarvis, W. B. G. (1996). Dispositional differences in cognitive motivation: The life and times of individuals varying in need for cognition. *Psychological Bulletin, 119*(2), 197.

17. Cacioppo et al., Dispositional differences in cognitive motivation, 197.

18. For a review, see Cacioppo et al., Dispositional differences in cognitive motivation, 197.

19. Zhang, Y. (1996). Responses to humorous advertising: The moderating effect of need for cognition. *Journal of Advertising, 25*(1), 15–32.

20. Mayer, J. M., Peev, P., & Kumar, P. (2016). Contingent effects of humor type and cognitive style on consumer attitudes. In *Let's get engaged! Crossing the threshold of marketing's engagement era*, 739–751. Springer International.

21. From Thorson, J. A., & Powell, F. C. (1993). Development and validation of a multidimensional sense of humor scale. *Journal of Clinical Psychology, 49*(1), 13–23.

22. Young, D. G., Bagozzi, B. E., Goldring, A., Poulsen, S., & Drouin, E. (2017). Psychology, political ideology, and humor appreciation: Why is satire so liberal? The psychology of popular media culture. doi: 10.1037/ppm0000157.

23. Ruch, W., & Hehl, F. J. (1993). Humour appreciation and needs: Evidence from questionnaire, self-, and peer-rating data. *Personality and Individual Differences, 15*(4), 433–445.

24. Ruch & Hehl, Humour appreciation and needs, 435.

25. Ruch & Hehl, Humour appreciation and needs, 434.

26. Ruch & Hehl, Humour appreciation and needs, 443.

27. Apter, M. J. (ed.) (2001). *Motivational styles in everyday life: A guide to reversal theory.* Washington, DC: American Psychological Association. Apter, M. J. (2007). *Reversal theory: The dynamics of motivation, emotion and personality.* 2nd ed. Oxford: Oneworld.

28. Zillmann, D., & Cantor, J. R. (1976). A disposition theory of humor and mirth. In *Humor and laughter: Theory, research, and application*, 93–115.

29. Becker, A. B. (2014). Humiliate my enemies or mock my friends? Applying disposition theory of humor to the study of political parody appreciation and attitudes toward candidates. *Human Communication Research*, 40(2), 137–160.

30. Thomas, C. A., & Esses, V. M. (2004). Individual differences in reactions to sexist humor. *Group Processes & Intergroup Relations*, 7(1), 89–100.

31. Thomas & Esses, Individual differences in reactions to sexist humor, 89.

32. Zillmann & Cantor, A disposition theory of humor and mirth.

33. Zillmann, & Cantor, A disposition theory of humor and mirth, 93.

34. Blake, A. (2017). Trump's continued, not-so-subtle suggestion of violence. *Washington Post.* July 28. https://www.washingtonpost.com/news/the-fix/wp/2017/07/28/president-trump-encourages-violence-yet-again-this-time-by-police/?utm_term=.db0318935904.

35. Manchester, J. (2017). Long Island police department responds to Trump: We don't tolerate roughing up prisoners. The Hill. July 28. http://thehill.com/blogs/blog-briefing-room/news/344402-long-island-police-department-responds-to-trump-we-dont.

36. Giora & Fein, Irony. Giora, Fein, & Schwartz, Irony.

37. Giora & Fein, Irony.

38. Seignovert, R. (2016). *De qui se moque-t-on.* Paris: Opportun.

39. Richardson, B., & Beck, P. (2007). The flow of political information: Personal discussants, the media, and partisans. In R. Gunther, J. Montero, & H. Puhle (eds.), *Democracy, intermediation, and voting on four continents*, 183–207. New York: Oxford University Press.

40. Stroud, N. J. (2011). *Niche news: The politics of news choice.* Oxford University Press on Demand.

41. Lear, Norman (2012). Interview. Chautauqua Institution. September 14. https://www.youtube.com/watch?v=FXAMWxYgBjk.

42. Vidmar, N., & Rokeach, M. (1974). Archie Bunker's bigotry: A study in selective perception and exposure. *Journal of Communication*, 24(1), 36–47.

43. Vidmar & Rokeach, Archie Bunker's bigotry, 46.

44. LaMarre, H. L., Landreville, K. D., & Beam, M. A. (2009). The irony of satire. *International Journal of Press/Politics*, 14(2), 212–231. doi: 10.1177/1940161208330904.

45. (2016). *Late Show* host says he has finally found his post–*Colbert Report* voice. *Fresh Air*. NPR. November 2. https://www.npr.org/2016/11/02/500303201/late-show-host-stephen-colbert-says-hes-finally-found-his-post-report-voice.

46. *Late Show* host says he has finally found his post–*Colbert Report* voice.

CHAPTER 6

1. Fechner, G. (1876). *Vorschule der Aesthetik*. Leipzig: Breitkopf & Hartel.

2. Palmer, S. E., Schloss, K. B., & Sammartino, J. (2013). Visual aesthetics and human preference. *Annual Review of Psychology*, 64, 82.

3. Palmer, Schloss, & Sammartino, Visual aesthetics and human preference, 82.

4. Zhang, Y. (1996). The effect of humor in advertising: An individual-difference perspective. *Psychology & Marketing*, 13(6),1–545.

5. Haugtvedt, C. P., Petty, R. E., & Cacioppo, J. T. (1992). Need for cognition and advertising: Understanding the role of personality variables in consumer behavior. *Journal of Consumer Psychology*, 1(3), 239–260.

6. Stokmans, M. J. (2003). How heterogeneity in cultural tastes is captured by psychological factors: A study of reading fiction. *Poetics*, 31(5–6), 423–439. Webster, D. M., & Kruglanski, A. W. (1997). Cognitive and social consequences of the need for cognitive closure. *European Review of Social Psychology*, 8(1), 133–173.

7. Webster, D. M., & Kruglanski, A. W. (1994). Individual differences in need for cognitive closure. *Journal of Personality and Social Psychology*, 67(6), 1049.

8. Kruglanski, A. W., Atash, M. N., De Grada, E., Mannetti, L., & Pierro, A. (2013). Need for Closure Scale (NFC). *Measurement Instrument Database for the Social Sciences*. www.midss.ie.

9. Kruglanski, A. W., Pierro, A., Mannetti, L., & De Grada, E. (2006). Groups as epistemic providers: Need for closure and the unfolding of group-centrism. *Psychological Review*, 113(1), 84.

10. Chirumbolo, A., Brizi, A., Mastandrea, S., & Mannetti, L. (2014). "Beauty is no quality in things themselves": Epistemic motivation affects implicit preferences for art. *PloS One*, 9(10), e110323.

11. Ostrofsky, J., & Shobe, E. (2015). The relationship between need for cognitive closure and the appreciation, understanding, and viewing times of realistic and nonrealistic figurative paintings. *Empirical Studies of the Arts*, 33(1), 106–113.

12. Chamorro-Premuzic, T., Reimers, S., Hsu, A., & Ahmetoglu, G. (2009). Who art thou? Personality predictors of artistic preferences in a large UK sample: The importance of openness. *British Journal of Psychology*, 100(3), 501–516, 501.

13. Wiersema, D. V., Van Der Schalk, J., & van Kleef, G. A. (2012). Who's afraid of red, yellow, and blue? Need for cognitive closure predicts aesthetic preferences. *Psychology of Aesthetics, Creativity, and the Arts*, 6(2), 168–174.

14. Wiersema, Van Der Schalk, & van Kleef, Who's afraid of red, yellow, and blue, 169.

15. Adorno, T. W., Frenkel-Brunswik, E., Levinson, D. J., & Sanford, R. N. (1950). *The authoritarian personality*. New York: Harper & Row.

16. Jost, J. T., Glaser, J., Kruglanski, A. W., & Sulloway, F. J. (2003). Political conservatism as motivated social cognition. *Psychological Bulletin*, 129(3), 339–375. Jost, J. T., Federico, C. M., & Napier, J. L. (2009). Political ideology: Its structure, functions, and elective affinities. *Annual Review of Psychology*, 60(1), 307–337. Leone, L., & Chirumbolo, A. (2008). Conservatism as motivated avoidance of affect: Need for affect scales predict conservatism measures. *Journal of Research in Personality*, 42(3), 755–762. Sargent, M. J. (2004). Less thought, more punishment: Need for cognition predicts support for punitive responses to crime. *Personality and Social Psychology Bulletin*, 30(11), 1485–1493. Stern, C., West, T. V., Jost, J. T., & Rule, N. O. (2012). The politics of Gaydar: Ideological differences in the use of gendered cues in categorizing sexual orientation. *Journal of Personality and Social Psychology*. December 31. doi: 10.1177/0146167204264481.

17. Sargent, Less thought, more punishment.

18. Sargent, Less thought, more punishment.

19. Stern et al., The politics of Gaydar.

20. Stern et al., The politics of Gaydar.

21. Amodio, D. M., Jost, J. T., Master, S. L., & Yee, C. M. (2007). Neurocognitive correlates of liberalism and conservatism. *Nature Neuroscience*, 10(10), 1246; Anderson, C. J., & Singer, M. M. (2008). The sensitive left and the impervious right: Multilevel models and the politics of inequality, ideology, and legitimacy in Europe. *Comparative Political Studies*, 41(4–5), 564–599. Jost, Federico, & Napier, Political ideology. Kemmelmeier, M. (1997). Need for closure and political orientation among German university students. *Journal of Social Psychology*, 137(6), 787–789.

22. Chirumbolo, A. (2002). The relationship between need for cognitive closure and political orientation: The mediating role of authoritarianism. *Personality and Individual Differences*, 32(4), 603–610. Ksiazkiewicz, A., Ludeke, S., & Krueger, R. (2016). The role of cognitive style in the link between genes and political ideology. *Political Psychology*, 37(6), 761–776. Onraet, E., Van Hiel, A., Roets, A., & Cornelis, I. (2011). The closed mind: "Experience" and "cognition" aspects of openness to experience and need for closure as psychological bases for right-wing attitudes. *European Journal of Personality*, 25(3), 184–197.

23. Jost et al., Political conservatism as motivated social cognition.

24. Jones, P. E., Brewer, P. R., Young, D. G., Lambe, J. L., & Hoffman, L. H. (2017). Explaining public opinion toward transgender people, rights, and candidates. *Public Opinion Quarterly*, 5.

25. Jones et al., Explaining public opinion toward transgender people, rights, and candidates, 5.

26. Jost et al., Political conservatism as motivated social cognition.

27. Jost et al., Political conservatism as motivated social cognition.
28. Malka, A., Lelkes, Y., & Holzer, N. (2017). Rethinking the rigidity of the right model: Three suboptimal methodological practices and their implications. In J. T. Crawford & L. Jussim (eds.), *Frontiers of social psychology: Politics of social psychology*, 116–135. New York: Psychology Press.
29. Jost, J. T., & Amodio, D. M. (2012). Political ideology as motivated social cognition: Behavioral and neuroscientific evidence. *Motivation and Emotion*, 36(1), 55–64.
30. Kanai, R., Feilden, T., Firth, C., & Rees, G. (2011). Political orientations are correlated with brain structure in young adults. *Current Biology*, 21(8), 677–680.
31. Jost et al., Political conservatism as motivated social cognition.
32. Jost & Amodio, Political ideology as motivated social cognition.
33. Amodio, D. M., Jost, J. T., Master, S. L., & Yee, C. M. (2007). Neurocognitive correlates of liberalism and conservatism. *Nature Neuroscience*, 10(10), 1246.
34. Kanai et al., Political orientations are correlated with brain structure in young adults.
35. Jost & Amodio, Political ideology as motivated social cognition, 61.
36. Jost et al., Political conservatism as motivated social cognition.
37. Fleischhauer, M., Enge, S., Brocke, B., Ullrich, J., Strobel, A., & Strobel, A. (2010). Same or different? Clarifying the relationship of need for cognition to personality and intelligence. *Personality and Social Psychology Bulletin*, 36(1), 82–96.
38. Hetherington, M., & Weiler, J. (2018). *Prius or pickup? How the answers to four simple questions explain America's great divide*. New York: Houghton Mifflin Harcourt.
39. Hetherington & Weiler, *Prius or pickup*, 14.
40. Schaller, M., & Duncan, L. A. (2007). The behavioral immune system: Its evolution and social psychological implications. In J. Forgas, M. G. Haselton, & W. von Hippel (eds.), *Sydney symposium of social psychology. Evolution and the social mind: Evolutionary psychology and social cognition*, 293–307. New York: Routledge. Schaller, M., & Park, J. H. (2011). The behavioral immune system (and why it matters). *Current Directions in Psychological Science*, 20(2), 99–103.
41. Oxley, D. R., Smith, K. B., Alford, J. R., Hibbing, M. V., Miller, J. L., Scalora, M., Hatemi, P., & Hibbing, J. (2008). Political attitudes vary with physiological traits. *Science*, 321(5896), 1668.
42. Oxley et al., Political attitudes vary with physiological traits.
43. Inbar, Y., Pizarro, D. A., & Bloom, P. (2009). Conservatives are more easily disgusted than liberals. *Cognition and Emotion*, 23, 714–725. Inbar, Y., Pizarro, D., Iyer, R., & Haidt, J. (2012). Disgust sensitivity, political conservatism, and voting. *Social Psychological and Personality Science*, 3(5), 537–544.
44. Rozin, P., Haidt, J., & McCauley, C. R. (2008). Disgust. In M. Lewis & J. Haviland (eds.), *Handbook of emotions*, 3rd ed., 757–776. New York: Guilford Press.

45. Haidt, J., Rozin, P., McCauley, C., & Imada, S. (1997). Body, psyche, and culture: The relationship of disgust to morality. *Psychology and Developing Societies*, 9, 107–131.

46. Inbar, Y., Pizarro, D., Iyer, R., & Haidt, J. (2012). Disgust sensitivity, political conservatism, and voting. *Social Psychological and Personality Science*, 3(5), 537–544.

47. Navarrete, C. D., & Fessler, D. M. T. (2006). Disease avoidance and ethnocentrism: The effects of disease vulnerability and disgust sensitivity on intergroup attitudes. *Evolution and Human Behavior*, 27, 270–282.

48. Terrizzi, J. A., Jr., Shook, N. J., & Ventis, W. L. (2010). Disgust: A predictor of social conservatism and prejudicial attitudes toward homosexuals. *Personality and individual differences*, 49(6), 590.

49. Terrizzi, Shook, & Ventis, Disgust, 590.

50. Aarøe, L., Petersen, M. B., & Arceneaux, K. (2017). The behavioral immune system shapes political intuitions: Why and how individual differences in disgust sensitivity underlie opposition to immigration. *American Political Science Review*, 111(2), 277–294.

51. Aarøe, Petersen, & Arceneaux, The behavioral immune system shapes political intuitions, 285.

52. Aarøe, Petersen, & Arceneaux, The behavioral immune system shapes political intuitions, 285.

53. Napier, J. L., Huang, J., Vonasch, A. J., & Bargh, J. A. (2018). Superheroes for change: Physical safety promotes socially (but not economically) progressive attitudes among conservatives. *European Journal of Social Psychology*, 48(2), 187–195.

54. Napier et al., Superheroes for change.

55. See Kruglanski, A. W. (1990). Lay epistemic theory in social-cognitive psychology. *Psychological Inquiry*, 1(3), 181–197.

56. Alford, J. R., Funk, C. L., & Hibbing, J. R. (2005). Are political orientations genetically transmitted? *American Political Science Review*, 99(2), 153–167.

57. Ksiazkiewicz, Ludeke, & Krueger, The role of cognitive style in the link between genes and political ideology.

58. Ksiazkiewicz, Ludeke, & Krueger, The role of cognitive style in the link between genes and political ideology, 767.

59. Alford, Funk, & Hibbing, Are political orientations genetically transmitted?

60. Alford, Funk, & Hibbing, Are political orientations genetically transmitted?, 165.

61. Alford, Funk, & Hibbing, Are political orientations genetically transmitted?, 163.

62. Smith, K. B., Oxley, D. R., Hibbing, M. V., Alford, J. R., & Hibbing, J. R. (2011). Linking genetics and political attitudes: Reconceptualizing political ideology. *Political Psychology*, 32(3), 369–397.

63. Smith et al., Linking genetics and political attitudes.

64. Smith et al., Linking genetics and political attitudes.

65. Kruglanski, A. W., & Mayseless, O. (1988). Contextual effects in hypothesis testing: The role of competing alternatives and epistemic motivations. *Social Cognition*, 6(1), 1–20. Ford, T. E., & Kruglanski, A. W. (1995). Effects of epistemic motivations on the use of accessible constructs in social judgment. *Personality and Social Psychology Bulletin*, 21(9), 950–962.

66. Ford & Kruglanski, Effects of epistemic motivations on the use of accessible constructs in social judgment, 953.

67. Ford & Kruglanski, Effects of epistemic motivations on the use of accessible constructs in social judgment, 959.

68. The worst part about this tendency: I am a bad judge of character. The people who I am most drawn to at first glance are often hucksters. And the people I'm sort of suspicious of at first, often end up becoming some of my closest friends over time.

69. Webster & Kruglanski, Cognitive and social consequences of the need for cognitive closure.

70. Dwyer, M. M., & Peters, C. K. (2004). The benefits of study abroad. *Transitions Abroad*, 37(5), 56–58.
    Zimmermann, J., & Neyer, F. J. (2013). Do we become a different person when hitting the road? Personality development of sojourners. *Journal of Personality and Social Psychology*, 105(3), 515.

71. Roche, M. W. (2010). *Why choose the liberal arts?* Notre Dame, IN: University of Notre Dame Press.

CHAPTER 7

1. Interview with George Schlatter (2017). WTF with Mark Maron. September 21. Episode 848. http://www.wtfpod.com/podcast/episode-848-george-schlatter.

2. Wilson, G. D., Ausman, J., & Mathews, T. R. (1973). Conservatism and art preferences. *Journal of Personality and Social Psychology*, 25(2), 286.

3. Feist, G. J., & Brady, T. R. (2004). Openness to experience, non-conformity, and the preference for abstract art. *Empirical Studies of the Arts*, 22(1), 77–89.

4. Feist & Brady, Openness to experience, non-conformity, and the preference for abstract art, 77.

5. Hibbing, J. R., Smith, K. B., & Alford, J. R. (2013). *Predisposed: Liberals, conservatives, and the biology of political differences.* New York: Routledge.

6. Hibbing, Smith, & Alford, *Predisposed.*

7. Hibbing, Smith, & Alford, *Predisposed*, 94.

8. Hibbing, Smith, & Alford, *Predisposed.*

9. Smith, K. (2018). Vexation in *Annihilation*. *National Review*. February 25. https://www.nationalreview.com/2018/02/annihilation-film-review-science-fiction-puzzler/.

10. Smith, Vexation in *Annihilation*.

11. Smith, Vexation in *Annihilation*.

12. Romain, L. (2018). The "Shimmer" and ending of *Annihilation* explained. Nerdist. February 26. https://nerdist.com/annihilation-shimmer-ending-explained/.

13. Van Hiel, A., & Mervielde, I. (2004). Openness to experience and boundaries in the mind: Relationships with cultural and economic conservative beliefs. *Journal of Personality*, 72(4), 659–686.

14. Hartmann, E. (1991). *Boundaries in the mind: A new psychology of personality differences*. New York: Basic Books.

15. Hartmann, *Boundaries in the mind*. As cited in Van Hiel & Mervielde, Openness to experience and boundaries in the mind.

16. Van Hiel & Mervielde, Openness to experience and boundaries in the mind.

17. Van Hiel & Mervielde, Openness to experience and boundaries in the mind, 660.

18. Van Hiel & Mervielde, Openness to experience and boundaries in the mind.

19. Ruch, W., & Hehl, F. J. (1993). Humour appreciation and needs: Evidence from questionnaire, self-, and peer-rating data. *Personality and Individual Differences*, 15(4), 433–445.

20. Forabosco, G., & Ruch, W. (1994). Sensation seeking, social attitudes and humor appreciation in Italy. *Personality and Individual Differences*, 16(4), 515–528.

21. Leggitt, J. S., & Gibbs, R. W. (2000). Emotional reactions to verbal irony. *Discourse Processes*, 29(1), 1–24, 5.

22. In the years after I conducted these experiments, Louis C.K. admitted to acts of sexual harassment—especially of younger female comics. This book doesn't deal with that, but it's difficult to talk about someone like Louis C.K. and not at least acknowledge that fact.

23. Bergson, H. (1911). *Laughter: An essay on the meaning of the comic*. New York: Macmillan, 127.

24. LaMarre, H. L., Landreville, K. D., & Beam, M. A. (2009). The irony of satire. *International Journal of Press/Politics*, 14(2), 212–231. doi: 10.1177/1940161208330904.

25. Vidmar, N., & Rokeach, M. (1974). Archie Bunker's bigotry: A study in selective perception and exposure. *Journal of Communication*, 24(1), 36–47.

26. Farley, C. (2005). Dave speaks. *Time*. May 14. http://content.time.com/time/printout/0,8816,1061512,00.html.

27. Brown, K., & Youmans, W. L. (2012). Intermedia framing and intercultural communication: How other media affect American antipathy toward Al Jazeera English. *Journal of Intercultural Communication Research*, 41(2), 178.

28. Farley, Dave speaks.

29. Thorson, J. A., & Powell, F. C. (1993). Development and validation of a multidimensional sense of humor scale. *Journal of Clinical Psychology*, 49(1), 13–23.

30. Howrigan, D. P., & MacDonald, K. B. (2008). Humor as a mental fitness indicator. *Evolutionary Psychology*, 6(4). doi: 1474704908006000411.

31. Raven, J. (2003). Raven Progressive Matrices. In R. S. McCallum (ed.), *Handbook of nonverbal assessment*. Boston: Springer.

32. Misch, D. (2017). Interview with author. October 10.

33. Howrigan & MacDonald, Humor as a mental fitness indicator.

34. Dagnes, A. (2012). *A conservative walks into a bar: The politics of political humor*. New York: Palgrave Macmillan, 133

35. Dagnes, *A conservative walks into a bar*, 148.

36. Dagnes, *A conservative walks into a bar*, 147.

37. Misch, D. (2017). Interview with author. October 10.

38. Black, A. (2018). Interview with author. January 5.

39. Black, A. (2018). Interview with author. January 5.

40. Bruce, L. (1992). *How to talk dirty and influence people*. New York: Simon and Schuster.

41. Black, A. (2018). Interview with author. January 5.

42. Black, A. (2018). Interview with author. January 5.

43. Spolin, V. (1999). *Improvisation for the theater: A handbook of teaching and directing techniques*. Evanston, IL: Northwestern University Press, liii.

44. Spolin, *Improvisation for the theater*, 8.

45. Spolin, *Improvisation for the theater*, liii.

46. Spolin, *Improvisation for the theater*. Italics in original.

47. Greengross, G., & Miller, G. F. (2009). The Big Five personality traits of professional comedians compared to amateur comedians, comedy writers, and college students. *Personality and Individual Differences*, 47(2), 79–83.

48. Wagner, A. (2016). Does Trump know how to laugh? *Atlantic*. September 28. https://www.theatlantic.com/politics/archive/2016/09/does-trump-know-how-to-laugh/501875/.

49. Thrush, G. (2016). What Chuck Todd gets about Trump. Politico's off message podcast. December 30. https://www.politico.com/story/2016/12/chuck-todd-donald-trump-off-message-podcast-233066.

50. Wagner, A. (2016). Does Trump know how to laugh?

51. Libit, D. (2016). The inside story of Donald Trump's Comedy Central roast is everything you thought it would be. *Huffington Post*. October 11. http://www.huffingtonpost.com/entry/the-inside-story-of-donald-trumps-comedy-central-roast-is-everything-you-thought-it-would-be_us_57fbed42e4b0e655ea b6c191.

52. Libit, The inside story of Donald Trump's Comedy Central roast is everything you thought it would be.

53. Nave, N. N., Shifman, L., & Tenenboim-Weinblatt, K. (2018). Talking it personally: Features of successful political posts on Facebook. *Social Media and Society*, July–September, 1–12. doi: 10.1177/2056305118784771.

54. Nave, Shifman, & Tenenboim-Weinblatt, Talking it personally, 8.

CHAPTER 8

1. Berry, J. M., & Sobieraj, S. (2014). *The outrage industry: Political opinion media and the new incivility.* New York: Oxford University Press.
2. Berry & Sobieraj, *The outrage industry*, 8.
3. Berry & Sobieraj, *The outrage industry*, 47.
4. Berry & Sobieraj, *The outrage industry*, 47.
5. Berry & Sobieraj, *The outrage industry*, 133.
6. Berry & Sobieraj, *The outrage industry*, 138.
7. Berry & Sobieraj, *The outrage industry*, 44.
8. Notably, one of the few content categories in which conservative outrage did not "outrank" liberal outrage was in their use of "mockery or sarcasm," where liberal and conservative shows scored about the same.
9. Joyella, M. (2018). MSNBC's Rachel Maddow hits no. 1 with long, complicated segments viewers love. *Forbes.* December 31.
10. Berry & Sobieraj, *The outrage industry*, 8.
11. Mutz, D. C. (2015). *In-your-face politics: The consequences of uncivil media.* Princeton: Princeton University Press, 148.
12. Hetherington, M. J., & Weiler, J. D. (2009). *Authoritarianism and polarization in American politics.* Cambridge: Cambridge University Press.
13. Berry & Sobieraj, *The outrage industry*, 99.
14. Pew's 2014 American Trends Panel is a national, probability-based online panel of adults in the United States living in households. Adults who use the internet participate in the panel via self-administered Web surveys, and adults who do not use the internet participate via computer-assisted telephone interviewing or mail. The survey was administered March 19–April 29, 2014. Respondents were shown a series of programming logos in a grid format and were asked: "Please click on all of the sources that you have heard of, regardless of whether you use them or not. If you are unsure, please DO NOT click it. You can click anywhere in each of the boxes." Of those sources that the respondents indicated having heard of, they were then asked: "Please click on all of the sources that you got news from about government and politics in the past week. This includes any way that you can get the source. If you are unsure, please DO NOT click it." The responses to this item resulted in the weighted Ns reflected in figures 8.1 and 8.2. The measures of party identification and ideology were based on the standard self-report.
15. O'Connell, M. (2013). TV ratings: MSNBC falls below HLN in May, Rachel Maddow hits lows. *Hollywood Reporter.* May 29. https://www.hollywoodreporter.com/live-feed/tv-ratings-msnbc-falls-below-559923.
16. "The Daily Show" and "The Colbert Report" finish 1Q 2013 as #1 and #2 among adults 18–49 and all key young demos. (2013). Futon Critic. April 4. http://www.thefutoncritic.com/ratings/2013/04/04/the-daily-show-and-the-colbert

-report-finish-1q-2013-as-number-1-and-number-2-among-adults-18-49-and-all
-key-young-demos-795303/20130404comedycentral01/.

17. The 2010 Media Consumption Survey, sponsored by the Pew Research Center,
obtained telephone interviews with a nationally representative sample of 3,006
adults living in the continental United States. The survey was conducted by
Princeton Survey Research, Associates International. The interviews were conducted in English by Princeton Data Source, June 8–28, 2010. Viewing estimates were obtained by asking respondents: "Now I'd like to ask you about
some television and radio programs. How often do you . . . [Watch/listen to X],
regularly, sometimes, hardly ever or never?" Ideology was asked with: "In general, would you describe your political views as . . . Very conservative, conservative, moderate, liberal, or very liberal?" Party identification was obtained with:
"In politics TODAY, do you consider yourself a Republican, Democrat or
Independent?" Percentages are based on weighted sample statistics.

18. March 2018 University of Delaware Poll conducted by the University of
Delaware's Center for Political Communication in collaboration with RABA
Research (N = 608), March 21–22, 2018. In certain analyses, due to missing
values and listwise deletion, the sample size drops to 601.

19. O'Connell, M. (2018). Maddow tops cable news demo ratings in January, but Fox
retains overall wins. *Hollywood Reporter.* January 30. https://www.hollywoodreporter
.com/news/cable-news-ratings-msnbcs-maddow-leads-but-fox-news
-is-still-top-1080124.

20. The 2015 data are based on a national online sample obtained by Qualtrics pan-
els in March 2015, designed to acquire 45 percent conservative, 45 percent liberal, and 10 percent moderate respondents to facilitate comparisons between
subgroups (N = 305). The 2018 data are from the University of Delaware Poll
conducted by the University of Delaware's Center for Political Communication
in collaboration with RABA Research (N = 608), March 21–22, 2018. In certain
analyses, due to missing values and listwise deletion, the sample size
drops to 601.

21. The tolerance for ambiguity measure is based on a measure from Kruglanski,
A. W., Peri, N., & Zakai, D. (1991). Interactive effects of need for closure and
initial confidence on social information seeking. *Social Cognition,* 9(2), 127–148.
Tolerance for ambiguity was measured with four items in 2015, coded from
strongly agree (1) to strongly disagree (5): I don't like situations that are uncertain; I dislike questions which could be answered in many different ways; When
a book or film ends and it's not clear what happens to the characters, I feel
upset; It's frustrating to listen to someone who cannot make up his or her mind.
Alpha = .60, *M* = 2.45, *SD* = .71. Measured with three items in 2018, coded from
strongly agree (1) to strongly disagree (5): I don't like situations that are uncertain; It's frustrating to listen to someone who cannot make up his or her mind;
When faced with a problem, I usually see the one best solution very quickly.

Alpha = .49, *M* = 2.48, *SD* = .65. Correlations were run between "Tolerance for Ambiguity" and self-reported viewing of various programs. Results for 2015: *Daily Show* with Jon Stewart (r = .21, $p < .001$), *Colbert Report* (r = .24, $p < .001$), *Oliver* (r = .15, $p < .01$), *O'Reilly* (r = −.04, $p < $ = n.s.), *Limbaugh* (r = .1, p = n.s.).

22. Results for 2018: *The Daily Show* with Trevor Noah (r = .09, $p < .04$), *The Late Show* with Stephen Colbert (r = .09, $p < .03$), *The Rachel Maddow Show* (r = .08, $p < .05$), *Hannity* (r = −.09, $p < .04$), *The Rush Limbaugh Show* (r = −.05, p = n.s.). *The Late Show* with Stephen Colbert (r = .1, $p < .01$), *The Rachel Maddow Show* (r = .1, $p < .02$), *Hannity* (r = −.06, p = n.s.), *The Rush Limbaugh Show* (r = −.05, p = n.s.).

23. In the model predicting exposure to Colbert (B for Tolerance for Ambiguity = .30, SE = .1, $p < .004$). In the model predicting exposure to *The Daily Show* (B for Tolerance for Ambiguity = .23, SE = .11, $p < .03$).

24. In OLS Regression predicting exposure to *The O'Reilly Factor* in the face of sociodemographic and political controls (Sense of Humor B = −.28, SE = .11, $p < .01$); predicting exposure to Rush Limbaugh (Sense of Humor B = −.24, SE = .11, $p < .02$).

25. While not perfect, a statistical test called mediation analysis can help researchers understand if the correlation between psychological traits and viewing preferences *is enacted* or *articulated* through political ideology. To test whether the correlation between tolerance for ambiguity and viewing preferences was partially explained by ideology, Hayes (2018) PROCESS macro was used. Hayes, A. F. (2018). *Introduction to mediation, moderation, and conditional process analysis: A regression-based approach.* 2nd ed. New York: Guilford Press. The macro allows researchers to test whether the effect of an independent variable on a dependent variable are partially explained by some other factor (m). Based on a 95 percent confidence interval, the models were consistent with a mechanism in which the effects of the psychological trait (tolerance for ambiguity) on consumption of satire and outrage programming were significantly mediated by political ideology, as indicated by the fact that these confidence intervals did not include zero. The results of running these tests on data from both 2015 and 2018 show that the relationship of tolerance for ambiguity with exposure to satire *and* outrage was significantly mediated by political ideology.

26. I explored these propositions using the data from the University of Delaware Poll conducted by the University of Delaware's Center for Political Communication in collaboration with RABA Research (N = 608), March 21–22, 2018. Included in the models predicting each program (*The Daily Show with Trevor Noah*, *The Late Show* with Stephen Colbert, *The Rachel Maddow Show*, *Hannity*, and *The Rush Limbaugh Show*) was an interaction of tolerance for ambiguity and political ideology. The tolerance for ambiguity X ideology interaction was statistically significant in three of the five models, predicting exposure to *The Daily Show*, *Hannity*, and *The Rush Limbaugh Show*. Regression models included the following

as predictors: tolerance for ambiguity, need for cognition, party, ideology, political interest, following politics, age, education, race, and gender. Predicting exposure to *The Daily Show*, adjusted R^2. = .24. N = 601 (drop in N due to listwise deletion). Standardized Beta for the interaction of ideology X tolerance for ambiguity = −.37, $p < .01$. Predicting exposure to *Hannity*, adjusted R^2. = .28. N = 601 (drop in N due to listwise deletion). Standardized Beta for interaction = −.52, $p < .001$. Predicting exposure to *The Rush Limbaugh Show*, adjusted R^2. = .24. N = 601 (drop in N due to listwise deletion). Standardized Beta for interaction = −.37, $p < .05$. In all three cases, visual interpretations illustrate the very mechanism I've outlined throughout this section: that tolerance for ambiguity drives liberals to satire and a lack of such tolerance drives conservatives to outrage. Note that in certain analyses, due to missing values and listwise deletion, the sample size drops to 601.

27. Berry & Sobieraj, *The outrage industry*, 229.

28. Delli Carpini, M. X., & Williams, B. A. (2001). Let us infotain you: Politics in the new media age. In W. L. Bennett & R. M. Entman (eds.), *Mediated politics: Communication in the future of democracy*, 160–181. Cambridge: Cambridge University Press.

29. Delli Carpini & Williams, Let us infotain you, 163.

30. Sobieraj, S. (2017). In-person interview with author. November 22.

31. Darcy, O. (2016). Fox News host Tucker Carlson's on-air war with elitism. Business Insider. December 5. http://www.businessinsider.com/tucker-carlson -tonight-show-fox-news-2016–12.

32. Song, J. (2015). John Oliver, a "disruptive comedian." CBSNews.com. October 30. https://www.cbsnews.com/news/last-week-tonight-john-oliver-effect -american-politics-donald-trump/.

33. Griggs, B. (2015) Jon Stewart, in his own words. CNN. August 20. https://www. cnn.com/2015/08/05/entertainment/jon-stewart-wit-wisdom-feat/ index.html.

34. Gay, V. (2004). Not necessarily the news; Meet the players who will influence coverage of the 2004 campaign; You might be surprised. *Newsday*. January 14. B6.

35. Sullivan, M. (2016). Samantha Bee says her show isn't influential. Don't believe her. *Washington Post*. July 27. https://www.washingtonpost.com/lifestyle/style/ samantha-bee-to-discontented-americans-canada-is-full/2016/07/27/25b7593a -5372-11e6-bbf5-957ad17b4385_story.html?utm_term=.9801cd418d72.

36. John Oliver finds humor in the news no one wants to hear about. (2018). *Fresh Air*. NPR. March 7. https://www.npr.org/programs/fresh-air/2018/03/07/ 591487621/fresh-air-for-march-7-2018-john-oliver.

37. John Oliver finds humor in the news no one wants to hear about.

38. John Oliver finds humor in the news no one wants to hear about.

39. Black, A. (2018). Interview with author. January 5.

40. Black, A. (2018). Interview with author. January 5.

41. Baym, G. (2017). Journalism and the hybrid condition: Long-form television drama at the intersections of news and narrative. *Journalism*, 18(1), 12.

42. D'Addario, D. (2018). Shep Smith has the hardest job on Fox News. *Time*. March 15. http://time.com/longform/shepard-smith-fox-news/.

43. Sobieraj, S. (2017). Interview with author. November 22.

44. Black, A. (2018). Interview with author. January 5.

45. Black, A. (2018). Interview with author. January 5.

46. Griggs, Jon Stewart, in his own words.

47. Bloom, E. A., & Bloom, L. D. (1979). *Satire's persuasive voice*. Ithaca: Cornell University Press, 38.

48. Sullivan, E. (2018). Laura Ingraham told LeBron James to shut up and dribble; He went to the hoop. NPR. February 19. https://www.npr.org/sections/thetwo-way/2018/02/19/587097707/laura-ingraham-told-lebron-james-to-shutup-and-dribble-he-went-to-the-hoop.

49. Greenwood, M. (2018). RBC Predicts low ratings for Oscars: "Americans aren't interested in Hollywood liberals." The Hill. February 28. http://thehill.com/blogs/blog-briefing-room/news/376178-rnc-predicts-low-ratings-for-oscars-americans-arent-interested.

50. For reasons that one could probably link to the underlying psychology of liberals and conservatives discussed throughout this book.

51. University of Delaware Poll conducted by the University of Delaware's Center for Political Communication in collaboration with RABA Research (N = 608), March 21–22, 2018.

52. "Tolerance for ambiguity" items included: "When faced with a problem, I usually see the one best solution very quickly," "I don't like situations that are uncertain," and "It's frustrating to listen to someone who cannot make up his or her mind." Response options included strongly agree (coded 1), agree (coded 2), neither agree nor disagree (coded 3), disagree (coded 4), strongly disagree (coded 5). These three items were averaged to create an individual tolerance for ambiguity score for each respondent. These scores can range from 1 to 5 (M = 3.52, SD = .65) (N = 608). "Need for cognition" items included: "Thinking is not my idea of fun (reverse coded)," "I only think as hard as I have to (reverse coded)," and "I would prefer complex to simple problems." Response options included strongly disagree (coded 1), disagree (coded 2), neither agree nor disagree (coded 3), agree (coded 4), strongly agree (coded 5). These three items were averaged to create an individual need for cognition score for each respondent. These scores can range from 1 to 5 (M = 3.76, SD = .72) (N = 608). In certain analyses, due to missing values and listwise deletion, the sample size drops to 601.

53. Again, the Hayes (2018) PROCESS macro was used. Hayes, *Introduction to mediation, moderation, and conditional process analysis*. The macro allows us to test whether the effects of an independent variable (the psychological trait

tolerance for ambiguity) on a dependent variable (support for celebrity political expression) is accounted for by some other factor (political ideology). In each case, the confidence interval surrounding the coefficient did not include zero, indicating that at least part of the association between tolerance for ambiguity and support for celebrity expression was captured by political ideology.

54. Hartenstein, M. (2010). Jon Stewart's Rally to Restore Sanity drew 200,000, beating estimated attendance at Glenn Beck's. *New York Daily News*. October 31. http://www.nydailynews.com/news/national/jon-stewart-rally-restore -sanity-drew-200-000-beating-estimated-attendance-glenn-beck-article-1 .188108.

55. *Jon Stewart & Stephen Colbert Sanity/Fear Press Conference*. (2011). National Press Club. June 24. https://www.youtube.com/watch?v=jyC8h6Oq1Eo.

56. *Hannity* (2018). Fox News. May 17.

CHAPTER 9

1. Katz, E., Blumler, J. G., & Gurevitch, M. (1973). Uses and gratifications research. *Public Opinion Quarterly*, 37(4), 509–523.

2. Rubin, A. M., & Perse, E. M. (1987). Audience activity and television news gratifications. *Communication Research*, 14(1), 58–84. Feldman, L. (2013). Learning about politics from *The Daily Show*: The role of viewer orientation and processing motivations. *Mass Communication and Society*, 16(4), 586–607.

3. The 2010 Media Consumption Survey, sponsored by the Pew Research Center, obtained telephone interviews with a nationally representative sample of 3,006 adults living in the continental United States. The survey was conducted by Princeton Survey Research Associates International. The interviews were conducted in English by Princeton Data Source, June 8–28, 2010. Viewing estimates were obtained by asking respondents: "Now I'd like to ask you about some television and radio programs. How often do you . . . [Watch/listen to X], regularly, sometimes, hardly ever or never?" To capture viewer motivations, respondents were asked: "We're interested in understanding WHY people use certain media sources. For example, earlier you said that you regularly turn to [program]. Do you turn to [program] MOSTLY . . . for the latest news and headlines, for in-depth reporting, for entertainment, or for interesting views and opinions?"

4. Lee, A. M. (2013). News audiences revisited: Theorizing the link between audience motivations and news consumption. *Journal of Broadcasting & Electronic Media*, 57(3), 300–317.

5. The survey asked: "Most of us have different reasons and motivations for reading/watching/listening to the news. Thinking back to the sources you get your news from, please indicate the extent to which the following statements describe why you read/watch/listen to the news . . ." Information motivations included:

"To find out what's going on in the world; to keep up with the way your government performs; to make yourself an informed citizen; because it helps you learn about others; to gain important new information; and to fulfill your "need to know." Social motivations included: "To keep up with what other people around you may be talking about; to appear informed to those around you; because most of your friends do; to make you more sociable; to have something to talk about with others; and to feel a part of a community." Lee, News audiences revisited, 306.

6. Entertainment motivations include "because it's exciting; for laughter; because it's a habit that you have; and when there is nothing better to do." Lee, News audiences revisited, 306.

7. Operationalized by Lee as "To help you form opinions on issues; to know about other people's opinions; for views from like-minded commentators; and to expose yourself to views that are different from your own." Lee, News audiences revisited, 306.

8. ANOVA exploring ideology as a function of "viewing for interesting views and opinions": *The Daily Show with Jon Stewart* (F = 31.19, p < .001). *The Colbert Report* (F = 8.85, p < .01). Note that because only 10 respondents reported watching Colbert for in-depth reporting, the ideological leaning of this small sample is excluded from the figure.

9. ANOVA tests of "viewing for entertainment" versus viewing for other reasons: *Glenn Beck* (F = 19.63, p < .001), *The O'Reilly Factor* (F = 12.429, p < .001), *Hannity* (F = 5.21, p < .03), *The Rush Limbaugh Show* (F = 1.99, p = .16).

10. For example, ANOVA tests of ideology as a function of viewing for "in depth reporting": *Glenn Beck* (F = 12.05, p< .001), *The O'Reilly Factor* (F = 12.74, p < .001).

11. "Daily Show" viewers knowledgeable about presidential campaign (2004). Annenberg Public Policy Center of the University of Pennsylvania. September 21. https://www.annenbergpublicpolicycenter.org/daily-show-viewers -knowledgeable-about-presidential-campaign/.

12. A content analysis of 52 episodes of *The Daily Show with Jon Stewart* from 2005 shows that 46 percent of all stories and 25 percent of guest interviews covered world affairs in some way. See Brewer, P. R., & Marquardt, E. (2007). Mock news and democracy: Analyzing *The Daily Show*. *Atlantic Journal of Communication*, 15(4), 249–267.

13. What you know depends on what you watch. (2012). Fairleigh Dickinson University's PublicMind Poll. May 3. http://publicmind.fdu.edu/2012/confirmed/.

14. Young, D. G., & Tisinger, R. M. (2006). Dispelling late-night myths: News consumption among late-night comedy viewers and the predictors of exposure to various late-night shows. *Harvard International Journal of Press/Politics*, 11(3), 113–134.

15. Since these studies are typically based on observational survey data, one can't be 100 percent sure that the high rates of knowledge aren't the result of some other

trait tied up with satire viewing, but I am at least making a case that satire might help contribute to these audiences' already high knowledge base.

16. While much of this research is based on observational survey data, experimental research confirms that satire is an effective educational tool, increasing audiences' knowledge about current events. See Young, D. G., & Hoffman, L. (2012). Acquisition of current-events knowledge from political satire programming: An experimental approach. *Atlantic Journal of Communication*, 20(5), 290–304.

17. Lowrey, A. (2011). The economics of Occupy Wall Street. Slate. October 5. http://www.slate.com/articles/business/moneybox/2011/10/occupy_wall_street _says_the_top_one_1_percent_of_americans_have_.html.

18. University of Delaware Newsroom (2012). Survey: Fox News viewers least informed, most negative about Occupy Wall Street. Press release. February 15. https://www.newswise.com/articles/survey-fox-news-viewers-least-informed-most -negative-about-occupy-wall-street.

19. Jones, J. P., Baym, G., & Day, A. (2012). Mr. Stewart and Mr. Colbert go to Washington: Television satirists outside the box. *Social Research*, 79, 50.

20. Hardy, B. W., Gottfried, J. A., Winneg, K. M., & Jamieson, K. H. (2014). Stephen Colbert's civics lesson: How Colbert Super PAC taught viewers about campaign finance. *Mass Communication and Society*, 17(3), 329–353. Lamarre, H. (2013). Breaking boundaries: When parody and reality collide: Examining the effects of Colbert's Super PAC satire on issue knowledge and policy engagement across media formats. *International Journal of Communication*, 7, 394–413.

21. Hardy et al., Stephen Colbert's civics lesson.

22. Net neutrality. (2014). *Last Week Tonight*. June 1. HBO. https://www.youtube .com/watch?v=fpbOEoRrHyU.

23. Becker, A. B., & Bode, L. (2018). Satire as a source for learning? The differential impact of news versus satire exposure on net neutrality knowledge gain. *Information, Communication & Society*, 21(4), 612–625.

24. Brewer, P. R., Young, D. G., Lambe, J. L., Hoffman, L. H., & Collier, J. (2018). "Seize your moment, my lovely trolls": News, satire, and public opinion about net neutrality. *International Journal of Communication*, 12, 23.

25. Poll results. (2015). CNN. September 12. http://i2.cdn.turner.com/cnn/2015/ images/09/12/iranpoll.pdf.

26. Gettier, E. L. (1963). Is justified true belief knowledge? *Analysis*, 23(6), 121–123.

27. Mitchell, A., Gottfried, J., Barthel, M., & Sumida, N. (2018). Distinguishing between factual and opinion statements in the news. Pew Research Center. June 18. http://www.journalism.org/2018/06/18/distinguishing-between-factual-and -opinion-statements-in-the-news/.

28. Kull, S., Ramsay, C., & Lewis, E. (2003). Misperceptions, the media, and the Iraq war. *Political Science Quarterly*, 118(4), 569–598.

29. Gershkoff, A., & Kushner, S. (2005). Shaping public opinion: The 9/11-Iraq connection in the Bush administration's rhetoric. *Perspectives on Politics*, 3(3), 525–537.

30. Sanburn, J. (2011). George W. Bush and the uranium. *Time*. January 25. http://
content.time.com/time/specials/packages/article/0,28804,2044176
_2044193_2044206,00.html.

31. Rendell, S., & Broughel, T. (2003). Amplifying officials, squelching dissent. Fairness
and Accuracy in Reporting. May/June. www.fair.org/extra/0305/warstudy.html.

32. Muddiman, A., Stroud, N. J., & McCombs, M. (2014). Media fragmentation,
attribute agenda setting, and political opinions about Iraq. *Journal of Broadcasting
& Electronic Media*, 58(2), 215–233.

33. Jamieson, K. H., & Cappella, J. N. (2008). *Echo chamber: Rush Limbaugh and the
conservative media establishment*. New York: Oxford University Press.

34. Jamieson & Cappella, *Echo chamber*, 195.

35. Jamieson & Cappella, *Echo chamber*, 197.

36. Schroeder, E., & Stone, D. F. (2015). Fox News and political knowledge. *Journal
of Public Economics*, 126, 52–63.

37. Schroeder & Stone, Fox News and political knowledge, 61.

38. See, for example, Hannity's repeated unverified claims from 2017 indicating
that DNC staffer Seth Rich was murdered by the Clinton organization.

39. Even after Fox News retracted the Seth Rich story and apologized, Hannity continued to cover the conspiracy theory, stating on his radio show: "I am not
FoxNews.com," and "I retract nothing": DePaolo, J. (2017). Hannity says he feels
"so badly" for Seth Rich's family while ignoring family's pleas to quit coverage.
Mediaite. May 23. For a summary of the conspiracy theory see Guo, J. (2017).
The bonkers Seth Rich conspiracy theory, explained. Vox. May 24. https://www
.vox.com/policy-and-politics/2017/5/24/15685560/seth-rich-conspiracy
-theory-explained-fox-news-hannity.

40. See, for example, Samantha Bee's 2017 inaccurate claim that an attendee of the
Conservative Political Action Conference had a "Nazi haircut" when it was later
discovered that he actually had brain cancer. The host and her program immediately apologized, reedited the segment to delete the young man from the
video, and pulled the footage from their website. Williams, D. (2017). Samantha
Bee's apology doesn't impress cancer patient. CNN. March 10.

41. *Jon Stewart and Stephen Colbert Sanity/Fear Press Conference*. (2010). National
Press Club. October 30. https://www.youtube.com/watch?v=jyC8h6Oq1Eo.

42. McCombs, M. E., & Shaw, D. L. (1972). The agenda-setting function of mass
media. *Public Opinion Quarterly*, 36(2), 176–187.

43. Iyengar, S., & Kinder, D. R. (2010). *News that matters: Television and American
opinion*. Chicago: University of Chicago Press.

44. Feldman, L., Maibach, E. W., Roser-Renouf, C., & Leiserowitz, A. (2011). Climate
on cable: The nature and impact of global warming coverage on Fox News,
CNN, and MSNBC. *International Journal of Press/Politics*, 17(1), 3–31. Searles, K.,
& Smith, G. (2016). Who's the boss? Setting the agenda in a fragmented media
environment. *International Journal of Communication*, 10, 22.

45. Stroud, N. J. (2011). *Niche news: The politics of news choice.* New York: Oxford University Press.
46. Searles & Smith, Who's the boss?
47. Young, D. G. (2006). Late-night comedy and the salience of the candidates' caricatured traits in the 2000 election. *Mass Communication & Society, 9*(3), 339–366.
48. McCombs, M. E., & Shaw, D. L. (1993). The evolution of agenda-setting research: Twenty-five years in the marketplace of ideas. *Journal of Communication, 43*(2), 65.
49. Entman, R. M. (1993). Framing: Toward clarification of a fractured paradigm. *Journal of Communication, 43*(4), 52.
50. Haigh, M. M., & Heresco, A. (2010). Late-night Iraq: Monologue joke content and tone from 2003 to 2007. *Mass Communication and Society, 13*(2), 157–173.
51. Blake, M. (2014). John Oliver rails against cable companies over net neutrality. *Los Angeles Times.* June 2. http://www.latimes.com/entertainment/tv/showtracker/la-et-st-john-oliver-rails-against-cable-companies-over-net-neutrality-20140602-story.html.
52. 2014 survey N = 812; 2015 survey N = 744.
53. Gandy, O. H., Jr. (1980). Information in health: Subsidised news. *Media, Culture & Society, 2*(2), 103–115, 104.
54. Brewer, P. R., Young, D. G., & Morreale, M. (2013). The impact of real news about "fake news": Intertextual processes and political satire. *International Journal of Public Opinion Research, 25*(3), 323–343.
55. Young, D. G. (2004). Late-night comedy in election 2000: Its influence on candidate trait ratings and the moderating effects of political knowledge and partisanship. *Journal of Broadcasting & Electronic Media, 48*(1), 1–22.
56. Baumgartner, J., & Morris, J. S. (2006). The *Daily Show* effect: Candidate evaluations, efficacy, and American youth. *American Politics Research, 34*(3), 341–367.
57. Morris, J. S. (2009). *The Daily Show* with Jon Stewart and audience attitude change during the 2004 party conventions. *Political Behavior, 31*(1), 79–102.
58. Feldman et al., Climate on cable.
59. Feldman et al., Climate on cable.
60. Muddiman, A., Stroud, N. J., & McCombs, M. (2014). Media fragmentation, attribute agenda setting, and political opinions about Iraq. *Journal of Broadcasting & Electronic Media, 58*(2), 215–233.
61. Muddiman, Stroud, & McCombs, Media fragmentation, attribute agenda setting, and political opinions about Iraq, 224.
62. Brewer et al., "Seize your moment, my lovely trolls," 23.
63. Brewer, P. R., Lambe, J. L., & Jones, P. E. (2017). The foundations of US public opinion about campaign finance in the post–*Citizens United* era. *Election Law Journal, 16*(1), 183–195, 191.
64. Hollander, B. A. (1996). Talk radio: Predictors of use and effects on attitudes about government. *Journalism & Mass Communication Quarterly, 73*(1), 102–113.

Hollander, B. (1996). The influence of talk radio on political efficacy and participation. *Journal of Radio Studies*, 23(3). Jamieson & Cappella, *Echo chamber*.

65. Brader, T. (2005). Striking a responsive chord: How political ads motivate and persuade voters by appealing to emotions. *American Journal of Political Science*, 49, 388–405. Brader, T. (2006). *Campaigning for hearts and minds*. Chicago: University of Chicago Press.

66. Brooks, D. J., & Geer, J. (2007). Beyond negativity: The effects of incivility on the electorate. *American Journal of Political Science*, 51, 1–16.

67. Martin, P. S. (2004). Inside the black box of negative campaign effects: Three reasons why negative campaigns mobilize. *Political Psychology*, 25(4), 545–562.

68. Ellul, J. (1973). *Propaganda: The formation of men's attitudes*. New York: Vintage Books.

69. Ellul, *Propaganda*, 73.

70. Valentino, N. A., Brader, T., Groenendyk, E. W., Gregorowicz, K., & Hutchings, V. L. (2011). Election night's alright for fighting: The role of emotions in political participation. *Journal of Politics*, 73(1), 156–170.

71. Valentino et al., Election night's alright for fighting, 159.

72. Ost, D. (2004). Politics as the mobilization of anger: Emotions in movements and in power. *European Journal of Social Theory*, 7(2), 229–244.

73. Ost, D. (2004). Politics as the mobilization of anger, 238.

74. Wagner, J. (2018). Trump uses Twitter to promote video of supporters chanting "CNN sucks." *Washington Post*. August 1. https://www.washingtonpost.com/politics/trump-uses-twitter-to-promote-video-of-supporters-chanting-cnn-sucks/2018/08/01/1bf288d4-9574-11e8-810c-5fa705927d54_story.html?utm_term=.4a146f367842.

75. Cao, X., & Brewer, P. R. (2008). Political comedy shows and public participation in politics. *International Journal of Public Opinion Research*, 20(1), 90–99.

76. Baumgartner, J. C., & Lockerbie, B. (2018). Maybe it is more than a joke: Satire, mobilization, and political participation. *Social Science Quarterly*, 99(3), 1060–1074.

77. Lee, H. (2012). Communication mediation model of late-night comedy: The mediating role of structural features of interpersonal talk between comedy viewing and political participation. *Mass Communication and Society*, 15(5), 647–671.

78. Hoffman, L. H., & Young, D. G. (2011). Satire, punch lines, and the nightly news: Untangling media effects on political participation. *Communication Research Reports*, 28(2), 159–168.

79. Baumgartner & Morris, The *Daily Show* effect. Brewer, Young, & Morreale, The impact of real news about "fake news."

80. Bennett, S. E. (1997). Knowledge of politics and sense of subjective political competence: The ambiguous connection. *American Politics Research*, 25, 230–240. doi: 10.1177/1532673X9702500205. Kenski, K., & Stroud, N. J. (2006). Connections between internet use and political efficacy, knowledge, and participation.

Journal of Broadcasting & Electronic Media, 50(2), 173–192. doi: 10.1207/s15506878jobem5002_1.

81. Young, D. G., & Esralew, S. (2011). Jon Stewart a heretic? Surely you jest: Political participation and discussion among viewers of late-night comedy programming. In A. Amarasinga (ed.), *The Stewart/Colbert effect: Essays on the real impact of fake news*, 99–116. Jefferson, NC: McFarland. .

82. Young, D. G., & Tisinger, R. (2006). Dispelling late-night myths: News consumption among late-night comedy viewers and the predictors of exposure to various late-night shows. *International Journal of Press/Politics*, 11, 113–134. Xenos, M. A., & Becker, A. B. (2009). Moments of Zen: Effects of *The Daily Show* on information seeking and political learning. *Political Communication*, 26(3), 317–332.

83. Feldman, L., & Young, D. G. (2008). Late-night comedy as a gateway to traditional news: An analysis of time trends in news attention among late-night comedy viewers during the 2004 presidential primaries. *Political Communication*, 25(4), 401–422.

84. Baum, M. A. (2003). Soft news and political knowledge: Evidence of absence or absence of evidence? *Political Communication*, 20, 173–190. Baum, M. A. (2003). *Soft news goes to war*. Princeton: Princeton University Press.

85. Gamson, W. (1968). *Power and discontent*. Homewood, IL: Dorsey. See also Hollander, B. A. (1997). Fuel to the fire: Talk radio and the Gamson hypothesis. *Political Communication*, 14(3), 355–369.

86. Johnson, T. J., & Kaye, B. K. (2013). Putting out fire with gasoline: Testing the Gamson hypothesis on media reliance and political activity. *Journal of Broadcasting & Electronic Media*, 57(4), 457. Gamson, *Power and discontent*.

87. Hollander, B. A. (1996). Talk radio: Predictors of use and effects on attitudes about government. *Journalism & Mass Communication Quarterly*, 73(1), 102–113.

88. Measured with "When something is run by government, it is usually inefficient and wasteful."

89. Hollander, Talk radio.

90. Baumgartner & Morris, The *Daily Show* effect, 34.

91. Hart, R. P., & Hartelius, E. J. (2007). The political sins of Jon Stewart. *Critical Studies in Media Communication*, 24(3), 263–272.

92. Hart & Hartelius, The political sins of Jon Stewart, 270.

93. Hart & Hartelius, The political sins of Jon Stewart, 270, 267.

94. See Young, D. G. (2013). Lighten up: How satire will make American politics relevant again. *Columbia Journalism Review* (July/August): 26–28. https://archives.cjr.org/cover_story/lighten_up.php.

95. Cao & Brewer, Political comedy shows and public participation in politics; Baumgartner & Lockerbie, Maybe it is more than a joke. Lee, Communication mediation model of late-night comedy.

96. Baumgartner & Morris, The *Daily Show* effect. Becker, A. B. (2011). Political humor as democratic relief? The effects of exposure to comedy and straight news on trust and efficacy. *Atlantic Journal of Communication*, 19(5), 235–250.

97. Baumgartner & Morris, The *Daily Show* effect.

98. Heimlich, R. (2011). *Hannity fans see bias in news*. Pew Research Center. January 14.

99. Shaer, M. (2017). *How far will Sean Hannity go? New York Times Magazine*. November 28.

100. Grynbaum, M. (2017). Trump calls the news media the "enemy of the American people." *New York Times*. February 17. https://www.nytimes.com/2017/02/17/business/trump-calls-the-news-media-the-enemy-of-the-people.html.

101. Ladd, J. M. (2010). The neglected power of elite opinion leadership to produce antipathy toward the news media: Evidence from a survey experiment. *Political Behavior*, 32(1), 29–50.

102. Holbert, R. L., Lambe, J., Dudo, A. D., & Carlton, K. A. (2007). Primacy effects of *The Daily Show* and national TV news viewing: Young viewers, political gratifications, and internal political self-efficacy. *Journal of Broadcasting & Electronic Media*, 51, 20–38. doi: 10.1080/08838150701308002; Littau, J., & Stewart, D. R. (2015). "Truthiness" and second-level agenda setting: Satire news and its influence on perceptions of television news credibility. *Electronic News*, 9, 122–136. doi: 10.1177/1931243115581416; Morris, J. S., & Baumgartner, J. C. (2008). *The Daily Show* and attitudes toward the news media. In J. C. Baumgartner & J. S. Morris (eds.), *Laughing matters: Humor and American politics in the Media Age*, 315–331. New York: Routledge.

103. Morris & Baumgartner, *The Daily Show* and attitudes toward the news media.

104. Peifer, J. T. (2017). Imitation as flattery: How TV news parody's media criticism can influence perceived news media importance and media trust. *Journalism & Mass Communication Quarterly*. doi:1077699017713002. Peifer, J. T. (2018). Liking the (funny) messenger: The influence of news parody exposure, mirth, and predispositions on media trust. *Media Psychology*, 1–29.

105. Peifer, Imitation as flattery, 738.

106. Peifer, Imitation as flattery, 739.

107. Peifer, Imitation as flattery, 739.

CHAPTER 10

1. Pressman, M. (2009). What ever happened to Air America? *Vanity Fair*. March. https://www.vanityfair.com/news/2009/03/what-ever-happened-to-air-america.

2. Lank, B. (2018). Interview with author. May 23.

3. A change in the editorial direction of the network came in 2007, closing the news division altogether and leaning instead in the direction of comedy-tinged outrage.

4. *Left of the dial.* 2005. HBO. Produced by P. Farrell and K. O'Callaghan.

5. *Left of the dial.*

6. Berry, J. M., & Sobieraj, S. (2014). *The outrage industry: Political opinion media and the new incivility.* New York: Oxford University Press.

7. Lank, B. (2018). Interview with author. May 23.

8. Corliss, R. (2010). Why Air America will be missed. *Time.* January 21. http://content.time.com/time/nation/article/0,8599,1955848,00.html. Lank, B. (2018). Interview with author. May 23.

9. *Q and A with Randi Rhodes* (2005). C-Span. December 13. https://www.c-span.org/video/?190377-1/qa-randi-rhodes.

10. Lank, B. (2018). Interview with author. May 23.

11. Corliss, Why Air America will be missed. Lank, B. (2018). Interview with author. May 23.

12. Air America host Randi Rhodes suspended for calling Hillary a "big f*cking whore." (2008). *Huffington Post.* April 11. https://www.huffingtonpost.com/2008/04/03/air-america-host-randi-rh_n_94863.html.

13. Glaister, D. (2007). Fox launches rightwing satire show. *Guardian.* February 16. https://www.theguardian.com/media/2007/feb/16/usnews.broadcasting.

14. Poniewozik, J. (2007). All-time 100 TV shows. *Time.* September 6. Stanley, Alessandra (2003). Television review; Countering terrorists, and a dense daughter. *New York Times.* October 28.

15. Stelter, B. (2013). Revival of "24" is more like "12." *New York Times.* May 13. https://www.nytim9es.com/2013/05/14/business/media/fox-to-bring-back-24-and-jack-bauer.html.

16. Green, A. (2005). Normalizing torture on "24." *New York Times.* May 22. https://www.nytimes.com/2005/05/22/arts/television/normalizing-torture-on-24.html.

17. Hewitt, H. (2007). "24" creator Joel Surnow on his new creation, the ½ Hour News Hour, and reacting to the hit piece in the *New Yorker.* HughHewitt.com. February 16. http://www.hughhewitt.com/24-creator-joel-surnow-on-his-new-creation-the-12-hour-news-hour-and-reacting-to-the-hit-piece-in-the-new-yorker/.

18. Hewitt, "24" creator Joel Surnow on his new creation.

19. Morrison, O. (2015). Waiting for the conservative Jon Stewart. *Atlantic.* February 14. https://www.theatlantic.com/entertainment/archive/2015/02/why-theres-no-conservative-jon-stewart/385480/.

20. Schimkowitz, M. (2013). "The ½ Hour News Hour": How Fox News's "Daily Show" did to comedy what Fox News does to news. *Splitsider.* September 23. http://www.vulture.com/2013/09/the-12-hour-news-hour-how-fox-newss-daily-show-did-to-comedy-what-fox-news-did-to-news.html.

21. Khanna, S. (2007). Fox's right-wing alternative to Daily Show fails. Think Progress. August 14. https://thinkprogress.org/foxs-right-wing-alternative-to-daily-show-fails-c468d7278fe7/.

22. Garron, B. (2007). The ½ Hour News Hour. *Hollywood Reporter.* February 15. https://www.hollywoodreporter.com/review/12-hour-news-hour-159093.

23. Griffin, J. (2017). The conservative "Daily Show": Fox News' failed foray into satire and why it matters. *Pop Matters.* November 6. https://www.popmatters.com/1-2-hour-news-hour-joel-surnow-fox-news-failed-foray-into-satire-2500322998.html.

24. Similar to when Trump revised the comedians' jokes at his Friar's Club roast. Remember how he removed the incongruity by deleting the punchlines?

25. Smith, C. (2016). *The Daily Show (the book): An oral history as told by Jon Stewart, the correspondents, staff and guests.* New York: Grand Central Publishing, 76.

26. Campbell, K. (2016). Jimmy Fallon speaks out about Orlando shooting in his opening monologue. *Us.* June 14. https://www.usmagazine.com/celebrity-news/news/jimmy-fallon-talks-about-orlando-shooting-in-opening-monologue-w209991/.

27. Caron, C. (2017). Heather Heyer, Charlottesville victim, is recalled as "a strong woman." *New York Times.* August 13. https://www.nytimes.com/2017/08/13/us/heather-heyer-charlottesville-victim.html?_r=0.

28. Jensen, E. (2017). An emotional Jimmy Fallon and an angry Seth Meyers address Charlottesville events. *USA Today.* August 15. https://www.usatoday.com/story/life/entertainthis/2017/08/15/jimmy-fallon-on-charlottesville-we-must-stand-against-what-wrong/567756001/.

29. Dessem, M. (2017). A teary-eyed Jimmy Kimmel talks about his infant son's heart disease, blasts Trumpcare. Slate. May 2. http://www.slate.com/blogs/browbeat/2017/05/02/a_teary_eyed_jimmy_kimmel_talks_about_his_infant_son_s_heart_disease.html.

30. Rao, S. (2018). "There's reason for hope": Stephen Colbert praises Parkland students' campaign for gun reform. *Washington Post.* February 21. https://www.washingtonpost.com/news/arts-and-entertainment/wp/2018/02/21/theres-reason-for-hope-stephen-colbert-praises-parkland-students-campaign-for-gun-reform/?utm_term=.4ecdc344976c.

31. Berry & Sobieraj, *The outrage industry.*

32. Haidt, J. (2012). *The righteous mind: Why good people are divided by politics and religion.* New York: Vintage Books.

33. Berry & Sobieraj, *The outrage industry,* 146.

34. Smith, K. B., Oxley, D. R., Hibbing, M. V., Alford, J. R., & Hibbing, J. R. (2011). Linking genetics and political attitudes: Reconceptualizing political ideology. *Political Psychology,* 32(3), 369.

35. Oxley, D. R., Smith, K. B., Alford, J. R., Hibbing, M. V., Miller, J. L., Scalora, M., Hatemi, P., & Hibbing, J. R. (2008). Political attitudes vary with physiological traits. *Science,* 321(5896), 1667–1670.

36. Personal correspondence with author, December 14, 2018.

37. Fox, J. D. (2017). Trump is one of the worst things ever to happen to comedy. Vulture. December 21. http://www.vulture.com/2017/12/donald-trump-jokes-bad-comedy.html.

38. Schaefer, S. (2017). Why Trump jokes aren't funny. *Scotland Herald*. July 29. http://www.heraldscotland.com/opinion/15442379.Why_Trump_jokes_aren_t_funny_American_stand_up_Sara_Schaefer_on_making_comedy_in_the_age_of_the_45th_US_president/.

39. Schaefer, Why Trump jokes aren't funny.

40. Kaling, M. (2017). Tweet from @mindykaling. October 2.

41. Wright, M. (2018). Samantha Bee to Ivanka Trump: "Do something about your dad's immigration practices, you feckless c*nt!" Vulture. May 31. http://www.vulture.com/2018/05/samantha-bee-calls-out-feckless-c-nt-ivanka-trump.html.

42. War of words: Why Samantha Bee survived controversy and Roseanne didn't. (2018). *NBC Nightly News with Lester Holt*. June 1. https://www.nbcnews.com/nightly-news/video/war-of-words-why-samantha-bee-survived-controversy-and-roseanne-didn-t-1246641219530.

43. Mazza, E. (2018). Trevor Noah reveals the real reason Jon Stewart left "The Daily Show." *Huffington Post*. June 12. https://www.huffingtonpost.com/entry/trevor-noah-jon-stewart-daily-show_us_5b1f3b35e4b0adfb826ced27.

44. Stambler, L. (2010). Dick and Tom Smothers: Hall of Fame tribute. Emmys.com. N.d. https://www.emmys.com/news/hall-fame/dick-smothers-tom-smothers-hall-fame-tribute.

45. Rubin, J. (2018). Journalists are at risk around the globe. Trump keeps adding fuel to the fire. *Washington Post*. July 30. https://www.washingtonpost.com/blogs/right-turn/wp/2018/07/30/journalists-are-at-risk-around-the-globe-trump-keeps-adding-fuel-to-the-fire/?utm_term=.c1d308efd028.

46. Sykes, C. (2017). A guide for frustrated conservatives in the age of Trump. NBCnews.com. October 23. https://www.nbcnews.com/think/opinion/guide-frustrated-conservatives-age-trump-ncna813226.

47. See the introduction.

48. Romano, N. (2017). Stephen Colbert *Late Show* monologue called "homophobic," incites #firecolbert campaign. *Entertainment Weekly*. May 3. 03/stephen-colbert-late-show-monologue-firecwolbert/.

49. Bradley, L. (2018). Colbert tears into Jeff Sessions for "evil" immigrant-children policy. *Vanity Fair*. June 15. https://www.vanityfair.com/hollywood/2018/06/colbert-immigrant-children-policy-sessions-bible-late-show.

50. Bradley, L. (2018). John Oliver rips into Trump's "objectively awful" immigrant children policy. *Vanity Fair*. June 18. https://www.vanityfair.com/hollywood/2018/06/immigrant-children-camps-detention-centers-border-separation-john-oliver.

51. Parker, N. (2018). Michelle Wolf went full meta on "The Break" and it was the best comedy moment all week. Salon.com. July 19. https://www.salon.com/2018/07/19/michelle-wolf-went-full-meta-on-the-break-and-it-was-the-best-comedy-moment-all-week/.

CHAPTER II

1. Jamieson, K. H. (2018). *Cyberwar: How Russian hackers and trolls helped elect a president: What we don't, can't, and do know.* New York: Oxford University Press.

2. Ellul, J. (1973). *Propaganda: The formation of men's attitudes.* New York: Vintage Books.

3. Ellul, *Propaganda,* 72.

4. Ellul, *Propaganda,* 63.

5. Colbert: "Re-becoming" the nation we always were. (2012). *Fresh Air.* NPR. October 4. https://www.npr.org/2012/10/04/162304439/colbert-re-becoming-the-nation-we-always-were.

6. Colbert: "Re-becoming" the nation we always were.

7. John Oliver is no one's friend on his new HBO show. (2014). *Fresh Air.* NPR. June 19.

8. *Jon Stewart & Stephen Colbert Sanity/Fear Press Conference.* (2011). National Press Club. June 24. https://www.youtube.com/watch?v=jyC8h6Oq1Eo.

9. Jensen, E. (2018). Michelle Wolf's White House correspondents' dinner remarks condemned by WHCA president. *USA Today.* April 30. https://www.usatoday.com/story/life/people/2018/04/30/michelle-wolf-white-house-correspondents-dinner-whca-president-margaret-talev/563835002/.

10. Lesser, F. (2017). "Trump claims no one cares about his taxes. The next mass protest should be on Tax Day to prove him wrong." Twitter. January 22, 2:37 p.m. https://twitter.com/sadmonsters/status/823298584409997312.

11. Lesser, F. (2017). Interview with author. October 31.

12. Lesser, F. (2017). Interview with author. October 31.

13. Curl, J. (2018). At star-studded rally, Trump makes closing argument: "Stop radical resistance in its tracks." Daily Wire. November 6. https://www.dailywire.com/news/38011/trumps-star-studded-closing-argument-stop-radical-joseph-curl.

14. Wemple, E. (2018). Fox News's Sean Hannity: Proud to be a Trump operative. *Washington Post.* November 6. https://www.washingtonpost.com/blogs/erik-wemple/wp/2018/11/06/fox-newss-sean-hannity-proud-to-be-a-trump-operative/?utm_term=.64f39932e7bc.

15. Pirro on "Russian collusion delusion": "Time for the Left to fold up their fantasy tents." (2018). Fox News. December 9. http://insider.foxnews.com/2018/12/09/judge-jeanine-pirro-rips-james-comey-and-russian-collusion-delusion-against-trump.

16. Curl, At star-studded rally, Trump makes closing argument.

Index

For the benefit of digital users, indexed terms that span two pages (e.g., 52–53) may, on occasion, appear on only one of those pages.